Peg Streep and
Alan B. Bernstein

GIVE UP
TO GET ON

How to master the art
of quitting in love, work and life

piatkus

PIATKUS

First published in the US in 2014 by De Capo Press,
a member of the Perseus Book Group
First published in Great Britain in 2014 by Piatkus

A CIP catalogue record for this book
is available from the British Library.

ISBN 978-0-349-40127-0

Designed by Jack Lenzo
Printed and bound in Great Britain by
Clays Ltd, St Ives plc

Papers used by Piatkus are from well-managed forests
and other responsible sources.

MIX
Paper from
responsible sources
FSC® C104740

Piatkus
An imprint of
Little, Brown Book Group
100 Victoria Embankment
London EC4Y 0DY

An Hachette UK Company
www.hachette.co.uk

www.piatkus.co.uk

Note: The information in this book is true and complete to the best of our knowledge. This
book is intended only as an informative guide for those wishing to improve their personal
or professional lives through better mental and psychological health. In no way is this book
intended to replace, countermand, or conflict with the advice given to you by a therapist,
life coach, or health professional. The ultimate decision concerning care should be made
between you and your own team of support. We strongly recommend you follow your own
counselor's or support team's advice. Information in this book is general and is offered with
no guarantees on the part of the authors or Da Capo Press. The authors and publisher dis-
claim all liability in connection with the use of this book. The names and identifying details
of people associated with events described in this book have been changed. Any similarity
to actual persons is coincidental.

For Alexandra Israel, best daughter,
and Craig Weatherly, best Beagle
—P. S.

Contents

INTRODUCTION

The Myth of the Little Engine

The premise of *Give Up to Get On* flies in the face of conventional wisdom because today's world doesn't have room for quitters. In fact, the only kind of giving up we collectively accept and support is quitting a bad habit like smoking or drinking. This book isn't about that.

Give Up to Get On proposes that the ability to give up or quit has a place alongside persistence and optimism and that its presence is necessary as a balance to both of those characteristics. Cultivating the ability to quit is especially important because, as we'll show, human beings are actually hardwired to persist, even when a goal is unreachable. Quitting not only frees us from the hopeless pursuit of the unattainable but permits us to commit to new and more satisfying goals. Learning how to quit is an important, conscious counterbalance to the built-in habits of mind, many of which are unconscious, which keep us committed to a path we would be better off abandoning.

Quitting isn't an end in and of itself. It's the necessary first step to rebooting and redefining your goals, and what you want from life.

We hope that *Give Up to Get On* will both help change individual attitudes toward quitting and provide a blueprint for those who need help either letting go of an unattainable goal or revising one that is no longer satisfying. The book presents a necessary corrective to a culture that only trumpets the virtue of staying the course.

The Balancing Act

As children, we fall asleep to the rhythms of the Little Engine's "I think I can, I think I can," which teaches us that both persistence and the power of positive thinking are the keys to success. From the get-go, we learn that "winners never quit and quitters never win," along with dozens of other sayings that make it clear that we must hang in and soldier on.

Seeing persistence as the key to success is also democratic. If hanging in there is what's required, then all the other characteristics and advantages one person might have over another—education, class, privilege—are taken off the table.

Where the ancient Greeks saw Sisyphus, we see a potential hero in the making.

The Little Engine and its grownup counterparts dominate the collective thinking so completely that we like our success stories mixed with at least a dash of failure and preferably a pinch of impossible odds so that in the telling, persistence comes to the fore. Would we admire Thomas Edison's invention of the light bulb as much if he'd succeeded on the first try? The answer is that we wouldn't because we admire people who come from behind, as witnessed by twenty-five years of Oprah, not to mention innumerable news stories, books, and movies. Persistence makes heroes of animals too—think of the unlikely champion racehorse Seabiscuit, or the occasional dog or cat that travels a thousand miles to find its way home.

In all of its iterations, the resolve-equals-success formula spawns other cultural tropes, not the least of which is that failure followed by renewed effort is intrinsic to success. It's not a surprise that the YouTube video "Famous Failures" has been watched millions of times and reposted on Web sites all over the Internet. Its message? If you haven't failed, you haven't lived.

It's a comforting thought. We put on these stories like a fighter's cape—Stephen King's thirty rejections and four unpublished novels, Steve Jobs's failed Next computer, and many others like them—when we set new goals for ourselves. We tell ourselves that the cultural hum in our heads—the mantra of "I think I can" combined with a chorus of "If at first you don't succeed, try, try again"—will see us through.

Our belief in the value of persistence colors the way we tell our own stories and the lessons we take away from the stories we're told. This belief is so interwoven into our way of looking at life that it's hard to see it any other way.

There's only one problem. No matter how many times we watch Rocky bound up those steps, persistence alone isn't a sure-fire formula for success. In fact, our reliance on tenacity narrows our field of vision in important ways because our brains are already wired to support it. In addition, each of us has innate habits of mind that steer us toward commitment and away from quitting, regardless of how remote the possibility of success.

Because our minds are geared to keep us going, when we think about the probability of achieving a goal, we're likely to err on the side of optimistic, even wishful thinking. As a result, we're not very good at judging whether a goal is actually attainable. That's not even the whole story. When a goal we've already achieved is no longer making us happy, both our habits of mind and the onus on quitting will get in the way of moving on with our lives and setting new goals. Persistence trips us up because when we do fail to reach a goal, we often don't give it up completely. Our persistence prevents us from moving on and setting new goals.

The ability to quit fully is as valuable a tool to living well as is persistence.

Accepting the value of quitting sounds weird, counterintuitive, boneheaded, and maybe subversive. We've all been taught that quitting is a sign of weakness and that quitters are losers.

But here it is in a nutshell: Successful and satisfied people know *both* how to persist *and* how to quit. Winners do quit but not in ways you think, and when they do, it's with authority and intelligence.

Despite the cultural folklore, knowing how and when to quit

is an important life skill—not a shameful last resort, as the culture dictates. Considering quitting yields a different perspective, one that is missing from what we've been taught and what we teach our children. It adds an important corrective to the way the human brain works, which is a deck already stacked on the side of persistence. Understanding why it is hard to quit artfully can give us insight into how much of our decision making is literally unconscious and what we can do to make it more conscious.

This book is based in science—what psychologists and researchers know about human behavior and motivation, and what scientists know about the brain. It looks at quitting as art that can be mastered and will help you understand how developing your ability to quit in balance with your ability to persist will make you happier and more satisfied with the decisions you've made. It will get you unstuck when you're stuck and help you move on in life. The only way to set new goals and open up new possibilities is to let go of old goals entirely.

The following simple observations apply to goals in all areas of life, including love, relationship, and work:

- People who ultimately reach their goals have to do more than learn from their failures. They have to give up on their failed goals fully and completely.
- Quitting frees the mind and spirit, and it's the act of quitting that permits growth and learning and promotes the ability to frame new goals. Failing without quitting diminishes the self and often incapacitates our ability to act. Without the ability to give up, most people will end up in a discouraging loop.
- The most satisfied people have the ability both to persist and to quit. They know when it's time to stop persisting and start quitting. And vice versa. When they quit, they really quit. Then they shift gears, set a new goal, and start persisting all over again. They don't look back.
- Some people are naturally better at both persisting and quitting. While that's not as democratic as believing in

doggedness, the good news is that anyone can master the art of quitting.

- Quitting is a healthy, adaptive response when a goal can't be reached or what appeared to be a life path turns out to be a blind alley or when life otherwise throws you a curve ball. Simply putting quitting on the table—seeing it as a possible plan of action—is a helpful corrective to the tunnel vision persistence often creates and a necessary first step to changing your perspective.
- To succeed, you need the ability to persist balanced by the ability to quit.

The psychological term for what we're talking about is *goal disengagement*, which is a series of interrelated steps, not a one-shot thing. What disengagement means and why it matters—how people who can quit are actually happier and more satisfied with their lives than people who can't—has been the focus of extensive research, most of which has been limited to academic circles. The well-being people feel is more literal than not; research has shown that being unable to disengage from an unattainable goal can actually make you sick.

Disengagement isn't the quitting associated with the off-the cuff, "screw you," slamming-of-the door kind, but is something else entirely. It's not the act of a coward or someone who doesn't have the energy to stick it out.

This book is a guide to the kind of disengagement that is mindful and intelligent and that takes place on all levels of the person. It alters how you think, feel, and behave. Done right, quitting will motivate you to set new goals and consider new possibilities.

CHAPTER ONE

The Psychology of Persistence

It's probably important at the outset to admit that both of us have quit major career paths. Strangely enough, we quit the same career path, though we each ended up in very different places and left for different reasons. In addition to Alan's years of work as a psychotherapist, our career changes give us an insider's view of what it means to quit, in terms of both the cost and the possibility.

A Tale of Two Quitters

Alan was in his late twenties, married and a father, and in graduate school on a track to earn a Ph.D. in literature. Having passed his oral exams, he was writing his thesis and was within sight of the goal: a Ph.D. and a position as a university professor. But while he liked teaching (and disliked research), he also realized that he was less interested in teaching Shakespeare's sonnets to his students than he was in listening to them talk about themselves, their goals, and their aspirations, which he had ample opportunity to do in a relaxed university setting in which students actually dropped in on, and spent time with, their teachers. The details of what Alan really loved to do emerged from these interactions at a time when he too was finding himself. He knew that he had a passion for his students as people and wanted to help them make positive choices in life more than he wanted to teach them about iambic pentameter. His calling wasn't literature but psychotherapy. He actually quit in the middle of his thesis.

Still, the transition from the prestige of a doctorate and a connection to a highly regarded academic institution to earning a master's degree in social work was hardly smooth at the time, in the early 1970s. It was accompanied by big doses of self-doubt and worry, something Alan remembers well even after many years of an immensely satisfying career: "Transition isn't from dark to light but more likely a process fraught with both hope and doubt, the two slugging it out through fifteen rounds."

What did quitting accomplish for him? It propelled him into finding and articulating a life's work that was truly satisfying and meaningful, helping people make the most important choices of their lives.

Peg, too, quit academia at a time when jobs were few and far between, and went into the world of publishing. She was on track to finish her dissertation, which was all that stood between her and a Ph.D. in literature, but the politics of academia made her feel that she had better things to do, much to the chagrin of her advisors. But to her surprise, corporate life was in some ways reminiscent of academia, and in her thirties, she decided she wanted to work for herself and set her own goals. In time, she became a writer, which has proved satisfying and permitted her to be a full-time mother while having a career—which she thinks is nothing short of a godsend.

Both of us understand not just the incredible leap of faith that giving up a long-held goal or dream entails, but also the doubt and worry that accompanies the first moment of free fall.

Why *Quitter* Is a Dirty Word

The kind of quitting we're talking about isn't what the word *quitter* brings to mind. As a corollary to the belief in persistence and the American Dream, *quitter* is one of the strongest epithets you can toss at someone. It connotes a deep-seated character flaw, an inability to commit to a course, and weakness in the face of challenge.

Look up *quitter* in the dictionary, and you'll read "one who quits, especially one who gives up too easily." The moral judgment is right there, up close and personal.

True goal disengagement isn't easily accomplished. It involves freeing the mind from its previous engagement, managing negative emotions, creating a new goal, and changing your behavior to line up with the new goal you've set. In contrast, the act of someone we call a quitter is decidedly different.

Take the case of Jason, thirty-two, who took six years to finish high school (his parents sent him to prep school for two extra years so he'd achieve more) and then six to finish college (after getting thrown out of the first prestigious college because he didn't do the work). His modus operandi throughout his twenties and thirties has been marked by quitting jobs, relationships, and even cities. He went to Spain to teach, although his goal wasn't teaching; he was just filling time. He moved to the West Coast to reinvent himself, quit that, and moved back east.

As he tells it, no job has ever been stimulating enough or worthy of his talents and abilities. He's always underappreciated. That's why he has never stayed at one job for longer than a year. He's still not sure what career path would work for him, and he doesn't seem to mind not knowing. He always quits an endeavor before he actually has to perform, which pretty much keeps him from ever failing—which may well be the point.

We've all met a Jason or two along the way, or a Jill, for that matter. He's the one who packs up when the hours get long, when the work gets tedious, or when he finds that he's in danger of failing. Collectively, we dislike a quitter because when we work as colleagues or teammates, he's the most likely to leave us holding the bag and we'll end up doing the work he was supposed to do.

What makes someone a quitter? It turns out there are lots of reasons. Quitters may not be able to commit. They may be afraid of success or afraid of failure. They may be hopelessly mired in self-defeating behaviors. They may be lazy or slackers or coasters on the lake of life.

This kind of quitting is equally based in avoidance and the inability to engage; it has nothing to do with the thoughtful kind of quitting we're talking about.

Before we turn to the right kind of quitting, let's look at how our reliance on persistence alone further skews our emotions and how we think about letting go.

The Emotional Push to Persist

Given the cultural and internal pressure to persist, it's pretty hard to overstate how emotionally charged the act of quitting actually is. On the simplest level, there's the problem of proving that you're not a quitter in conventional terms—the person who reacted emotionally, who didn't have the gumption to hang in there, who lacked the inner resources to see a situation through to the end, the one weakling in the pack. That's a lot to take on, and a pretty good incentive to keep on going.

As a group, we see quitting as proactive only when it involves giving up a bad habit. The rest of the time, quitting is viewed as reactive, and not a very good reaction at that. For those reasons, anyone who even contemplates quitting is going to find himself or herself in a fair amount of emotional turmoil, not to mention a defensive crouch. The cultural context demands that we justify the act of quitting, both publicly and personally, which involves taking on a boatload of emotional baggage. It shouldn't be a surprise that's one way we're emotionally encouraged to persist.

There's an equally important reason we shy away from quitting. By and large, human beings are more avoidant than not, especially when it comes to emotional or physical pain. When people are stuck in a toxic or stressful situation—it could be in the realm of career or relationship—they're much more likely to continue coping with the emotional pain they know than to take on the emotional turmoil they don't, the terra incognita they'll have to explore if they decide to quit and leave. Therapists' offices are filled with people who are stuck in this way, choosing to persist in situations that make them actively unhappy but that are known to them. Moreover, persisting won't involve any of the feelings of shame, powerlessness, or failure we broadly associate with the wrong kind of quitting.

Because staying the course is seen as a virtue, there's a certain amount of emotional equanimity associated with it, and none of the upheaval that is part of letting go. This, too, gives an emotional boost to persistence.

While the kind of quitting this book advocates and explains is decidedly different, it too has an emotional quotient. Artful quitting, by definition, involves letting go of the familiar, staking out new territory, living through a period of ambiguity, and dealing with the emotional fallout of letting go of something important. By definition, this is all difficult emotional terrain to navigate, but in the end, it promises greater emotional rewards. Managing your emotions is an important part not just of artful quitting but of the process of resetting new goals. The emphasis on persistence—keeping us in place—paradoxically doesn't teach us to manage our emotions but to contain them. In that sense, mastering the art of quitting involves an emotional education as well. As one woman, now in her sixties, who has had four separate career paths during her lifetime says, "Quitting takes courage; deciding to take the chance isn't always easy. Something I like about myself is that I manage to find that courage and then go ahead and make the leap anyway, even when I don't know where I will land. A tremendous amount of trust is involved when you risk going off into the wild unknown and assume that this will probably turn out just fine."

In the end, though, it's neither our mere avoidance of the emotional cost of quitting nor the cultural shame of letting go of a long-term goal that keeps us persisting. It's also about how our minds are geared to persist.

The Brain and Persistence

What makes artful quitting difficult is, in part, a consequence of how our brain processes the information it's given by our senses. Both the cultural pressure to persist and the workings of the brain collude in ways that keep many of us in hot pursuit of goals that aren't attainable in the end.

We pursue our goals believing that the process is orderly, logical, and conscious, but in reality, our brains function using strategies that can be valuable if the goal is easily reached and, equally, detrimental if the goal is unattainable. Scientists have delineated two overlapping systems of thought, or cognition. One, called *intuition*, is fast and relatively effortless. It works by association and is often emotionally laden. The other system depends on reasoning; it's much slower, deliberate, and conscious. Since a human being's overall capacity for mental processing is limited, the more effortful thinking processes tend to interrupt each other. In contrast, the intuitive kind of thinking proceeds without interruption when combined with other tasks. As a result, when we think about more than one thing at once, the easy answer—the one offered up by the intuitive system—is the most likely to come to mind. Of course, we're not aware that this is happening, and we tend to ascribe reasoning and deliberateness to all of our thoughts.

Intuitive thinking was once extremely useful to human beings, most usually in contexts that involved physical pursuits like hunting or physical prowess, when both quick response and sheer persistence were necessary to survival. In the twenty-first century, our minds still employ these strategies, which have nothing to do with logic or reason.

The ways in which most people react to a hard-to-reach goal is universal enough that the various ways have actually been named and studied by researchers. In some cases, we've renamed them for clarity but we give the scientific terms as well. These are all common habits of mind we need to recognize and understand because they get to the heart of why persistence needs to be tempered by the ability to quit. All of these innate behaviors are nourished by our cultural myths and the injunctions against quitting.

The story of Jennifer is a case in point. Jennifer is thirty-two, the daughter of a lawyer, and now an associate in a small but prestigious law firm. She'd set becoming a lawyer as her goal in college, and she'd been a gifted and dedicated student in law school. She brought the same committed energy to her work, and for the first four years, she'd loved practicing law, despite the long hours she put in. Then her immediate superior left to join another firm.

Her new boss was something else. Even though her clients and the other members of the law firm seemed to like her, he was extremely critical of her and her work. But, in the hierarchy of the firm, his evaluation of her mattered.

She adopted new ways to please him, and from time to time, she was encouraged by his response. At those moments, she could reassure herself that she was on the verge of winning him over. But in the end, nothing she did was good enough for him.

Over time, she began to dread going to work. Whatever pleasure she'd derived from her practice was fast fading. She was anxious and depressed and had no idea what to do. Everyone she spoke to—her husband, her parents, her friends—counseled her to hang in.

She had too much time and effort invested to quit—three years of law school and almost four at the firm. She still had a shot at making partner and was hopeful she could win her boss over eventually. If she quit, the boss would win. In a bad economy, with more lawyers than there were jobs, she might never get work as a lawyer again. Quitting would make her look bad, as though she couldn't handle pressure. A bad reference from her boss might dog her for years. If she hung in, she'd have more control over what would happen next than if she simply bailed.

Jennifer's story isn't unusual. You can substitute the particulars in her story for others—change her profession, her goal, the bad boss scenario, etc.—and you'll still have the kind of quandary our singular reliance on tenacity creates. It could easily be a story of a relationship or even a marriage where the dilemma is to stay or to leave, and both the voice in our head and the chorus outside are telling us to hang on.

As we'll see, in the face of obstacles to a goal, we may believe that we are reacting consciously and rationally but something else is actually going on.

Seeing the Near Win

Fed by the myth of persistence, when people fall just shy of achieving their goal, they're much more likely to see it as a near win than a loss or a failure. There's a reason for that.

The human brain is wired to respond to the near win because when it comes to physical skills, the near win is actually a good predictor of success. Say you're trying to hunt down an animal for food, shoot a target, or hit a baseball—any physical activity that involves real skill and expertise—and you almost succeed. The near win signals that you're getting closer to achieving your goal—that if you just hone your skills a little bit more, you're very likely to succeed. In academic pursuits, the near win—falling just short of the grade you've set as a goal for yourself—is also reliable. Studying harder and longer the next time will probably do the trick.

Unfortunately, neither human beings nor their brains are uniformly good at figuring when the near win is applicable and when it isn't. A British study on gambling took a bunch of ordinary people, matched them up with slot machines, and then measured their brain activity when they played. Winning at the slots, of course, isn't a matter of skill at all, but the researchers found that players and their brains responded to the near win exactly as they would when skill was actually involved. The pleasure and reward parts of their brains lit up for a near win almost as brightly as when they actually won money. Moreover, the near win was enough to keep them playing, even though they'd actually lost money and what they perceived as a near win was totally useless as a predictor of a real win. It didn't matter. Not surprisingly, the near win plays a big part in the lives of those who become compulsive gamblers.

But we don't have to be playing the slots to be affected by the near win. Even when it doesn't apply to the situation we're in, the near win reinforces our positive beliefs and kicks up our capacity for wishful thinking. It often results in our staying in relationships and situations long past their expiration date, even when it's obvious to the rest of the world that we're very unlikely to succeed. Our belief in persistence encourages us to reframe what's actually a miss as a near win.

In Jennifer's story, the near win at work comes into play when she tries new ways of eliciting her boss' praise and begins to read any response that isn't downright dismissive as a sign that she's getting closer to winning him over. Just the word *okay*, instead of a withering criticism, is enough to make her feel she's making progress.

The near win influences us not just because of the wiring in our brains but also because of the cultural injunctions against quitting. If letting go of a goal isn't an option, we're that much more open to its seductions, whether it's in the realm of business, relationship, or love. Understanding the power of this particular habit of mind and identifying our individual tendency to recast a loss as a near win are important first steps on the way to the perspective we need to be able to quit.

Listening to Anecdote

When you're deciding whether something is likely to happen to you or whether one event is likely to lead to another, you're going to sit down, apply the rules of logic, and make your most considered decision, right? Actually not. What's much more likely is that your brain will work from the examples or anecdotes that spring most readily to mind, and you'll decide on that basis.

This psychological phenomenon, with the tongue-twisting name *availability heuristic*, is another mental proclivity that gives the myth of persistence a big boost. This kind of thinking—drawing from the most available and vivid example—was originally extremely valuable to human survival. Say you're a Paleolithic caribou hunter and you've been taking the shortest route to the lake where the deer gather. Then you hear that three men have been attacked by bears on this very same route. The information lets you connect the dots—short route equals bears equals danger—and you decide instead to take a longer route that may make hunting harder but will allow you to live longer. Similarly, without knowing anything about internal temperatures or trichinosis, many ancient cultures and religions heeded the anecdotes about people dying after eating pork and prohibited it as a food.

Alas, in today's world, the power of anecdote to persuade isn't universally beneficial. The easy availability of an example—the lottery winners we see on television and read about, the people who persisted beyond all odds and achieved lofty goals as showcased on talk shows—can have us believing, "Why not me?" even if there's absolutely no evidence at all that it *will* be you. In a media-saturated world, hearing some examples over and over can have us connecting the dots when there aren't any to connect. It has us believing that some things—both good and bad—are more probable than they really are. That's true both for the persistence-equals-success stories and everything else.

For example, take the media attention focused on dangers such as school shootings and shark attacks. As a result of this attention, people, no matter how smart they are, attribute greater likelihood to these events simply because the examples are more easily pulled up out of memory. The more vivid or emotionally compelling the example, the more likely it will be readily available.

To prove the point, psychologist Scott Plous asked subjects whether a person was more likely to be killed by falling airplane parts or by a shark attack. Think a minute, and answer it yourself.

Because shark attacks get more publicity, most people will answer "shark attack," even though you're thirty times more likely to die from pieces of aircraft falling from the sky—an unlikely event, to be sure, but a better bet than a shark attack. That's the availability heuristic at work.

Our cultural assumptions about persistence—and the many examples the media extols and delivers in the form of story—make us especially vulnerable to the power the anecdote has over our thinking. There's nothing wrong with inspiration, of course, and stories of persistence can and do inspire people. The problem is that when our decisions are being shaped by the first things that come to mind, we're not likely to be asking the right questions. And the right question, for sure, isn't usually, "Why not me?"

The availability heuristic, alas, makes us lousy at predicting success or anything else, for that matter. Taking stock of how we chose to persist in an effort—while keeping the availability heuristic in mind—is one important way of keeping the hounds of persistence at bay and beginning to take an honest look at whether quitting is what we need to do.

The Power of Intermittent Reinforcement

Unwarranted persistence can also be fed by what's called *intermittent reinforcement*, and if the phrase reminds you of something you once heard in Psych 101, then you've got a damn good memory. Intermittent reinforcement is relevant because it turns out that what happens to rats also happens to human beings. (And to refresh your memory, the guy who did the work was B. F. Skinner.)

Picture three hungry rats in three separate cages, each of which has a lever. In the first cage, the rat pushes the lever and gets a pellet of food every time. It doesn't take the rat long to realize that the lever is a reliable source of food, and the creature is free to do whatever rats do, like run the wheel, dig up sawdust, and the like. The rat is a happy camper because it knows where its food is coming from.

In the third cage, though, the rat pushes the lever and nothing happens. It pushes again and again, and nothing happens. Because there's no food reward, the rat gives up on the lever and goes about its business looking for food.

The rat in the second cage, though, is in real trouble. When it hits the lever, sometimes it gets a pellet and sometimes it doesn't. Even for a rat, hope springs eternal and the animal becomes fixated on the lever, continuing to push, frustrated and rewarded by turns. The intermittent reinforcement keeps the rat parked by the lever day and night. In other words, of the three rats, the rat whose lever delivered only some of the time ends up being the most persistent.

There's no doubt that intermittent reinforcement was useful at times in human history, especially when it came to hunting, fishing, and foraging. Getting what you needed at least some of the time reinforced the persistence you needed to survive. Alas, when applied to other situations, intermittent reinforcement may not be such a good thing. That's certainly true of the unattainable goal.

Say your goal is to try to make the line of communication between you and someone else more open and responsive. (You can fill in parent, sibling, spouse, lover, friend, colleague, or boss as you wish. You can also switch the "he" in the story to "she.") You have numerous heart-to-hearts and a couple of screaming matches, and every time, you explain to the person that he isn't empathetic enough or listening to what you have to say. Nothing about his behavior changes, and you're actually considering packing it in when, suddenly out of nowhere, he opens up to you. Miracle of miracles, he's actually listening and every hesitation you had about staying in the relationship flies out of your head.

Life goes on and so does he—and his behavior goes back to what it was before. You repeat the serious conversations and the screaming matches, and—lo and behold—he's suddenly open, understanding, and attentive. Again, you decide to persist.

That's intermittent reinforcement. Perhaps the classic example of intermittent reinforcement in a relationship was played out between Carrie Bradshaw and Mr. Big on *Sex in the City* for six seasons.

But intermittent reinforcement works outside the realm of relationship too. Temporary resolutions to a problem blocking a goal can reinforce unwarranted tenacity the same way.

For example, Julie's passion was making jewelry, and she'd always dreamed of being her own boss and creating a life in which she did what she loved. She saved her money and went into business by subleasing space in a store in New Jersey. "To turn a profit," she says, "I had to sell three thousand dollars' worth of jewelry a week at retail if I were open six days a week. Most weeks, I didn't make my goal, but now and again—say, one week out of four—I would actually meet it or exceed it. That kept me thinking that I was just a step or two from success. I stayed on the merry-go-round for two years, depleting most of my savings, until I finally faced the music."

Intermittent reinforcement feeds persistence even when it isn't connected to any real progress that might bring a goal to fruition and keeps the individual from adopting new behaviors that might help him or her to disengage. It's another reason why the reliance on tenacity alone isn't a good idea, and why we need to step back and ask ourselves whether our habits of mind are actually driving the bus.

Trapped in the Escalation of Commitment

There's some dispute about who actually said, "When the going gets tough, the tough get going," but it turns out to be true in unexpected ways. In the broader culture, the saying summons up noble persistence—think D-day and the beaches of Normandy or Rocky bounding up those steps—but the truth is something else entirely. *Escalation of commitment*, as it's called, is a favorite of researchers for reasons that will soon be clear. In a nutshell, scientists have found that people actually increase their commitment to a goal when it's foundering or even unsalvageable and they do it without prompting or even a prayer to Saint Jude, the patron saint of lost causes.

The escalation of commitment is fascinating for a variety of reasons. First, it's universal and operates in every culture around the globe, no matter how different the cultures. Second, being smart or well educated doesn't protect you from falling into the trap of escalation. Third, everyone except the one redoubling his or her efforts knows that the escalation is irrational. And finally, escalation of commitment tells us a lot about the human beings and their brains, motivations, and actions.

Needless to say, the near win, the availability heuristic, and intermittent reinforcement can all contribute to the escalation of commitment. But there are other reasons too—biases in thinking, various innate or social behaviors, and, of course, the onus on quitting—that make us amp up the volume even when failure is in plain sight.

One major contributor to the phenomenon is basic to human nature: our inability to assess ourselves and our talents realistically. While self-help books and television shows tend to focus on our collective lack of self-esteem, most of us actually have oversized visions of how skilled or talented we are compared with others. Again, at some point in human history, this bias in thinking probably served a purpose—giving our Paleolithic forebear the extra oomph and self-confidence to become the leader the clan needed or the psychological edge that pushed him to hunt better than his peers. Nowadays, though, it's more like a set of blinders than not.

The *above-average effect* describes how, when people are asked to measure their capacities against those of their peers, the majority will rate themselves as above average. This appraisal holds true across many categories, including driving skills, athletic prowess, health, managerial ability, and character traits like kindness and generosity. Most famously, one enormous study of a million high school students by the College Board showed that 70 percent of them rated themselves as above average in leadership abilities! Even more astonishing, when asked to rate their ability to get along with others, each person rated his or her ability as at least average while 60 percent awarded themselves the top tenth percentile and a full 25 percent placed themselves in the first percentile! Put another way, of one million people, only 15 percent judged their ability as average.

Bluntly put, we may fall into the escalation trap because we are bad judges of whether our skills are good enough to achieve the goal or even whether they're a good fit. If we're in a competitive situation, we're more likely to overstate our abilities and underestimate those of the competition. We tend to be overconfident.

And there's more. Writing in the *Harvard Business Review*, Dan Lovallo and Daniel Kahneman pointed out that the above-average effect has another corollary or two. First, we tend to be overly optimistic about outcomes, exaggerating their probability in much the same way we do our talents. Mind you, under the right circumstances, optimism is a very good thing, as is tenacity. Optimism fuels our efforts when we're in the right place, with the right skills, and the right goal. And without optimism, few of us would succeed at anything. But—yes, there is a *but*—in the free fall that escalation of commitment ultimately becomes, delusional optimism just speeds up the cascade. It's not just that we tend collectively to be optimistic about the future; it's also that we don't necessarily look at past experience as an indicator of how the future will play out. Human beings look forward in abstract and general terms, uncluttered by the sometimes spotty details of past experiences.

Lovallo and Kahneman also explain that our tendency to exaggerate our abilities is amplified by how we attribute cause to success and failure. While people take credit for positive outcomes, they also tend to attribute negative ones to external factors, which they see as out of their personal control. These two ways of thinking are factors in the escalation of commitment, the more so because quitting isn't a consideration but is only a last resort.

And one more thing: for all that we tend to overrate our skills, human beings are also very, very touchy about having that point of view readjusted. That's another reason that people will escalate their commitment under fire. As many studies have shown, when people receive a bunch of bad news or negative feedback about a venture they've committed to, they're far more likely to escalate their effort than they are to scale down or pull out, no matter how persuasive or negative the feedback.

We've already seen some of the ways the mind recasts the situation for persistence, but it actually goes beyond all of that. The more money, time, energy, and effort a human being has invested and the greater the personal responsibility he or she feels for the initial decision, the more likely he or she is to persist. Justifying the initial decision trumps all and by investing even more in it, the person feels as though he is actually validating himself and his initial reasoning.

It doesn't make a lot of sense, but people do it all the time, in their personal and business lives, individually and collectively. Studies show that a manager who was personally responsible for hiring an underperforming employee is far less likely to fire the employee than a manager who had nothing to do with the hiring. Instead, the manager will escalate his or her commitment to the initial decision to hire the employee. On a corporate level, where teams of people make decisions, bad news is usually greeted the same way. People do it with failing marriages and even with old cars they've decided to hang on to.

The car that ultimately becomes a clunker is the perfect example of how the "reasoning" behind the escalation of commitment works. Patrick and his wife Barbara disagree on whether to buy a new car or maintain an old one. Patrick wants to keep the old car. He wins the argument and begins to spend money maintaining the car—new tires, new brakes, new muffler, and whatever else the mechanic says it needs. Typically, as the expenses mount up, he's more likely than not to be hopeful that this—whatever "this" is—will be the last repair he has to make. The more money he pours into the car, the more likely he is to continue investing in it since his focus shifts from the piece of metal in front of him to the dollars he's sunk into it.

The fancy name for that is the *sunk-cost fallacy* and it's yet another engine for persistence.

Giving In to the Sunk-Cost Fallacy

The *sunk-cost fallacy* is a mouthful and its name makes it sound more complicated and esoteric than it actually is. Basically, when we let what we've already invested in a situation dictate our decision about whether to keep going, we're invoking the sunk-cost fallacy. For Patrick, it's the car; for Jennifer, our unhappy lawyer, it's the time, money, and effort that went into her law degree, the four years she's spent at the firm, and the potential promise of making partner. The term *sunk-cost fallacy* comes out of economics, where it describes how investors decide whether to go forward on a problematic venture that has already had a significant investment of money.

The sunk-cost fallacy is so prevalent in our thinking that we can see it at work in how our leaders talk about war or military efforts and how ordinary people talk about everything from investments and jobs to real estate and marriages. The sunk-cost fallacy is persistence's cheerleader and the naysayer to quitting.

Take, for example, the logic that pervaded the thinking of America's leadership about sending troops to Vietnam even as it acknowledged that winning, in the conventional sense, was impossible. Leaders invoked the sunk-cost fallacy by saying that if the country quit, the loss of life already incurred would be wasted.

On the face of it, this argument is illogical—how could the possibility of more people dying justify the deaths of others who came before?—but many people actually justify persisting in situations because of what they've already invested. This kind of thinking trumps the adage "Don't throw good money after bad" because people are generally hesitant and unwilling to (1) admit that what they invested is lost and (2) take the risk of quitting prematurely. They're often more willing to invest even more before they concede the loss, largely on the off chance that hanging in longer will reap the big payoff. Both the culture of persistence and the onus on quitting keep the sunk-cost fallacy going.

The investment of time and energy—and the unwillingness to quit and call it a lost cause—keeps people in place. It also stops them from reframing the situation they find themselves in, imagining a new goal, and reinventing themselves. The sunk-cost fallacy influences decision-making when people think about leaving a long-term marriage, a job or career to which they've devoted much time and effort, and many other situations, large and small.

The Bird in the Hand

You know the expression "A bird in the hand is worth two in the bush"? Scientific research shows not only that the saying accurately describes how people behave but also that human beings are willing to do just about anything to hold on to that bird.

Stories often emphasize how people are more inclined to be risk takers when there's the possibility of gain—mortgaging their house and the like—but it turns out not to be true. As Nobel Prize winners Daniel Kahneman and Amos Tversky discovered, when we weigh our future prospects, the scales aren't evenly balanced. As surprising as it may sound, when weighing possible gains against possible losses, human beings are a very conservative lot. People are far less inclined to take a risk in the name of gain, but they are willing to do almost anything to avoid a certain loss. Paradoxically, their *loss aversion*, as it's called, encourages them to become risk takers. Loss aversion is a key component in human psychology when it comes to judgments about whether to persist in an effort.

How sensitive people are to losses or cuts was demonstrated by a completely counterintuitive but remarkably revelatory research experiment in which people were asked which job they would prefer. The first one paid $30,000 to start, $40,000 at year two, and $50,000 the third year. The other choice was one that paid $60,000 the first year, $50,000 the second, and $40,000 the third. Despite the easy math, people actually preferred the job with the increases, even though it actually paid less.

Not surprisingly, loss aversion amps up the escalation of commitment, as the following story shows. A professional in the communications industry, Robert had been very successful at bringing teams of disparate people together to work on commercial projects, but he'd never worked on anything that was both personally and professionally satisfying. Finding such a project became an important goal. A dedicated environmentalist, he conceived of putting together a consortium of experts who would pool their knowledge and create a national platform on sustainable living. For six years, he worked on recruiting both individuals and groups of scientists, engineers, farmers, chefs, and others who were already committed to sustainability to participate. He envisioned a bank of information on the subject—a go-to source of books, videos, and Web information. It took time to get everyone on board, more time to sign a contract, and even more time to come up with a sustainability platform everyone could agree on. His investors were signed on.

Two of the professional groups suddenly changed their minds. They now wanted to showcase their members, not the principles of sustainability. This wasn't, of course, what they'd agreed to, but Robert made whatever concessions he could to keep the venture going. The more concessions they demanded, the more Robert escalated his commitment and the more fractious the in-fighting became. But time after time, the concessions weren't enough.

Robert was well aware that the project had veered off its original course. Even so, he still thought he could make it work. Then he learned that the groups had solicited the other experts because they wanted to take the project over for themselves. Even worse, Robert's investors were talking to them. His project had been hijacked.

There were lots of arguments to justify tenacity. He had a track record of success in communications, and it didn't seem likely that the other participants, no matter how vocal they were, had the expertise to pull it off. The idea for the project had been his, and he'd acted in good faith. He had countless hours, not to mention years, tied up in the project. He had every reason to believe that succeeding at the project would further his career. He wouldn't and couldn't let all he'd put into the project go to waste.

Until Robert put quitting on the table, he wasn't able to see that his commitment was taking up all the mental and emotional energy he had, even though that commitment was, in fact, getting him no closer to getting what he wanted. He continued to escalate his commitment for months until his hand was forced and he had to consider giving up.

The Perceived Value Conundrum

When we embark on a goal, few of us anticipate every obstacle, and unfortunately, realistic or clear thinking and persistence aren't necessarily good bedfellows or even teammates. Researchers have found that when problems plague the pursuit of a goal, people will weigh two factors to decide whether to continue on. The first factor is how valuable the goal is. Not surprisingly, the more valuable the goal is perceived to be, the more inclined the person will be to persist. The second factor is the strength of the expectation of success. Again, the stronger the belief in success, the more likely the person is to stay the course.

All of this sounds straightforward enough on the surface, but once again, human nature intervenes. As researchers have found, the frustration caused by being thwarted can actually make the goal appear even more valuable than it was initially. Up to a point, the level of commitment rises in proportion to both how unavailable—and, hence, valuable—the goal appears to be. As in the Greek myth of Tantalus, who is punished by never being able to grasp the fruit dangling from the branch just above his head, the goal becomes literally more tantalizing by virtue of its being out of reach.

This phenomenon shows up in all walks of life and in almost every circumstance. Anything unattainable—the lover, the dream house, the ideal job—becomes that much more valuable to the beholder because it can't be had. Again, the conscious act of considering quitting opens up possibilities that can't be looked at otherwise: the recognition that the energy and the emotional investment we've committed to the impossible dream could be put into the service of a goal that might actually make us happy.

The Problem with White Bears

As if it isn't enough to discover that when we think we're thinking logically and hard when we're really not, it's also true that we don't act just on the basis of conscious thought or motivation either. We're motivated to act by unconscious thoughts as well. The *unconscious* here isn't the term made famous by Freud—all those repressed childhood memories and experiences—but something else entirely. Despite all the human brain's amazing capacities—it writes sonnets, puts a man on the moon, invents the iPhone!— it doesn't work the way we think it does. Or as Daniel Wegner explains, "The slowness of consciousness suggests that much of what we see and do involves the operation of *preconscious* mental process." Yes, this sounds as though your brain is thinking without your knowing it is and that you're going about your business in the world, doing what you're doing, on the basis of thought processes you don't even know about. While it may make you uncomfortable thinking about human "will" in those terms, that's pretty much the case. Let us explain.

Take the pursuit of a goal. It can be any goal—getting a promotion, taking Friday off and playing golf, keeping the peace at a family gathering—and if you had to write down what pursuing that goal would look like on paper, you might do it like this:

A. Define the goal.
B. Think about how to achieve it.
C. Formulate actions and strategies.
D. Act.
E. Reflect on how actions are bringing the goal closer.

Most people assume that steps A through E are conscious in the literal sense of the word and accompanied by thought processes that are totally deliberate.

The truth, though, is a bit more complicated than that, in part because of the brain's limited capacities. Some of what it does has to be on automatic because, if these processes weren't, they would take up too much of the brain's attentional capacity. Some actions are intentionally automatic. Take backing the car out of the driveway. If you can remember the first time you actually did this, the memory you'll summon up is doubtless a nervous and frazzled you, trying desperately to concentrate, twisting your head. The likelihood is that when you back out now, you're probably doing other things as you do—turning on the radio, talking on the phone, thinking about what you need to do first thing. We don't need to argue the usefulness of that kind of automaticity. But there is another equally automatic process, which lies beyond our conscious perception, in which choices in situations are automatic as well. That's the process by which "goals and motives will be automatically activated by situations," even though we're unaware that they have been.

There's the influence of *priming* on decisions we make. Research has shown that all kinds of cues, or primes, in the environment influence our thoughts, attitudes, and behaviors without our being conscious of those cues. Among other things, primes such as the smell of a cleaning fluid have been shown to make people more prone to clean up after themselves. Evoking the mental representation of a library, on the other hand, makes people more prone to lower their voices to a whisper. Other experiments, especially those conducted by John A. Bargh and Tanya L. Chartrand, point to a much more direct influence between primes and behavior. For example, in one experiment, participants completed sentences with words which were either rude (such as "aggressively," "bold," "annoying"), polite ("respect," "honor," "courteous") or neutral. The participants primed with the rude words were, in another part of the experiment, more apt to act rudely than either those primed with polite words or neutral words.

But perhaps even more salient to the discussion about goals and quitting are the experiments with mundane physical objects and the mental representations and behaviors they evoked. Bargh and his colleagues conducted several experiments with objects meant to signify the capitalistic business world (such as briefcases, a conference table, fountain pens, dress shoes, suits, etc.). The idea was to see if these primers would activate the construct of competition, and indeed they did. In one experiment, participants were asked to complete word fragments, one of which was *c_ _ p_ _ _ tive*. While

70 percent of those primed with business representations completed the word as *competitive*, only 42 percent of the unprimed participants did. Note that the other possible word to be made from the fragment was *cooperative*.

The most clear-cut experiment on the effect of priming involved the "ultimatum game," in which one person proposes a division of a sum of money (in this case, $10), which the other person can take or leave. The key is that the player with the money had to divest himself or herself of a portion of it so the strategy is normally how little can you give away while appearing fair at the same time. In one experiment, while 100 percent of the group unprimed by business symbols offered a fifty-fifty split, or $5 apiece, only 50 percent of those primed did. In a second experiment, only 33 percent of those primed split fifty-fifty, as compared with 91 percent of those who were unprimed. The business-equals-competition primes in the environment changed not only the participants' understanding of the goal but also how they behaved.

Similar experiments, as well as brain scans, showed no difference between goals that are consciously chosen and automatic ones. As Bargh and his coauthors explain, not only can goals be activated by external, environmental information, but "once they are put into motion, they operate just as if they had been consciously intended, even to the point of producing changes in mood and in self-efficacy beliefs, depending on one's degree of success or failure in reaching the goal." In other words, we react emotionally in the same ways to goals that are unconsciously chosen as we do to those that are consciously pursued. A later chapter will return to this idea to show how this propensity gets in the way of artful quitting.

And as if all this unconscious activation weren't enough, there's the matter of white bears, another aspect of automaticity. Psychologist Daniel Wegner set out to answer one of life's most vexing questions: Why is that when we're trying *not* think of something, the thought keeps barging in like an unwelcome guest? Why is it so hard not to think of cookies the minute we decide to diet, or why can't we stop thinking about the lover who has spurned us, or why do we keep second-guessing our decision to quit? In other words, why do thoughts we're actively trying to suppress keep intruding on us anyway? Wegner discovered what he called "ironic processes of mental control," but he boiled it down to this: "The mind actually appears to search unconsciously and automatically for whatever thought, action, or emotion the person is actually trying to control." Yes, this discovery is another blow to whatever notion we might have about free will.

Wegner and others initially showed how this worked in a series of experiments in which participants were told, while they were performing other tasks, *not* to think of white bears. Another group was instructed to think of white bears first and then *not* think of them. Participants who were told not to think about them nonetheless thought about them more than once a minute! And in the second group, participants actually thought about white bears more often when they were told to suppress the thought than they did when they were instructed to think about them.

It turns out that thought suppression and the effort to control thoughts act as primes for the opposite effect. This presents a real problem for people who decide to disengage from a goal, especially one that has been central to their sense of self and identity and that has great emotional meaning.

Persistence and Personal Experience

In addition to the habits of mind covered in these pages—habits that can distort our thinking when the going gets rough—each of us brings our personal histories and experiences to the framing of goals, the assessment of probable success, and our willingness to persist. Sometimes, positive reinforcement, whether intermittent or not, will make people try even harder. Paradoxically, though, others are just as likely to persist when the circumstances evoke difficult or painful feelings and behaviors that they remember from their childhoods. Because these feeling are familiar, they create a comfort zone for the individual, even though the feelings themselves may be stressful or painful. This sounds totally counterintuitive, but it's nonetheless true.

Comfort zones have to do with how the developing human brain is shaped by experience during infancy and childhood. A later chapter will go into more detail about how this works and why it matters, but the most salient point is that each of us is most comfortable with the emotional patterns we're familiar with—whether they make us happy or not. Overall, the known trumps the unknown, whether the known makes us happy or not. These responses aren't conscious but influence our perceptions in myriad ways.

People who grow up in emotionally healthy environments with attuned and loving parents are much less likely to fall into the comfort-zone trap. They're better than others at reacting relatively quickly to abusive or destructive environments. Nevertheless, most of us have psychological histories that are more of a mixed bag than not, so the comfort-zone trap is likely to keep us persisting at least some of the time.

Persistence and Inflexibility

Persistence gets in the way when the goals we've already achieved, particularly long-held ones, need updating or relinquishing because they no longer serve us or make us happy. Our belief in staying the course doesn't take into account that who we are and what we want may change over time. Perhaps the trade-offs we were willing to make initially to achieve a goal don't end up working for us in the long term. Or perhaps the life we end up living isn't the life our older self wants after all. These major goals may be ones we've chosen for ourselves or those we've inherited from our parents, but in either case, revising them is always difficult.

Because of the cultural and personal pressure, the hardest goals to give up on are those that look successful on the surface but leave us feeling dead and soulless or make us unhappy in other ways.

Sometimes, a goal will become outworn because it doesn't deliver what we expected or because it conflicts with new priorities. As we've already seen, the greater the investment of time, the harder it will be to even consider disengaging, thanks to the sunk-cost fallacy. Other times, the struggle entails not just letting go of a major goal but a definition of self.

When persistence isn't coupled with the ability to disengage, there's no solution in sight and no chance of imagining a different future.

How Quitting Balances the Scales

Because the decision to disengage from a goal is a conscious choice, considering quitting diminishes the effect of the brain's unconscious processes and allows us to reframe and reassess the goal at hand. Consciously putting quitting into the mix alters our perspective in meaningful ways and begins a process that will ultimately permit us both to let go of an unattainable goal and to articulate new goals that will enrich our lives.

You won't be surprised to learn that all of the stories about unattainable goals were ultimately resolved when the individual considered quitting as a viable choice. Each woman and man made the decision thoughtfully and, as they tell it, went through the process of what it means to quit. In some cases, the necessary steps took months, if not years.

For Jennifer, the process began when she started to consider using her legal experience in different ways. She networked and sought out others who had given up the practice of law but were using these skills in another context. Once she began to consider quitting, she was able to stop seeing the years she'd invested as a loss. That shift in her vision freed her to explore other opportunities she would never have considered otherwise. She's happy and productive in a nonprofit organization where her skills and her attitude are appreciated.

Julie the jewelry designer closed her shop and came to the realization that she wasn't cut out to be an entrepreneur. She saw that financial stability and peace of mind were more important goals than being her own boss and more than compensated for the loss of her dream. She worked hard at marketing her design skills and got a job at a clothing manufacturer. She still makes jewelry but she looks at it as more of a creative outlet than not. She sells to friends and acquaintances through her Web site and at craft fairs.

Robert finally walked away from the sustainability platform he'd created and went back to corporate communications, which he saw as a short-term solution. This time, though, he focused on finding a firm that served a variety of clients. His specialty has become green industries. Although he's still looking for a suitable new project that will meet his long-term goal, he says that if he finds one, he'll pay much closer attention to the interaction of personalities and long-term vision.

All of these people acknowledge that, initially, it was difficult to come to terms with quitting and what they first saw as a loss of time and energy and, in some cases, money. Even more important, each of them admits that the cultural pressure to persist made disengagement much harder. While some of them found support for their decision to quit in their circle of friends and family, others did not. Through the acts of quitting and then setting new goals, each of them gained a new perspective on what they really wanted and what made them happy.

One aim of this book is to change how you think about quitting so that you can see how being able to let go can increase your sense of well-being. Another is to help you evaluate whether your goals are working for or against you and whether you need to rechart certain aspects of your life. Implicit in every chapter is the acknowledgment that while goals give our lives meaning and structure, it is rare that any of us will achieve *all* of them. Disappointment and regrouping are part of everyone's life script. In no small part, mastering the art of quitting is about learning to be flexible when you need to so that you can meet whatever challenge you're facing. By permitting ourselves to quit, we can achieve a flexibility of mind and spirit that ultimately yields to greater life satisfaction.

In addition, we think that the lessons contained in these pages will help when we need to cope with and recover from an unanticipated life reversal that forces us to revise or let go of goals we've set for ourselves. These reversals may be in the realm of career, personal relationship, health, or economics. In those instances, even though we've not chosen to change paths, the ability to quit those initial goals artfully will determine how well we recover from their loss and how we're able to commit to scaled-down or new goals that offer the promise of happiness and satisfaction. It's yet another reason why mastering the art of quitting is important.

Having looked at how people are geared to persist, we'll turn next to why quitting in the conventional sense—which is nothing like true goal disengagement—doesn't work.

Persistence Profile

Take a look at the following statements. Answer yes or no, trying to be as honest as possible, to gauge your level of persistence.

1. I believe that things usually work out for the best.
2. I think quitting is a last resort.
3. I'm energized by challenges other people find daunting.
4. I worry a lot when things go off track.
5. When I can't get what I want, I want it even more.
6. I'd rather stay in a situation or relationship too long than leave it too soon.
7. I never walk out of something I've paid for, even if it's boring or dull.
8. I'm an optimist by nature.
9. I believe in staying the course.
10. I tend to second-guess myself.
11. I spend a lot of time talking about my failed relationships.
12. What people think of me is very important.
13. If I lose something, I can't stop thinking about it or looking for it.
14. I won't settle, but I will shop until I find exactly what I want.
15. Succeeding is very important to me.
16. I have trouble compromising.
17. I make to-do lists and complete them all the time.
18. I'm not good at distracting myself when I'm stressed.
19. I consider myself more focused than other people.
20. I think giving up is a sign of weakness.

The more items you agree with, the more likely you are to err on the side of persistence, even when it's unwarranted, and the harder it may be for you to consider quitting. This profile is an informal way of looking at your personal attitudes toward persistence.

CHAPTER TWO

Unsuccessful Quitting

It may come as a surprise that in addition to not knowing why they're thinking what they're thinking much of the time, people are relatively clueless about both what will make them happy and how happy they'll be. Many of us will set goals for ourselves, only to discover that what we once wanted isn't enough. Given the absence of a reliable crystal ball, being able to decide whether to disengage from a goal and then the ability to let go and start over are essential life skills.

Please note the word *disengage*. *Disengagement* or *artful quitting* has nothing to do with the emotionally fueled quitting that many, if not all of us, have indulged in at one point or another in our lives. Some of us may actually have a signature quitting style, and if you have one, it's worth identifying this first before you begin learning how to quit artfully.

The following styles of quitting aren't scientific descriptions of how people quit, of course; they're meant to be evocative enough so that you can recognize aspects of your own behavior and quitting style.

The Slacker Quit

We've already mentioned the habitual quitter in the first chapter but it's worth revisiting since the *slacker quit* is what comes to mind when the word *quit* is mentioned. This style of quitting—invoked when the going gets rough or when the situation appears to put more demands on the person that he or she anticipated—is as much about not engaging as it is about quitting. This kind of quitting actually can become a pattern in a person's life and fans out over a broad range of activities. As a rule, these folks rarely finish anything.

The O.K. Corral

The *O.K. Corral* type of quitting refers to the posturing, winner-take-all kind of quit. This approach usually tries to show the quitter in the best possible light, making the act of quitting part of a moral or another imperative. Its narrative is framed to put the emphasis on what might have been lost had the person persisted, as in "I quit because my integrity was more important to me." You can substitute any number of other nouns for the word *integrity* in that sentence, but the gist will remain the same. Because this style of quitting invokes an ethical high ground, one of its appeals is that it blunts the cultural onus on quitting.

A good contemporary and public example of the O.K. Corral is that of Greg Smith, the Goldman Sachs manager who quit on the op-ed pages of the *New York Times* after "discovering," some twelve years into the job, that the investment bank cared more about its own profits than its clients' interests. In Smith's case, the op-ed quit got him a seven-figure book advance, but for most people, the O.K. Corral approach, while momentarily very satisfying and ego-boosting, can do enormous damage to a career. If you're counting on referrals or staying in the same industry, it's a bridge burner and not a very smart move.

In the area of personal relationships, especially divorce, the O.K. Corral pretty much guarantees widespread collateral damage since the other person will, of necessity, be cast as the bad guy and the middle ground will most certainly disappear. Celebrity divorces often devolve into the O.K. Corral mode, with each party trying to work the cycle of publicity and spin to his or her advantage. If you'd like to see the O.K. Corral in action as black comedy, just rent the movie *The War of the Roses*.

Emotional dishonesty is, by definition, built into this style of quitting since the person quitting doesn't have to take any responsibility for the actions or behaviors that preceded the moment of quitting, or for the quit itself. It's all whitewashed in the name of the higher value that "forced" the quit. As a result, the O.K. Corral approach isn't likely to yield real personal growth or much happiness and is unlikely to open up new opportunities. Cleaning up after the shoot-out is real work.

The Faux Quit

The *faux quit* isn't a single quitting style but has many variations on a similar theme. But all versions of the faux quit, while appearing to move the person toward the exit, actually keep him or her in place. The person may actually go through various motions that suggest disengagement, such as temporarily severing a relationship, setting new boundaries, or suggesting different courses of action, but he or she will ultimately retreat from them. There's plenty of room to spare for this brand of quitting in the areas of long-term goals, career, and relationships. The faux quit sustains, rather than ends, conflict.

Stressed familial relationships—between mothers and daughters, fathers and sons, siblings—sometimes develop a cyclical pattern of faux quitting, which effectively keeps either an emotional resolution or even a détente out of reach. Conflicting desires— being dissatisfied with a partner but being unwilling to be alone, hating the work but liking the pay, and other similar contradictory or conflicting emotions—can turn the faux quit into an incomplete quit that leaves the person feeling utterly stymied or seemingly paralyzed. For all that she or he may be completely articulate about the need and desire to quit, the person nonetheless remains unable to do it. Faux quitting often becomes a holding pattern, leaving the person suspended, unable either to commit to a course of action fully or to give it up in the absence of therapy. And sometimes, not even therapy can resolve the conflict.

The faux or incomplete quit also describes what happens when a person leaves a situation or a relationship or abandons a long-term life goal but continues to think and ruminate about it as much as he or she did before. Think of the divorcée who spends hours talking about her ex-husband on dates with other men, the person who's been fired and bad-mouths his former employers in every interview, or the person who gives up a pursuit but remains so emotionally entangled in it that he lacks the energy to move forward. Long and heavily litigated divorce cases are often the result of one or even two incomplete quits; despite appearing to be finalizing their split, the parties are nonetheless fully engaged, each looking to "win." By definition, the faux quit keeps you engaged.

The Threatening Quit

The *threatening quit* could be called the "If you don't do this, then I'll quit" stance. What "this" stands for in that sentence is entirely up to you. The threatening quit isn't a real quit at all; it's a manipulation by way of a threat to quit. Often, the person who is doing the threatening really has no intention of ending whatever interaction is involved. This style of quitting is familiar to managers in the workplace, where it's sometimes used as a ploy to get a raise or promotion. Threatening to quit does sometimes work in the short term, but it's never a good long-term strategy; eventually, someone will take the person up on the threat. In personal relationships, threatening to quit is often part of a pattern of passive-aggressive behavior, with one person palliating the other, temporarily at least. The threatening quit is usually about power. Strictly speaking, this approach is a not-too-healthy way of engaging.

The Disappearing Act

While the *disappearing act* is an actual quit characterized by slinking, the person who's quitting or leaving offers no reason for his or her decision. Although the disappearing act is sometimes meant to devastate ("You're not even worth confronting!") or punish ("Wait until the team has to pick up the slack I've left them!"), most of the time the disappearing act simply betrays the disappearing person's lack of either courage or intention. This style tends to confirm every negative the culture holds about quitting generally. It also doesn't bode well for the person quitting, since the gesture is self-serving and does little to move him or her forward into new territory. The person may have disappeared but has plenty of baggage in tow.

With the advent of digital communications, the disappearing act has become the preferred method of relationship breakups for teenagers all over the country, so much so that there are seminars being given to middle school and high school students on why the text or Facebook breakup is unhealthy. Members of the perpetually connected and wired millennial generation, too, sometimes avail themselves of text and e-mail when disappearing from jobs or relationships since this electronic approach is an easy way of avoiding confrontation. This is not good news since the disappearing act tends to leave the quitter with reams of unfinished business.

The Big Bang

This is the "enough is enough" moment—that straw that famously broke the camel's back—and when it comes to work, love, and life, probably the most self-destructive quitting style of all since it's totally reactive, emotionally fueled, and devoid of planning or conscious thought. With or without the slamming of a door or other grandiose gestures, the big bang leaves the quitter with a mess to clean up and a future path littered with emotional and other debris, even if he or she is finally out of there. Some managers who are dissatisfied with an employee's performance but who shrink from actually firing people or are motivated by avoiding paying unemployment insurance will sometimes try to engineer a big bang reaction. A corporate power play by one executive may try to evoke a big bang response from another.

While the big bang *does* release you from whatever prison you've found yourself trapped in, it leaves you with no clear path ahead and no fallback position. Because the big-bang quit usually follows (and is often the result of) a long period of stress, frustration, and high emotion, this explosive style of quitting often leaves you vulnerable to a long period of second-guessing, rumination, and, sometimes, remorse. In most ways, it is the opposite of true goal disengagement and is a contender for the worst quitting style along with the O.K. Corral.

The Stealth Quit

We could also call the *stealth quit* the "liar, liar, pants on fire" style since this kind of quitting entails pretending not to quit and perhaps even pledging renewed effort while the person is actually heading for the door. Collaborative projects—from the shared social-studies report in middle school to business partnerships in the adult world—are often plagued by the stealth quit, which is usually driven by the quitter's unwillingness to own up to wanting out. The cultural onus on quitting is, in part, to blame for the stealth quit, but there are other motivators as well.

Why This Kind of Quitting Fails

None of these quitting styles is close to artful quitting or goal disengagement. At their best, they manage to sever the person from the pursuit of the goal on the surface at least, but leave in place all the mechanisms that keep humans persisting in one form or another. None provides any forward motion toward the creation of new goals and possibilities.

Most important, these styles of quitting fail to address or effectively counteract all the habits of mind (and brain) that keep us persisting at and engaging in goals, pursuits, and relationships long past their expiration date and wrestling with those intrusive thoughts we can't control. These quitting styles effectively leave us stuck in one way or another; they don't change our ways of looking at things. They do nothing to resolve conflicts of interest. Nor do they help us manage the emotions that may flood us when we give up on something we genuinely thought would make us happy. They don't stop us from ruminating about how things might have gone differently, or second-guessing ourselves. They don't open a pathway to motivating ourselves to set new goals and to cut bait on old goals that can get in the way of new ones. They don't help us recalibrate and start over.

True goal disengagement does all of that, and more.

Stumbling Blocks

Even when we do quit an endeavor, the first question people will ask is whether we've tried to make it work. For example, when a person mentions an impending divorce (something roughly half of us will face), friends and strangers alike will ask if the couple has gone to counseling. The culturally acceptable answer is yes, which attests to our efforts to persist despite the union's ultimate failure and takes a bit of the onus off. Answer it in the negative, though, and see what people think and say. Many of us are so conditioned to feel ashamed if we show any lack of persistence or—heaven forbid—actually decide to quit, that we're likely to feel as though we have to explain ourselves. Unfortunately, we may find ourselves inadvertently sabotaging our effort to move forward in life.

That was certainly the case for Tim, a man close to thirty who was a graduate of an Ivy League college and law school. He had going for him all the things that successful people need in a corporate culture—a great education, charm, intelligence, and, from college sports, a reputation for being a team player. But after four years on a partnership track, he realized that while he loved certain aspects of his work—traveling and talking to clients who were forging new businesses—he most definitely didn't like the nuts and bolts of drafting the contracts that were, in fact, his main job description. He found himself wishing he were on the other side of the desk, creating new business, on the one hand, while he worried that his bosses might ferret out his dissatisfaction, on the other. He sought a therapist's counsel, and at the counselor's suggestion, Tim started going on informational interviews, learning what he could about where to head next. He had plenty of good contacts—a wide circle of friends, acquaintances, and friends of friends—and it all seemed promising.

Oddly enough, these informational interviews—which usually evolve into other meet and greets and then actual interviews and offers of employment—were pretty much dead ends. People just weren't referring him onto the next level. Why was that? It turned out that during these conversations, Tim always worked in a comment or two about how it had been an enormous mistake going to law school and then wasting another four years and how he had screwed up his career path. In other words, he was both apologizing for and presenting himself as a quitter, instead of promoting himself as a potential resource for a company, given his background. Tim wasn't doing this consciously, of course; he was, without realizing it, expressing his own doubts about quitting.

Once Tim became aware of what he was doing and stopped thinking of himself as a quitter, he began to get referrals and then interviews until he was finally able to redirect his career in the way he wanted. Tim's behavior is hardly unique: Cultural pressures may be invisible, but they are powerful and omnipresent nonetheless.

A Bit of Clarification

Although we all use the word *goal*, a more specific discussion of the term is in order. What are goals anyway, and why are they important? Since goals direct our actions, human beings, by definition, are goal oriented. At the beginning, the original human goals—which we all continue to share—were simpler than the ones that crowd our minds in the twenty-first century. The human to-do list was once short but essential and focused on staying alive; finding food, water, and shelter; having sex; and belonging to a group. Now, at any given moment, each of us has an array of goals to which we devote varying degrees of attention. Some of them are so simple that we perform them without even consciously thinking about them. (If the goal is to drive to work, we have a series of interim goals— getting out of bed, showering, getting dressed, grabbing some coffee or breakfast, gathering the things we need for the day, locking the door, starting the car—that help propel us forward to achieving this goal.)

A goal may be intrinsic or extrinsic. An *intrinsic goal* emanates from within the individual—sparked by the mental image we have or want to have of ourselves as well as our own immediate desires. As Richard M. Ryan and Edward L. Deci write, "The most basic distinction is between *intrinsic motivation*, which refers to doing something because it is inherently interesting or enjoyable, and *extrinsic motivation*, which refers to doing something because it leads to a separable outcome." Not surprisingly, intrinsically motivated goals garner the lion's share of creativity and effort.

These intrinsic goals can be abstract personal strivings and pertain to the development of the self (goals such as becoming more empathetic, standing up for oneself, making new friends, becoming more cultured, and achieving inner peace) or concrete (e.g., the goal of acting in such a way as to be perceived as intelligent or as a good worker). Extrinsic goals, on the other hand, have their origin in the outside world. They may be things someone else wants us to do (be a conscientious student, become a lawyer like Dad, be a better spouse) or may emanate from other nonsocial cues in the environment. As Ryan and Deci note, "Extrinsic motivation has typically been characterized as a pale and impoverished (even if powerful) form of motivation that contrasts with intrinsic motivation." In later chapters, when we focus on mapping goals, answering the question of whether a goal is intrinsic or extrinsic to you will be key to your understanding of whether you need to quit and, more important, where you want to head next.

Some goals are short term and decidedly concrete (pick up dry cleaning, buy cat litter, drive kids to school, send Uncle Dave a birthday card, pay bills). Others are mid-term goals, sometimes combining concrete and abstract goals (get more exercise to stay healthier, save money to move to a better school district, work on controlling temper so family dinners go more smoothly). Still others are long-term achievement goals (go to law school and become a partner in a firm, make lots of money, buy a boat and sail to Fiji, find the right mate for the rest of one's life). Psychological theory has classified achievement goals by dividing them into three useful categories: Mastery goals are focused on the development of a skill or an area of competence or expertise. Performance-approach goals focus on attaining competence or expertise relative to other people. Performance-avoidance goals avoid incompetence in comparison with others.

Each of us, over the course of life, will have a mix of both performance-approach and performance-avoidance goals. We choose some goals because of the promise they hold—some desired state or outcome. These are called approach goals because we initiate actions to effect or get closer to that desired outcome. The formula here is "If I do X, then Y will happen," with X and Y being, respectively, whatever action and whatever result you wish. Approach goals can be either concrete ("If I smile at her and engage her interest, she'll go out with me") or abstract ("If I learn another language, people will think I am more cultured"). Similarly, we choose avoidance goals to dodge an unwanted outcome. The formula here is "If I don't do X, then Y won't happen." It's why some people never smoke and others stop, for example. Both approach and avoidance goals play an important role in human life, not to mention the lives of lower species, including the dog or cat that may be sitting at your feet as you read, or the gazelle that decides to stay thirsty when it sees the lion at the watering hole. As John A. Bargh and his colleagues' work has shown, for the most part, human beings automatically and often without consciousness classify and evaluate whatever comes into view on a positive or negative dimension; it's built into the survival of our own species and that of other species.

Andrew J. Elliot and Todd M. Thrash have suggested that approach and avoidance could equally be used to describe a person's temperament. Doing so yields a different and perhaps more effective model of personality when it comes to goals than the "big five" characteristics used in psychology. Elliot and Thrash argue that people with approach temperaments have a sensitivity to positive and desirable goals, show emotional and behavioral receptivity to these positive goals, and are inclined to pursue them. People with avoidance temperaments, on the other hand, are inclined to respond to the negatives inherent in any situation, choose goals on the basis of avoidance, and focus on the negative cues in their environments.

Approach and avoidance temperaments aren't synonyms for looking at the glass as half full or half empty—an optimistic or pessimistic point of view—but a much broader life approach that operates across affective, cognitive, and behavioral responses to situations, events, and even people and relationships in the world. In fact, the orientation—either approach or avoidance—is so fixed that it actually crosses over from one domain to another, as can be seen in a series of experiments Elliot and his colleagues conducted and are consistent across the life span.

Imagine two people, each of whom has the goal of forging a friendship. One of them is motivated by approach, drawn to the goal of making a friend because of the satisfying social connection, the shared intimacy, the way friends help open up a person's social and emotional understanding. The other person is motivated by avoidance; he or she seeks friendship to avoid the social isolation of being alone, not wanting to feel unpopular, rejected, or out of sync in a world where people have friends. If these two people were to try to forge a friendship with each other, what would follow is a reasonably predictable script of misunderstandings and disappointments. Even though the goal (making friends) is ostensibly the same, the "why" behind the goal is startlingly different. Shift this example to a more intimate relationship—boyfriend and girlfriend, lovers, or husband and wife—and the importance of the motivation becomes all the more apparent.

The distinction between these two motivations and what happens to the people with one orientation or the other is enormous. As Elliot notes, "avoidance motivation is limited in a structural sense, in that by its very nature it can only lead to the absence of a negative outcome (when effective) or the presence of a negative outcome (when ineffective)." More tellingly (and perhaps depressingly), "thus, avoidance motivation is designed to facilitate surviving, while approach motivation is designed to facilitate thriving."

Switching into "survival mode," even when there's no danger—thinking the lion might be at the watering hole can leave you dying of thirst—not only can mean lost opportunities for growth and development but may even propel a person or an animal closer to the very thing he or she seeks to avoid.

What makes some people approach-oriented and others governed by avoidance? The answer, friends, is childhood—yes, back to the nursery—and upbringing, especially attachment to parents or caregivers. We'll return to this subject in the next chapter.

Conflicting Goals

Given the complexity of human nature and desires, all goals are, unfortunately, not created equal; nor are they always compatible with each other. For women and men alike, the ongoing cultural dialogue about having it all is, of course, about conflicting goals—balancing the need or desire to work with the goal of being an attentive and available parent, fulfilling one satisfying aspect of life without sacrificing another, being in close relationships without losing sight of ourselves and our own needs. Understanding the harmful effects of conflicting goals—such as emotional distress, the loss of general well-being, and a negative impact on health—is another reason that being able to consider real goal disengagement is an important life skill.

Psychologists Robert Emmons and Laura King conducted a series of experiments to examine the effect of conflicting personal goals. Participants were asked to compile a list of fifteen goals, which could be motivated by either approach or avoidance. (Examples of avoidance goals given by the participants, who were college students, included avoiding dependence on a boyfriend and avoiding spreading malicious gossip.) Lists in hand, they were then asked to answer which goals were in conflict and, then, whether succeeding in one goal "had a helpful, harmful, or no effect on another striving." Finally, the participants were asked about ambivalence—whether succeeding at one goal over another would make them unhappy. Emmons and King followed up with this group a year later.

Not surprisingly, the results revealed that people were most ambivalent about goals that were in conflict with other goals. Both conflict and ambivalence were associated with loss of psychological well-being and health problems.

In a second experiment, after they filled out the goal lists and noted conflicts and ambivalences, the participants filled out mood reports twice a day for twenty-one days. They listed both positive (happy, joyful, pleased) and negative (unhappy, angry, anxious) emotions. These were then correlated with self-reports on health as well as health records from the prior and current years. A third experiment had the original participants from the first study report on their thoughts and actions, prompted by beepers that went off at random intervals.

What Emmons and King found reflects on both the cost of conflicting goals and the value of goal disengagement. First, they found that when there's conflict between personal goals, people ruminate more, but do less, about the goals—another variation on the "stuck" theme: "Conflict appeared to have an immobilizing effect on action and was associated with lowered well-being." As the researchers explained, besides leaving people stuck, conflict between goals also hurt people's psychological and physical health.

It turns out that conflict between goals without disengagement can literally make you sick, not to mention profoundly unhappy. The story of Linda and George demonstrates what conflicting goals look like in real life.

Linda, age sixty-two, and George, sixty-five, have been married for eighteen years, and while their living arrangement is unconventional—she lives in San Diego and he's in San Francisco, so they've always commuted—it's hardly unique. They own a place in Colorado together. It was a second marriage for each of them, and when it started, both still had children under the age of majority where they lived. The children are now grown, but Linda's and George's work and habits still keep each partner in his or her own home base. They live parallel lives that connect for weekends, long vacations, phone calls, and e-mails. Their plan, though, is to live together when they both retire.

Although their life together is free of the daily stresses that most couples living together are familiar with, it's hardly stress-free. While George spends freely, Linda is much more focused on saving and the future. Over the years, their different attitudes toward money have sparked enormous arguments. Linda initiates these confrontations, usually after she has discovered a financial matter that George decided on his own. (He has sold off furniture and other valuables, used money earmarked for retirement for other purposes, and overspent on his hobbies and other interests). In the past, Linda has been momentarily energized to find a solution, but she gets tired of fighting with him and life goes on, which leaves the conflict between them unresolved. But as retirement nears, these tensions have become more constant, particularly once Linda discovered the enormous amount of credit card debt—over six figures' worth—George had accumulated. He is strapped for cash because of the high cost of interest on this debt.

Linda has tried a number of approaches—going to a counselor, among them—but George remains resistant to her suggestions. Since he has earned this money, he wants to be free to spend it as he sees fit. He gets angry if Linda suggests that they have mutual oversight on spending. She is frightened for the financial future, is worried about retirement, and suffers a great deal of emotional distress. But her striving for financial security isn't her only goal; emotional connection and being part of a family are important to her as well. She is also afraid of spending the rest of her life without a partner. So, when she considers leaving George, those other goals pop into play and she remains effectively stuck—still made actively unhappy by her fears and his actions, but unable to do anything about it.

Conflicting goals leave people stuck without the hope of resolution unless disengagement is a possibility. The particulars of Linda's conflicting goals can be switched with others—work satisfaction versus monetary reward, family stability versus having your emotional needs met by a true partner—but it all comes down to the same thing.

Without the ability to disengage, people will continue to live in conflict, unhappily and unhealthily. Luckily, true goal disengagement is a skill that can be cultivated and learned.

CHAPTER THREE

Quitting As an Art

By now, you've realized that while the culture says that quitting is the easy way out, genuine disengagement isn't. Goal disengagement takes place on what might be thought of as four levels simultaneously: cognitive, affective, motivational, and behavioral. In plain language, those are the levels of thought, feeling, motivation, and action. As we describe and explain these levels, it will become clear that modifying motivation and behavior are wholly dependent on achieving cognitive and affective disengagement.

For disengagement to work, it must subvert many of the automatic and habitual processes of the mind that keep us persisting no matter what, along with battling cultural pressure. Letting go on every level, it would seem, isn't as easy it looks.

Cognitive Disengagement

The part of disengagement that requires us to clear the mind (the working memory, to be more precise) of intrusive thoughts is called cognitive disengagement. Here the white-bear problem, the automatic process mentioned in Chapter 1, comes into play, along with other forms of rumination that effectively keep our thoughts going round on the carousel instead of in a new direction. To let go on a cognitive level, we need to manage those intrusive, white-bear thoughts. These thoughts might be a preoccupation with how we might have succeeded if we'd only persisted or various other second guesses or variations on the theme. Have you ever had a filling fall out or a loose tooth? You know how your tongue, no matter how you try to stop yourself, keeps going back to the tooth, feeling the rough edges? White-bear thoughts are just like that, and they happen automatically. Daniel Wegner explains that since the mind searches for whatever thought, action, or emotion the person is trying to control, the "ironic monitoring" process can actually create the mental contents for which it is searching. That's why the unwanted thought rebounds into the mind.

Wegner and his colleagues conducted numerous experiments to see what, if anything, could stop those thoughts of white bears from coming back. Their findings are pertinent to the strategies for cognitive disengagement we'll be suggesting, and they underscore (even though it hardly needs more emphasis) why those intrusive thoughts are so damn hard to get rid of. The researchers tested whether focusing on a *distractor*—another thought brought to mind—would end the return of the intrusive white bear. Some participants who were asked to suppress the thought of a white bear were told to focus on a red Volkswagen whenever the white bear came to mind. While thinking about the red VW didn't help suppress their white-bear thoughts, it did stop them from becoming preoccupied with the white bear later. The focused distraction—honing in on a red VW—instead of a focus on random things stopped the white bear from getting linked to the VW. The focused distractor stopped the rebound effect that researchers had noted before.

What's the lesson here? Wegner explains: "If we wish to suppress a thought, it's necessary to become absorbed in another thought. The distractor we seek should be intrinsically interesting and engaging to us, and even if it is unpleasant, it should not be boring or confusing." As we'll see in the next chapter, being able to focus not just on a distractor but also on a new goal or aspiration—that is, beginning to reengage in a new goal as you disengage from another—is key to the whole process.

Alas, the white bear isn't the only immediate problem. It turns out that any energy you invest in ridding yourself of those distracting thoughts will actually lessen the amount of energy you have to spend on other tasks. *Ego depletion* is the term Roy Baumeister coined for this phenomenon, but it might just as easily be called *willpower*, as he does in his popular book of the same name. Whether you call it *ego*, *self*, or *willpower*, it is not an infinite resource. When we humans seek to regulate an impulse or a thought, we do so at the cost of reducing our ability to control other impulses, thoughts, or actions. Ego or self is more like a limited source of energy—brain energy, as it happens—than not. While it has become fashionable for the media to insist that human beings are good multitaskers, Baumeister's work and that of others suggests the very opposite.

The experiment conducted by Baumeister and his colleagues was simple in its design. Researchers asked participants to fast before they showed up, and then ushered them into a room that smelled of freshly baked chocolate chip cookies. There were bowls of cookies and radishes on the table. Some students were told they could eat the cookies, others were told they couldn't eat the cookies but had to eat at least three radishes, and the rest were told they could eat nothing. Then the students were instructed to solve a puzzle that, unbeknownst to them, was in fact insoluble. The folks who had to both resist the cookies and eat the radishes gave up on the puzzle first—in fact, much more quickly than the students who'd eaten the cookies and those who'd eaten nothing. The students who had to do double duty resisting something yummy and eating something unpleasant also reported being more tired. Baumeister concluded that the energy used to control one impulse leaves less energy to regulate other choices and actions.

Baumeister and his colleagues ran additional experiments, all of which confirmed a pattern of ego depletion that resulted from not just exercising self-control (not eating cookies or eating radishes) but making choices. Participants in one experiment were divided into three groups, one of which was required to read a speech advocating a rise in tuition at the university. Given that the participants were students, it's fair to assume that no one was for a tuition hike. The second group (called the "high choice") was handed folders that contained speeches either for tuition raises or against; they were told it would be appreciated if they would read the pro-hike speech but that the choice was entirely up to them. The third control group didn't have to read any speech. The participants were then given the same puzzle—the one that couldn't be solved—as the one given in the resisting-temptation experiment. Although the participants who'd been given no choice (having to read a speech they most certainly disagreed with) and those with no speech to read persisted in trying to solve the puzzle, those who had to choose between speeches gave up on the puzzle much faster. This led Baumeister and colleagues to conclude that "acts of choice draw on the same limited resource used for self-control."

Other experiments showed that suppressing emotion resulted in ego depletion too—something else to keep in mind when you consider the effort artful quitting entails. The following experiment has implications not just for letting go on the cognitive level but also for the management of emotions—an undertaking that is an important part of artful quitting as well. Baumeister and coworkers had half of the participants watch a video and told them to suppress their emotions; the participants were also told that their expressions would be videotaped as they watched. Those in the control group were also told that they would be videotaped but were instructed to "let their emotions flow." Half in both groups watched a Robin Williams riff, while the remainder watched the tearjerker scene in which the daughter is dying of cancer in *Terms of Endearment*. After a ten-minute break, all of the participants were asked how hard it had been to comply with the instructions and then were given thirteen anagrams to unscramble. Not only did the group that tried to suppress emotion report that it had been hard to do so, but this group also fared significantly worse on the anagram test.

Ego depletion isn't just a theoretical concept, as shown by a recent study of the brains of participants who had engaged in acts of self-control. We'll turn to this study in greater detail later, but for now, we note some findings by Dylan D. Wagner and Todd F. Heatherton at Dartmouth. The researchers found that the MRIs of the brains of participants who had tried to self-regulate showed increased activity in the amygdala, the part of the brain—along with the prefrontal cortex—responsible for managing emotion.

The brain's wiring for persistence also gets in the way of cognitive disengagement on a completely unconscious level. It's what's called the *Zeigarnik effect*. Bluma Zeigarnik's experiment, conducted in 1927, was the first to demonstrate how the brain deals with unfinished business—specifically a goal that was consciously selected and then unselected—but its results have been replicated many times since. The experimenters told people to work on jigsaw puzzles and to keep at it until they finished. But some of the participants weren't permitted to finish, and even though they were put to work at other tasks—to distract them from the initial goal and to substitute another in its place—when these participants were tested, they had thought about the unfinished task with twice as much frequency as the other tasks, even though they were told not to think about it. The Zeigarnik effect explains why so many people get stuck in a loop when they quit a goal or situation; it's as though the unconscious is nudging them to go back and finish what they started.

Again, this doesn't mean that letting go of intrusive thoughts is impossible; it simply underscores that the habits of the mind need to be dealt with systematically. While we'll explore how to manage intrusive thoughts in later chapters, the recent work of E. J. Masicampo and Roy Baumeister sheds new light on the Zeigarnik effect and how it can be moderated. Their first experiment tested whether intrusive thoughts could be eliminated. The researchers had one group write about two important tasks that needed to be completed in the next few days, along with an explanation of what would happen if they weren't completed. The participants also assigned a numerical value indicating the importance of the task, ranging from 1 to 7. The second group was given the same instructions as the first but was also told to come up with a plan to complete the two tasks. The third (control) group simply wrote about completed tasks. All of the participants were then given a section of a popular novel to read and were tested on it.

Masicampo and Baumeister found that participants who made plans weren't distracted by intrusive thoughts; in fact, they reported no more intrusive thoughts than the participants in the control group who had only reflected on completed tasks. More important, those with a plan performed better on the reading tests, showing greater focus and less distraction than those who had detailed incomplete tasks alone. The key is that no plans were actually implemented, nor did the participants actually move any closer to completing the tasks. Apparently, just making a plan, without making real progress, is enough to reduce the Zeigarnik effect.

Further studies explored how accessible the goal remained to the unconscious; again, planning reduced the number of intrusive thoughts. Another experiment showed that when people made plans to complete the goal that they were actually going to implement, they had fewer intrusive thoughts even when they were working on an unrelated task. But while planning helped manage unwanted, intrusive thoughts, two other experiments found that planning did little to alleviate the emotional stress and anxiety associated with unfulfilled goals.

Importantly, while making plans to fulfill goals—even ones that were meant to be implemented—did help tamp intrusive thoughts, the action did nothing to change the emotional content. Planning does, however, begin the motivational and behavioral process.

It turns out that when it comes to managing emotions, human beings are drawing on the same limited resources as those they use for managing self-control and thought.

Affective Disengagement

Affective disengagement, one aspect of artful quitting, involves the management and regulation of the unwanted emotions that are a common consequence of abandoning or quitting a goal. We've already seen how, in Tim's case, his own negative feelings about quitting colored how he talked about his experience and how he presented himself to potential employers. Feelings of frustration, a sense of inadequacy, and even depression accompany the act of quitting so regularly that it's been suggested that being depressed is actually not just a component of goal disengagement but a normal one.

In his seminal 1975 article, Eric Klinger argued that a coherent and predictable cycle of emotions accompanies giving up a goal, just as the striving for a goal produces its own cycle. He identified four consequences of goal setting, explaining that the consequences affect "actions, the contents of thoughts and dreams, sensitization to goal-related cues, and perceptual qualities (or at least memories and interpretations of those qualities) of goal-related stimuli." He asserted that there was equally a coherent cycle of disengagement, instead of random or highly individualized responses to letting go of a goal. The disengagement cycle goes as follows: a reinvigoration of efforts (renewed activity accompanied by disbelief that the goal is unattainable); aggression (protesting the loss of the goal or assigning blame for its loss); and then depression followed by recovery and acting on new goals. These aren't completely discrete stages; nor do they necessarily follow this precise sequence. But they are coherent. He also pointed out that these cycles of disengagement could vary greatly in duration and intensity, ranging from minor disappointments that you can quickly recover from ("Because my 5 PM meeting ran late, I will miss Billy's soccer game") to those that can last for months ("The love of my life has left me and I am bereft" or "I've lost my job and I'm worried about my future"). Klinger wrote that "in most cases depression is a normal, adaptive, nonpathological [sic] process which, despite its being a nuisance, need cause little concern for the psychological viability of the depressed individual." He went even further to say that depression could be seen "as an important kind of information from which one can deduce new plans for self-fulfillment."

Our point here isn't to marginalize or understate the debilitating effect of clinical depression; it's to point out that sadness is, in fact, a normal response to letting go of a goal, and that the "put on a happy face" stance—showing that quitting was the best thing that ever happened to you—is both unhealthy and counterproductive. Artful and conscious quitting requires that we permit ourselves to feel the loss of a goal—hence Klinger's identification of depression as a necessary component—and then work to regulate those feelings, rather than suppress them.

The bigger point is that suppressing our emotions doesn't work. We've already seen how exercising self-control in one area, including suppressing emotion, lessened the ability to perform in another. This brings us back to the recent findings of what happens to the brain when we do. Dylan D. Wagner and Todd F. Heatherton tested the limited-resource model of self-regulation by having participants undergo functional neuroimaging while emotionally valenced movies (positive, negative, and neutral) which were then followed by a difficult attention-control task (ignoring distractor words that were flashed on the screen while watching a movie). Half of the participants were told they had to ignore the words; the other half could read them. Then all the participants watched another series of emotional scenes. The researchers found that ego depletion increased reactions in the amygdala, especially in response to negative emotions. But others have argued that further research and neuroimaging may show that it's not just negative emotion that is affected by depletion and causes the amygdala to light up.

That's precisely what a series of experiments conducted by Kathleen D. Vohs, Roy F. Baumeister, and others suggest. While previous studies found that efforts at self-regulation weakened the ability to exercise restraint, researchers assumed that emotions and feelings stayed the same. New work, however, challenges that thinking; as Vohs et al. write, "ego depletion may not change what you feel as much as how strongly you feel it." The statement is, of course, completely in sync with the neuroimaging results that showed increased activity in the amygdala after an exercise in self-control.

What this means is that impulses and restraint might, in fact, be "causally intertwined." It may be that when restraint is weakened through depletion, emotions and desires are felt more strongly. Ironically then, trying to exert self-control—a strategy for managing and regulating emotions—may, in the moment, simply heighten them. In a later chapter, we'll turn to alternative strategies for regulating emotion.

Motivational Disengagement

This aspect of disengagement involves both cognitive and emotional regulation. *Motivational disengagement* might as well be called "getting back on the horse" or "putting your ducks in a row," as you are motivated to let go of one goal and begin thinking about pursuing another. This step requires that you actively reject goals that are either unattainable or don't serve your inner needs—that is, consciously rejecting extrinsic goals—and focusing on those that are attainable or tied to inner imperatives.

Behavioral Disengagement

Behavioral disengagement works in the sphere of real-world choices, in which the person acts to quit the old goal and exhibits new behaviors oriented toward the achievement of the new goal. Among other things, behavioral disengagement requires flexibility and renewed focus. Because life has a way of throwing some of us curveballs that have nothing to do with drive or talent, sometimes even the most intrinsically motivated and satisfying goals must be given up for reasons that are beyond the individual's control. At moments like these, knowing how to quit artfully is a valuable skill.

That was certainly the case for Deidre, now twenty-eight, whose journey might have been different and a bit easier had she not been so persistent. She began swimming competitively at the age of seven, and the sport defined her childhood and early adolescence both literally and metaphorically. Other than going to school,

swimming is what she did—she had to give up practically everything else in its pursuit—and it defined who she was. She loved
how she felt when she swam. Even now, all these years later, she is
wistful, recalling "an incomparable feeling of exhaustion, of exhilaration, of feeling alive" in the pool. She dreamed of going to college
on scholarship and then on to the Olympics, but unlike so many
young people's dreams, hers were based in the possible.

Then, the summer before high school, she developed shoul-
der pain while she was training for the nationals. The diagnosis
was chronic tendonitis in both of her shoulders, and the doctors
recommended that she quit swimming at least temporarily, if not
permanently. Her coach, though, wanted her to swim through the
pain and so she did; it was the triumph of "quitters never win and
winners never quit" and "when the going gets tough, the tough get
going" over medical advice. Her condition worsened. She switched
teams and, this time, her new coach encouraged her to take time
off, which she did. Her physical symptoms were plain to see—she
couldn't raise her hand in class, brushing her hair was torture, and
she could barely manage getting dressed—but the invisible psychological pain of trying to let go was much harder.

Who was she if she weren't swimming? "If I weren't a swimmer," she explains, "I didn't know who I was. My self-esteem, my
sense of myself, my self-worth were all wrapped up in it and so
much more." So she went back to swimming after three months,
and as she says, "I suffered along for a while. I couldn't make it past
five hundred yards, which is nothing more than a short warm-up,
without it causing a flare-up. I wasn't able to do the things I loved
about swimming—that amazing feeling of a good workout, flying
through the water, pushing myself to go faster."

Deidre quit. She felt devastated, empty, and literally at a loss
about what to do with herself. She worked hard at shifting her focus
and identity—getting involved in acting and theater and other
activities—and although she wasn't happy, she was beginning to be
okay with not swimming. She was young, after all.

But the sirens of the water were still calling, and she hadn't stopped being receptive. That's precisely what happens when a satisfying and self-fulfilling goal slips from your grasp. She spent her junior year of high school abroad and, acting on a friend's encouragement, joined the swim team. She was, predictably enough, so much faster than anyone else that she won all the meets, even in her worst strokes. But the pain was back. She quit again, this time not just because of the pain but because that "good burning feeling" she'd once had wasn't there. Winning alone wasn't enough.

But she still wasn't done with swimming. Not surprisingly, the swim coach of the small liberal-arts college she attended was eager to have her and cut her slack about practices. She was fast enough that even without practices, she broke records and placed well in her school's conference. "It felt good to be appreciated so much," she says. By junior year, though, the game was up; the inflammation got worse and she finally stopped swimming, though she stayed with the team as captain. After college, she still wasn't ready and worked at a local pool, teaching swimming and coaching the team. But finally, she had to quit that, too, because the small amount of swimming required to teach irritated her shoulders. Six years after her problems began, she finally quit for good.

The physical damage is still with her. "I have pain if I sleep on my arm," she says. "And I can feel it when the weather changes, like an old war vet. I have a nearly constant reminder that it is okay to let go and say, enough is enough—that quitting is good sometimes and persevering can be damaging. I'm not naturally inclined to quit things, and I obviously needed a big wake-up before I got it. It's a lesson I carry with me."

Deidre's reflections on her struggle to quit an important and self-defining goal that gave her pleasure offer an insight into why letting go can be both so difficult and valuable. She acknowledges both the internal and the external pressure to continue competing: "Swimming in college was probably a bad call for me physically, even though I loved being on the team. Yes, I was pressured by friends and my coach, but in the end, I was easy to persuade. Swimming is a competitive sport (against the clock and your opponents) with a lot of pressure to always push yourself hard. I did worry that people would think I was wussing out. In the end, it was me who had the hardest time with my quitting."

Wisely, she points out there is a "before" and an "after" connected to quitting: "Letting go of something that was so much a part of my life and my identity was in itself formative. But overall, quitting made me a more interesting and varied person than I might have been if I had continued swimming. I had so many experiences I wouldn't have had if I hadn't quit."

Deidre has put what she has learned to good use as a therapist working with victims of domestic abuse, most of whom have trouble leaving their situations. "I can see what they're dealing with through the lens of my experience," she says. "In a way, I'm able to use the personal lessons I learned. I truly understand how difficult it is to leave, even when you hurt. I can identify with how hard it is."

Giving up something that has made you happy in the past is never easy. And happiness, after all, is the biggest goal all of us share.

The Pursuit of Happiness

If you were around for the Clinton-Gore presidential campaign, you doubtless remember the song that contains the line "Don't stop thinking about tomorrow." Well, it turns out that no one needs to have worried, since human beings *can't* stop thinking about tomorrow or the future. In his book *Stumbling on Happiness*, psychologist Daniel Gilbert notes that approximately 12 percent of our daily thoughts are about the future: "In other words, every eight hours of thinking include an hour about things that are yet to happen."

Why do we spend so much time thinking about the future? First and foremost, it's pleasurable, as Gilbert points out. We can imagine that tomorrow will be very different from today and that it will fulfill our hearts' desires in ways that today doesn't. But—yes, there is a *but*—human beings aren't very good at assessing either the likelihood that the dream will come true or, more important, whether, if it did, the dream would actually make them happier.

Just for fun, before you continue reading, finish the following sentence, either in your imagination or on a piece of paper: "I would be happier if ___." Then imagine a goal or a plan that would make that moment happen. It could include buying a winning lottery ticket, getting a promotion, becoming a writer or a stock trader, finding the right mate, or anything else that would float your boat into sunny climes. There are, obviously, as many answers to that question as there are shells on Florida's Sanibel Island. Are you sure about your answer, that whatever you filled the blank with would truly deliver bliss? After you've nodded but before you pat yourself on the back and reassure yourself that you will be the exception to the rule, that you're not likely to overstate your chances of achieving happiness, and that you actually do know what will make you happy, continue reading.

Remember the above-average effect? How everyone thinks he or she is above average and therefore more likely to succeed at achieving a goal than other people? There are a number of corollaries to that effect. One of them is described by Daniel Gilbert: "Americans of all ages expect their futures to be an improvement on their presents." In addition, as Emily Pronin, Daniel Lin, and Lee Ross note in their article "The Bias Blind Spot," when people reflect on themselves and their views of the world, they tend to think that they are more objective and see things more realistically than other people do. We apparently have a blind spot when it comes to our own biases in thinking, but we are generous when we attribute those biases to others.

The above-average effect isn't, as it might seem, a gloss on American narcissism. But perhaps, as Gilbert suggests, it reflects our tendency (or even our need) to think of ourselves as more unlike other people than we actually are. As he puts it, "we don't always see ourselves as *superior* but we almost always see ourselves as *unique*."

Part of this attitude is a function of the human condition, of course; we know our thoughts and emotions intimately, firsthand, and from the inside while we can only glean what others (even significant others) feel and think by their actions and words from the outside. Moreover, as Gilbert notes, we like thinking of ourselves as unique; because we value our uniqueness, we overestimate how unique we are. And by the same token, we ascribe that same degree of uniqueness to others. This appreciation of individual difference—as opposed to seeing others as more like us than not—begins very early in life because even kindergarteners exhibit it. Alas, all of this means that not only are we likely to have overwrought confidence in knowing how we'll react tomorrow, but we're also unlikely to learn from or use the experiences of others to gauge how we might feel, because, well, they're too "different" to be of any use.

There's another glitch as well. Curiously, even though we are always thinking about tomorrow, we—and our brains—are actually tethered to today. (The word *tethered* is a deliberate choice, since human beings aren't, by nature, either grounded or present in today, in the Buddhist sense.) That's the problem with predicting future happiness; other biases get in the way of what the experts call *affective forecasting*, that is, knowing what we'll feel like tomorrow or in the future.

Timothy Wilson and Daniel Gilbert delineate four aspects of predicting our happiness: the valence of our future feelings (whether they will be positive or negative); the specific emotions that we expect to experience; the intensity of those feelings; and how long those emotions will last. As soothsayers, we are better at some parts of predicting than others. In general, we are better at estimating whether a future event will make us feel great, good, lousy, or awful—so we're pretty much on target on the first aspect of valence. But when it comes to predicting the specific emotions we'll feel at some future event—it could be anything from moving into a new apartment to starting a new job, graduating from school, or getting married—people tend to oversimplify the emotions they'll feel, seemingly oblivious to the fact that most situations evoke a mix of emotions. (You can be very happy about your new job, thrilled by your upward mobility, and excited about the pay but worried about succeeding in it, fretting about the transition, and stressing about changing your routines.)

When we think about how happy a future event will make us—say, getting married or having a baby—our imaginings are oversimplified as well, especially when it comes to the details that will evoke emotion. You're imagining yourself, serene in your white dress, on the day you've dreamed about, with your guy waiting for you at the altar. What you're not anticipating is the groomsman's boorish toast, the way your about-to-be sister-in-law is making snide remarks about everything, and the like. You catch our drift?

The other problem is that people also tend to oversimplify and overestimate how they imagine themselves reacting to a future, hypothetical situation. Our projections of how we will act and what we will feel are often very different from what will actually transpire when and if the situation does arise. Our predictions are aided and abetted by the above-average effect. When we look into the future, we fully expect that our most admirable (and most above-average) self will show up, as a fascinating study on sexual harassment showed.

Researchers Julia Woodzicka and Marianne LaFrance first asked 197 women between the ages of eighteen and twenty-one how they would react if a male interviewer, age thirty-two, asked them the following questions during a job interview for a research assistant position: (1) Do you have a boyfriend? (2) Do people find you desirable? (3) Do you think it is important for women to wear bras to work? (Women readers might want to ask themselves how they would respond to the interviewer. Men might want to consider it as well.)

Not surprisingly, 62 percent of the women imagined taking the interviewer on—either confronting him about why he was asking or telling him the question was out of line. Of the respondents, 28 percent said they'd either walk out or confront the interviewer. And 68 percent asserted that they would refuse to answer at least one of the questions. Most of the women said they would be angry or enraged if they found themselves in this situation; only 2 percent thought they would be afraid.

The researchers then created a lab setting with an actual interview, with the participants believing they were really up for a research position. The three questions used in the theoretical experiment were used for half of the participants. The control group was asked strange and rather random questions, but ones that weren't harassing: (1) Do you have a best friend? (2) Do people find you morbid? (3) Do you think it important for people to believe in God?

The difference between how women imagined themselves reacting in a harassing scenario and how they actually reacted was remarkable. Every woman answered every question. Not one woman walked out. None of them confronted the interviewer—or even told him that "it was none of his business." In fact, 52 percent of the women ignored the harassing nature of the questions; they simply answered them without comment. Although 36 percent of the women did ask why the question or questions were being posed, 80 percent of those who asked only did so at the very end of the interview, not when the question was being asked. Most important, while the women imagining the situation said they'd be angry, only 16 percent of the women thrust into the situation were. But 40 percent of them did feel afraid.

This experiment underscores why it's relatively easy to predict how we will react emotionally to an uncomplicated event ("I got an A in chemistry" or "I flunked my English exam") but much more difficult when we are predicting a more complicated, more emotionally nuanced life situation. Presumably how students reacted was influenced by their desire for the research position (they thought it was real, after all), their need to please, perhaps their own temerity or insecurity, or any number of other things that—in the course of life—produce a very different emotional state from the one we've predicted for ourselves. Other studies confirm much the same thing.

The problem with tomorrow, after all, is that we haven't been there yet. This explains why the scenarios we have in our heads as we contemplate quitting or other stressful moments of decision may not play out the way we anticipate and may make us feel disappointed in ourselves. It also explains our general tendencies to second-guess ourselves.

According to Wilson and Gilbert, in addition to overestimating the impact of future events on their lives, people don't have a bead on how long their emotions will last. Taken together, this phenomenon is called the *impact bias*. Wilson and Gilbert argue that "people make sense of their worlds in a way that speeds recovery from emotional events and that this sense-making process is largely automatic and unconscious. Humans inexorably explain and understand events that were initially surprising and unpredictable and this process lowers the intensity of emotional reaction to the event." There's both good and bad news here. Let's consider the bad news first.

The bad news is that people overestimate how long a wished-for result or event will actually make them happy. The goal could be making partner or getting a promotion or numerous other events. The stress and anxiety you feel as you inch toward your goal make you absolutely sure that once you achieve the goal, you will be happy for a long, long time. But unfortunately, the extraordinary moment—the one you've dreamed of—becomes, in time, part of the ordinary scheme of things and thus rarely delivers the lasting cascade of happiness you were anticipating.

The good news, though, is that people also overestimate how long a dreaded event will make them unhappy. While the good stuff doesn't keep us happy for as long as we anticipate, the bad stuff won't keep us down for as long as we think, either. Most of you reading this page will remember a time in your life when you were recovering from one loss or another—it could be in any area of life. You may remember thinking, "I'll never get over this," or "I'll never be happy again." But you were happy again, weren't you? This is a function of what Wilson and Gilbert call "the psychological immune system," which works to ameliorate the impact of negative information, again on a largely unconscious basis. Our psychological defenses help us feel better by making sense of a negative event

and by restructuring our thoughts about it (put plainly, rationalizing it). The system defends us more completely if we're unaware
we're doing it.

Here's an example of how this works. It's similar to one that
Wilson and Gilbert use. Say you've been unceremoniously dumped
by a lover or spouse. At first, everything you remember about him
or her is lovable and excruciatingly painful. But then, other, much
more negative details and memories begin to fill in the empty space:
the way he always took slugs directly out of the juice container, or
the endless clutter of her makeup by the sink; his penchant for controlling a conversation, or her inability to be on time; or how he'd
suddenly fly off the handle for no apparent reason, or her habit of
constantly interrupting. You get the picture.

The genius of this kind of self-protection is that we're not consciously aware that we're doing it. The person who has spurned you
hasn't changed, of course; you've just adapted your mental image of
him or her. So too the awful humiliation of being fired by the boss
without warning is replaced by the recognition that the guy was a
jerk, the job was enormously boring, and the company dysfunc-
tional anyway.

What remains is the question of what possible evolutionary
advantage there is to having such an imprecise notion of what will
make us happy. (Gilbert's own book is called *Stumbling on Happiness* for a reason.)

About Positive Thinking

Paradoxically, while positive thinking and an optimistic outlook
has been shown to have many benefits—people who think positively tend to be motivated and perform better than those who
approach goal-related tasks with a negative point of view—some
forms of positive thinking actually work to a person's detriment.
Before you're tempted to toss your entire shelf of self-help books
out the window—along with all of those affirmations you've been

faithfully reciting all these years and your library of inspirational quotes—there's an important distinction to be made.

In an important series of experiments, psychologists Lauren B. Alloy and Lyn Y. Abramson showed that depressed students' view of the amount of control they had over an outcome was more accurate than that of their nondepressed counterparts, who were not just more optimistic but overestimated the amount of agency and control they had. Participants were asked to press (or to refrain from pressing) a button and then to observe whether a green light went on. They were then asked to estimate the amount of control—expressed as a percentage—they had over the light's going on. The truth was that the light was actually being manipulated by an experimenter. But that didn't stop some of the participants from inferring a sense of their own agency from the results.

Alloy and Abramson found that depressed students were more likely to gauge accurately how their actions affected the outcome; nondepressed participants, on the other hand, were more likely to overstate their own agency. These 1979 findings—and what has come to be called *depressive realism*—have been hotly debated in psychological circles ever since, as they are out of sync with the prevailing understanding of depressives as distorting reality since they view the world and events in it through a negative lens. Without taking sides in the debate, what's pertinent to our discussion is that, generally, healthy people tend toward overoptimism (sometimes referred to as *optimistic bias*) when it comes to goals and achievements. The takeaway lesson here is that while positive thinking is, in some instances, useful, it isn't *always* a trusty ally.

The Zen of Expectation

All over America, every day and every week, millions line up to buy a lottery ticket. Women and men, young and old, of every race and creed, well-off and struggling, buy tickets alone or in groups. The New York State Lottery's motto is "Hey, You Never Know," and it seems that many people agree with that statement (yes, it's the availability heuristic at work). So they play lucky or random numbers, birthdays, and secret combinations all in the hopes that "today will be my lucky day." The irony, of course, is that people who win the lottery are rarely happier than they were the day they bought the ticket. That's the problem with "tomorrow" again and the ability to forecast the future; people don't forecast the moochers who'll come out of the woodwork, the long-lost relatives or so-called friends begging for a piece, the advisors who will prey on their financial ignorance, the need to move or get an unlisted phone to live a normal, hassle-free life. Worse still, even when none of that awfulness happened, the winners' experience of ordinary pleasures was also diminished. As Timothy D. Wilson writes, after citing study after study that shows the sorry truth about most lottery winners, "if people knew that winning the lottery would not make them any happier and might even cause substantial misery, they might think twice before plunking down their hard-earned dollars for lottery tickets." (The people who do best with lottery winnings are those who had money, along with investment experience, to begin with and didn't need the lottery to make their dreams come true.)

So if winning the lottery is a pipe dream, what's the difference between a pipe dream and the expectation of a bright future? (The word *pipe dream* came into the American lexicon in the nineteenth century, when smoking opium and the resulting hallucinations were all the rage.) Are all daydreams created equal? Is there a distinction between a possibly inspiring daydream and pure fantasy?

It won't come as a huge surprise that this is a pertinent question both for setting goals and for deciding when and whether to quit them. The guy who dreams about fame and writing the Great American Novel but never writes a word is an easy one to label. But what about the twenty-nine-year-old, stay-at-home mother of three who hadn't written a word since college but who woke up from a dream filled with a cast of characters she couldn't get out of her head? Pipe dream?

Even she had her doubts: "Though I had a million things to do, I stayed in bed, thinking about the dream. Unwillingly, I eventually got up and did the immediate necessities and then put everything that I possibly could on the back burner and sat down at the computer to write—something I hadn't done in so long that I wondered why I was bothering." By her own account, she wasn't writing for any other audience but herself; she wanted to know how the story came out. But something else happened; she discovered writing made her happy: "Once I got started within that day, I was completely hooked on writing and this was something brand new to me." She then did a reality check on how she could make this work, along with taking care of her kids.

She finished the manuscript and sent out fifteen letters to literary agents. She was turned down by nine of them and didn't even hear from five. But she did hear back from one agent, who was enthusiastic. Was it a pipe dream or a possibility? Does the result determine which it is?

Not surprisingly, psychologists have tried to answer that question. Dreaming is, after all, a part of setting goals; if you can't imagine or dream it, you can't go after it. But what kind of expectations about tomorrow—remember that Dan Gilbert tells us that we spend one hour out of every eight thinking about tomorrow—ensure success? Psychologists Gabriele Oettingen and Doris Mayer distinguish between beliefs about the future (expectations) and images depicting future events (fantasies). Expectations rely on past performance to evaluate the future; fantasies, on the other hand, bear little relationship to past events and usually picture that rosy future as progressing smoothly and effortlessly. Moreover, a fantasy has you enjoying the fruits of the future in the here and now; you aren't thinking about the many hours of work it will take you to actually finish that novel or worrying that you might fail at the effort because there just aren't enough hours in the day or you simply don't have the talent. Instead, your thought process cuts right to seeing your name at the top of the best-seller list or, better still, walking the red carpet when your novel is made into the hit movie of the year.

Consistent with other findings about unadulterated positive thinking, just a smidge of pessimism mixed with a dash of realism is what's really needed to distinguish the kind of dreaming that is helpful from the kind that isn't. What Oettingen calls *mental contrasting* is essential not just to dreaming about achieving a goal but also to figuring out whether it is actually feasible. Mental contrasting involves envisioning the desired future and then reflecting on the possible negatives associated with attaining it and is distinguished from three other mental strategies that pertain to goal setting. Mental contrasting alone is a strategy aimed at solving problems. It permits you to evaluate the obstacles that stand in the way of achieving the goal, all the while keeping the goal in mind—almost as if you were watching a television with a split screen. The contrast permits you to plan and act to fix what stands in the way of achievement, while you remain highly motivated by the vision of the desired goal.

Other possible but ultimately ineffective strategies include what Oettingen calls *indulging*, which involves bringing up a mental image of that rosy future or desired end in great detail and returning to that mental image frequently to add detail or elaborate. Then there's *dwelling*, where the person stays fixed on the current situation, reflecting largely on its negatives. Even though dwelling is very different from indulging, neither motivates the person to act. Finally, there is what Oettingen calls *reverse contrasting*, where the person focuses first on the present reality and then on the desired future, without considering the two in relation to each other. Unlike mental contrasting, these other ways of imaging leave the person stuck, if for different reasons, unable to gear up, on the one hand, or to disengage, on the other.

One experiment by Oettingen and her colleagues asked participants to name their most important interpersonal problem. Among those mentioned were "getting to know someone I like," "improve my relationship with my partner," and "understand my mother better." The participants were asked to rank on a scale of one to seven their expectation of how successful they'd be at resolving the problem. They were then also asked to rate how important resolution was to them, again on a scale of one to seven. All the participants were then asked to list four positive outcomes they associated with a happy resolution and then to list four negative aspects of reality that stood in the way of the resolution. The participants were then divided into three groups, and the tasks they were given mirrored the mental contrasting, indulging, and dwelling conditions. Participants in the mental contrast group were asked to mentally elaborate on two positive and two negative aspects, the indulging group was asked to elaborate on four positives, and the dwelling group on four negatives. Of the groups, only the mental contrasting participants made plans and took responsibility for their actions when they had a high expectation of success; when their expectations were low, they took no actions.

These findings were confirmed by a second experiment that used the same interpersonal theme and procedure but went on to measure which of the groups would initiate action to achieve the goals. Participants were asked to rate how they felt (energetic, active, or empty) and then were told to come back in two weeks and report on which day they had initiated the two most difficult steps to implement. Again, the participants who used mental contrasting *and* had high expectations of success initiated action more quickly.

A later chapter will discuss mental contrasting in more detail, but it's important to acknowledge here that it's hard work. As the poet T. S. Eliot wrote, "Human kind can't bear very much reality," and that, alas, is true. Our fondness for pipe dreams—which can range from having six-pack abs to leapfrogging from manager to CEO in a flash to becoming rich and famous—doubtless is bolstered because a pipe dream doesn't require that we acknowledge very much, if any, reality. It's way easier just to picture how great you'd look with those abs without letting in thoughts about all the sit-ups you'd have to do, the foods you'd have to give up, the time you'd be spending at the gym, not to mention the real possibility of failure. While picturing those wished-for abs is happy-making, considering the realistic to-do list that accompanies the goal is something else entirely. People, to be blunt, prefer purely happy thoughts.

Which brings us back to the homemaker who woke up from a dream with an idea. The likelihood is that with three small kids in the house, she had to do some mental contrasting and figure out the obstacles that stood in the way of her sitting down at the computer, much less finishing her novel. And in case you were wondering, the woman's name was Stephenie Meyer and the book that came to her was titled *Twilight*.

Taking First Steps

By any estimation, Jamie, age twenty-nine, has done well. She has been writing for a small but well-regarded newspaper on the West Coast for over two years and has been a journalist since she graduated from a prestigious liberal arts college six years ago. Being a writer has been her intended goal since she was in middle school, but she didn't focus on journalism until after college, and then only at the suggestion of her college mentor. She took a job as a reporter, thinking it would serve as a kind of writing boot camp. "That had been my advisor's idea," Jamie says. "He thought that reporting would demystify writing, teach me to sit down day after day, develop discipline, and hone my craft." He wasn't wrong; all of that has happened and more.

But it has come at a price Jamie didn't expect; the day-to-day work of newspaper journalism doesn't make her happy. It isn't the kind of writing she wants to do—she'd like to try something more creative—and she knows this isn't the life she wants to live. "I can't remember the last time I didn't have to work (or worry about my work) over the weekend. I dread getting up in the morning. I feel mentally, physically, and spiritually hollow when I leave my office at the end of the day. My neck hurts. My shoulders hurt. I don't even get excited about the stories I write. I don't even really enjoy seeing my name in print anymore."

But she still hasn't quit. Some of that has to do with the loyalty she feels to her bosses and colleagues, and to the newspaper itself. She's unsure because she has felt this kind of restlessness before at the first two newspaper jobs she'd held, but then, she'd thought she just wasn't cut out to be a writer. Now she knows she wants to continue writing but with a different focus and under different circumstances. "I've worried that this means that I'm a failure who can't really stick with anything," she says. "But then, other people remind me and I remind myself that I've stuck to the journalism path for six years." Jamie has spent months trying to make sense of what she should do. "I've thought this thing to death. I've considered it from every angle. I drive myself crazy trying to figure out which decision is more cowardly. Am I a coward to leave this job, to give up on a career that I'm really quite good at, just because it's hard and exhausting? Or am I a coward if I put up with the status quo and sink into the outline of a job that makes me deeply unhappy?"

At the moment, she has put off deciding whether to quit and is taking a leave of absence from her job to travel and write before she makes up her mind. She believes that a freelance career, writing on various topics, might give her a sense of freedom and of owning her time and the ability to reflect when she needs to. "I want flexibility, you see. I'm not sure I want to do just one thing in life." Even though she knows rationally that this is the right moment in her life to make a leap—she's married but doesn't have a mortgage or other financial encumbrances and isn't quite ready to have a child—she's still unsure. "I'm an expert ruminator," she says. "I second-guess everything. When I'm trying to put a positive spin on it, I say that I'm an incredibly open-minded, empathetic person who can really see an issue from any perspective. But that, of course, means I agonize over every little decision."

Interestingly, Jamie's newly minted goal of becoming a freelance writer is one of the first career goals she has actually set for herself since she graduated from college. "I don't think I've been terribly goal-oriented," she admits. "So far, I've made it through life just sort of heading in one general direction, seeing which doors will open themselves to me. I'm getting closer to knowing where I want to go next, and that makes me happier. I hope that I'm taking a step toward the life I want to live."

Even though Jamie hasn't quit, she's working on garnering editorial contacts for the articles and essays that she plans to write during her leave and that hopefully will be published. In short, she's beginning to master the art of quitting.

In the next chapter, we'll look at what a talent for quitting entails.

You and Your Goals

This list of statements is meant to prompt a consideration of how you set goals for yourself, how you approach them, and how you deal with potential setbacks. Please agree or disagree with each.

1. I'm most motivated to work hard when there's a financial or another tangible reward.
2. It's important to me that I feel stimulated and creative and I actively pursue those opportunities.
3. Conflict often paralyzes me, and I end up doing nothing.
4. When I'm feeling conflicted about what to do next, I think about what matters most and choose.
5. Give me an opportunity to procrastinate or waste time, and I'm there.
6. I'm very disciplined and good at controlling my impulses.
7. I spend a lot of time worrying about unfinished tasks.
8. I'm a planner. I do what I can, but if I can't do it all, I don't worry.
9. I'm definitely proactive. I think along the lines of "If I do this, then that won't happen."
10. I'm motivated by the positive. I usually think "If I do this, then that will happen."
11. I feel a lot of pressure to measure up to what others have accomplished.
12. I'm usually focused on what will make me happy.
13. I don't like being around sad people, and I hate being a downer myself.
14. Sadness is a part of life. I deal with it by talking about it.
15. I'm the only person who can fix what's ailing me.
16. It's valuable to find out how other people deal with things in times of crisis.
17. If someone criticizes me or my work, I can't stop thinking about it.
18. I try to take criticism in stride. I consider the source and whether it's true.
19. If a task is frustrating me, I'll just keep going, no matter what.
20. If something's driving me crazy, I'll take five and consider whether I should continue or not.
21. I think it's important to put a positive spin on things, no matter what.
22. Sometimes I have to let myself consider that things aren't working out as I'd hoped.

The more odd-numbered statements you've agreed with, the more likely it is that many of your goals are extrinsic or avoidant.

CHAPTER FOUR

A Talent for Quitting

There's a tradition followed at Harvard Law School and other institutions of higher learning. The dean or someone else in authority gathers all the first-year students into a room and tells each of them, "Look to your right and your left, because one of you won't be here next year." The truth is that we could, with a straight face and no intention of intimidating, ask you to do precisely the same thing the next time you find yourself in a group. One of you won't be "here" next year, because one of you is better at quitting than the others.

What qualities or characteristics keep some of us so intensely hidebound, resistant or sensitive to change, unable to let go even when holding on is making us deeply unhappy? Why do some of us only see a chasm of negative possibilities when we're confronted with a leap of faith and remain rooted to the spot? Why do some of us approach life's challenges in a defensive crouch, always looking for a way to cut our potential losses? Why do some of us seem to lack an OFF button when it comes to managing negative feelings? Why do some of us keep persisting, no matter what?

What gives some of us the grace and skill of a yoga master when it comes to moving from one thing to another in life, whether it's a relationship, a job, or an aspiration? What does a human being need to be able to imagine a new flight plan, complete with a successful landing? Why is it easier for some people to find the right balance of realism and optimism, and how do they come by the skill? Do they know a secret that eludes the rest of us, or do they have some kind of internal thermostat? How do they leave one thing and go on to find something else that really makes them happy? How do they bounce back from losses? Why do some of us have a talent for quitting while others of us don't?

That's the question at hand, and in the pages that follow, we'll be talking about those qualities and the people who have them and what you can do to polish yours or, if need be, begin to acquire them if you don't. The talent for quitting is distinct from those unproductive, emotionally fueled styles of quitting covered earlier. What we have to say is founded on science, but let's begin with a small disclaimer anyway. No single measure or how-to formula can possibly address the question of the right time to quit. There are simply too many variables in any situation. Disengaging from a goal or a life path in the real world is often a complicated affair, which differentiates it from a laboratory setting, where hypotheses are set forth and tested. Deciding to change paths may be easier at certain times of life because there are fewer real-world consequences; it's safe to say that the more financial and emotional obligations you have to others, the more difficult it may be to find the right time to quit a relationship, job, or career path. In addition, the time may be right for you, but not for the other people in your life.

Quitting is easier at certain stages of life—young adulthood, for example—than it is at others, both because there's less cultural disapproval and there are usually fewer real-life complications. The risks of starting a new business or any other entrepreneurial activity are more easily tolerated early in your career, as is resetting goals if the venture fails. You're allowed to change your mind about your path when you're young, especially if you're relatively free of responsibility. The millennial generation—those born between 1977 and 1992—has appeared to embrace fluidity for the moment at least, even in a bad economy. They are getting married later (the average age is now twenty-eight) and spend only two years in a job (as opposed to baby boomers, who spend at least five). Quitting at a later stage of life takes on a different complexity, not simply because of personal obligations but because long-held goals and perhaps a diminishing sense of what's possible may also come into play.

But that said, once you understand your own talent for quitting (or the lack of it), the habits of mind that are keeping you in place, and your ability to assess and prioritize your own goals, the question of timing will become clearer to you. You'll know and feel with some certainty when the time is right. Studies show that while persistence is valuable, knowing when to fold them—to borrow a term from poker—is absolutely invaluable. One of our aims in this chapter is to encourage you, the reader, to take your own measure of not just your goals and persistence but also your innate ability to quit.

Seizing the Moment

The postcollege years, the third decade of life, are widely understood to be the time to build the foundation for the life you'll be living in your thirties and forties. This cultural understanding can make quitting one arc that is stable and predictable for one that is decidedly more risky a difficult balancing act. That was certainly true for James, twenty-seven, who graduated from college in 2009 and since then strove to maintain both the demands of a full-time job in the financial industry and the training required to pursue his passion, rowing. Unlike other sports such as tennis, skiing, or football, rowing is by its very nature an "amateur" sport that carries with it none of the perquisites—endorsements and money—that other sports do. Still, it was something James wanted to do—to see if he could compete at the highest levels of national and international competition, including the Olympics. Rowing had long been his passion—since ninth grade, in fact—but was relegated, out of necessity, to a secondary status, something he fit in around his working schedule.

He was finding it increasingly stressful to put in the number of hours of training he needed, some sixteen to twenty a week, alongside the demands of a forty-hour work week. But he enjoyed the collegial atmosphere of the firm, even as it became clear to him that finance—something a number of family members had traditionally been involved with—wasn't the career path he would follow. Then, an opportunity to train at an elite level of rowing presented itself; it came with the added benefits of housing, insurance, clothing, and food.

But while rowing competitively was a deeply held goal that James was passionate about, it wasn't precisely a career. Moreover, even if he succeeded at reaching the highest level of competition, what lay beyond that was unclear, except perhaps a coaching job. He was giving up a steady job that paid well in a weak economy to pursue a dream that, most likely, wouldn't enhance his ability to earn a steady living. Not everyone was thrilled with his decision, but as he says, "Quitting is a very personal decision. I was really the only person who could fully understand my motivation to quit." Another complication was his three-year relationship with his girlfriend, who was, understandably, upset about his making his training a priority over their relationship as he moved hundreds of miles away.

The decision to go forward, quit one path, and take on another has required James to manage a complex range of feelings. He feels responsible for his girlfriend's turmoil, has worked hard at being sensitive to and understanding of her feelings, and appreciates how hard it is for her to be supportive. But when he's asked what happens if he fails at this goal—if he discovers that he simply doesn't have the talent or ability—his voice is confident: "I'm not sure it matters, because I'm not focused on the end; I'm focused on what I'm doing and trying to focus on being the best that I can be. It's hard to shift your mind-set, to become completely engrossed in a single task with full mindfulness. You have to get yourself from being very good to being exceptional, and that takes a great deal of focused clarity." He doesn't see this as a detour or as something that will put him behind his peers who are following a more traditional career arc. "The lessons I learn in rowing are easily transferable, and I would venture to say that few people are willing to work as hard as elite long-endurance athletes." In addition, he's confident that when he finds a career that is as pleasurable and sustaining as rowing, he'll know where he needs to go, and he'll have the persistence to get there. He isn't worried about taking his time to get there.

Evaluating Your Talent

Different psychological theories have offered answers to what personality traits or temperaments make one person better at setting goals, evaluating them, and then disengaging from them, if necessary, than another individual. We'll take a number of perspectives to get as complete a picture of what the talent for quitting looks like. While there's some congruency between these theories, each offers a slightly different point of view.

Please think about yourself as you read, and decide where your talent for quitting fits into the scheme of things. No matter where you find yourself, this chapter and the ones that follow will offer you strategies to build your skill set for quitting.

As we mentioned, one perspective has been suggested by Andrew J. Elliot and Todd M. Thrash, who examine people in terms of their basic motives and goals as being either *approach* or *avoidant* in character. The basic urge to approach (i.e., to secure a positive end) and to avoid (i.e., to avert negative or painful consequences) is built into the human species, as well as across many other animal groups, including one-celled animals. Their theory, though, goes further and identifies approach and avoidance motivation as a key component of personality; early socialization plays an important role in determining which of these two temperaments describe how you navigate life and goal-setting.

If you've ever spent any time in a playground or schoolyard, you've probably seen what approach and avoidance temperaments look like in real life. There's the little girl who climbs to the top of the slide, confident and smiling, and sails down, waving at her mother, making eye contact. Then there's the other child, who picks his way through the other kids and equipment as if the playground is hostile terrain. His mother sits nearby, talking on her cell phone, but the little boy doesn't look up or gesture at her. He shuns the slide, afraid of stumbling on the steps, and avoids the jungle gym out of fear of getting stuck and looking dumb. He's content to sit on terra firma in the sandbox, by himself, avoiding contact with the other children. One child approaches the playground with nothing but positive motivation; the other, though, sees a different landscape. Are these approaches inborn or has each of these children been shaped by his or her environments? What happens to these children when they reach adulthood? Will their temperaments remain consistent?

Andrew J. Elliot and Harry T. Reis suggest that indeed they will. Their 2003 study specifically connected familial patterns of relationship as explained by attachment theory to the exploration and formation of goals in adulthood. Understanding attachment theory—and how you were attached to your parents—is a stepping-stone for understanding your ability both to persevere and to quit in life generally but especially in relationships. Attachment theory also helps explain how *comfort zones*—situations that are emotionally familiar and hence feel comfortable in that sense but actually make you unhappy—function in your life.

Attachment theory grew out of a series of experiments conducted by Mary Ainsworth. The experiments have been replicated hundreds of times since and focused on the character of the mother-infant relationship. The model, called the *strange situation*, looked at how a baby reacted when, after arriving at the lab with his or her mother, the mother left and a stranger entered the room. Ainsworth focused on the child's response when the mother returned. As she expected, most children fussed and cried when they were left but were immediately reassured by their mothers' return. They reconnected to their mother by reaching for her, establishing eye contact, cooing, and becoming content. Ainsworth labeled these children "securely attached" and deduced that their mothers were attuned to the children's needs and consistently responsive to the infants.

But not all children responded to the strange situation in this way. Some babies showed little emotion or distress when their mother left, and weren't comforted when she returned. Others showed no emotion when the mother left, and they avoided contact when she returned. Ainsworth categorized these babies as "insecurely attached" and refined insecure attachment into three types: avoidant, ambivalent or anxious, or disorganized. *Avoidant attachment* is a result of a mother's unavailability to the baby or her rejection of her baby's approaches; the child adapts by avoiding emotional and physical proximity to her. Unreliable or unpredictable maternal behavior results in *ambivalent attachment*; the child never knows whether the mother will be attuned or dismissive, so he or she adapts to the unreliability. The last and most damaging category of insecure attachment is called *disorganized attachment*, because it creates within these children a conflict between the need to have their wants met and their fear or apprehension of their mother. This last category is usually the result of maternal behavior that is physically or emotionally abusive.

Patterns of childhood attachment are reliable predictors of how we handle adult relationships, including romantic ones, handle stress, and regulate our emotions. Securely attached children grow up to be adults able to pick romantic partners who are attuned and loving, and are able to regulate emotions better than their insecurely attached counterparts. Why are these patterns of attachment so enduring? Human infants are wired to adapt to the circumstances in which they find themselves, thus increasing their chances of survival. Because these early attachments yield the mental images and neurological templates for how relationships work in the world, they also form the basis for motivation and action.

How an infant depends on the signals he or she receives from the mother and learns to react to them was demonstrated by one fascinating experiment called the *visual cliff*, which has often been replicated with some variations. With the baby's mother visible at the far end, a baby who is able to crawl is put on a countertop that is half solid and half clear Plexiglas. Once the baby reaches the edge of the Plexiglas, it looks like a sheer drop down (the baby doesn't know about the wonders of Plexiglas, after all). The baby stops dead in his or her tracks and looks up to scan the mother's face and waits for the answer: Safe or dangerous? Go or stop? The child is skilled at reading his or her mother's expressions by now—thanks to the limbic brain and evolution—and a smile or some happy expression will keep the baby crawling, no matter what the drop looks like. But if the mother expresses negative affect, the baby will respond very differently.

In one visual-cliff experiment conducted by James F. Sorce and others, mothers were instructed to pose with either a happy face or a frightened one. None of the babies crossed the cliff when they saw fear on their mothers' faces, and most of them actually retreated to where they'd started. Next, the mothers posed with either an interested expression or an angry one. While most of the babies crossed the cliff on cue with the interested expression, only two of the eighteen babies ventured forth when their mothers' faces looked angry. When mothers looked sad, only one-third of the babies crossed. Keep in mind that the expression of fearfulness stopped *every* infant.

As infants and children, we all learn how to regulate our emotions and direct our behaviors through our connections to our primary caregivers. It all begins in the nursery. That's why other studies have argued that an infant's ability to explore and open up his or her horizons, both literally and figuratively, is connected to how securely (or insecurely) attached the child is, and that this disposition would stay constant through adulthood.

Elliot and Ries hypothesized that securely attached adults would see achievement goals as a positive challenge that would make them feel competent. Moreover, the researchers argued that these adults would be able to respond with relative equanimity to the possibility of failing at the task. Their insecurely attached counterparts, on the other hand, would regard an achievement goal as a possible threat, given the possibility of failure, and would "self-protectively seek to avoid incompetence," as the researchers put it. In their first experiment, they measured attachment in romantic relationships; 50 percent of the participants identified themselves as securely attached, 30 percent as avoidant, and 20 percent as anxious/ambivalent. The participants then completed an achievement goal questionnaire. By presenting statements with which the subjects had to disagree or agree, the questionnaire assessed the participants' approach or avoidant stances. For example, "It was important for me to understand the content of the course as thoroughly as possible" (mastery-approach); "It's important for me to do well compared to others in this class" (performance-approach); "I just want to avoid doing poorly in this course" (performance-avoidance). The participants also made a list of eight personal goals.

What the researchers found in this and other subsequent experiments was that securely attached people needed high achievement, had a low fear of failure, and had strong personal-approach goals and mastery-approach goals. Put plainly, they were highly motivated to expand in the areas of relationship, skill, and achievement. In contrast, insecurely attached participants had a low need for achievement and a high fear of failure; their goals were largely avoidant in both the areas of mastery and performance. One point, though, should be emphasized: while both participants who identified themselves as anxious/ambivalent and those who were avoidant shared a fear of failure, the anxious/ambivalent used avoidance goals, but the avoidant group did not. The category of anxious/ambivalent is important when it comes to the talent for quitting: "Anxious attachment undermines optimal achievement motivation because it impels individuals to view achievement tasks in terms of losses and to feel a heightened need to do well, both of which produce a defensive focus on avoiding negative outcomes."

People with the anxious/ambivalent stance have a particular problem. While they're inclined to focus on failure, they also want to succeed. It sounds like a contradiction, but then again, ambivalence by definition is contradictory. These people have a great deal of difficulty quitting anything, especially relationships. They are preoccupied with relationships, suffer from highs and lows in feeling, and are unable to quit, no matter what. People with avoidant attachment—as the term implies—fear intimacy and, more than anything else, suffer from an inability to engage.

An in-depth analysis by Philip R. Shaver and Mario Mikulincer sheds even more light on how these attachment models connect to the work of goal engagement and the stress involved with changing course. The problem is clear: The ability to quit artfully requires the regulation of thought and emotion first, which then leads to motivational and behavior change and the formulation of new goals. Securely attached people are good at regulating their emotions when they are distressed. They can get angry without being hostile and are quick to adopt constructive goals aimed at repairing a relationship under stress. They are open on a cognitive level, too, and don't have to rely on distortion to feel good about themselves.

Anxiously attached individuals use strategies that tend to exacerbate, rather than relieve, the effect of stressful events; they ruminate and thus, by focusing on the negative emotion, find themselves more deeply embroiled in it. The same thing happens on a cognitive level when they try but fail to suppress intrusive thoughts. People with avoidant attachment distance themselves from stress consciously—they react to threats by inflating their positive views of themselves—but they also cut themselves off emotionally. By armoring themselves in this way, they also lose access to all the positive feelings and connections that might actually help them cope. To paraphrase Shaver and Mikulincer, the strategy has a very high price and leaves them deprived of and without access to positive cues in situations that might actually get them through the crisis by making them feel better. Needless to say, this strategy does nothing to resolve the turmoil they feel.

How those initial childhood attachments affect our abilities to persevere *and* to quit makes perfect sense. Securely attached individuals are grounded and more capable of managing emotion and seeking support when an endeavor begins to falter or even fail. Their insecurely attached counterparts, on the other hand, are mostly motivated by the negative. The ambivalently or anxiously attached who want nothing more than *not* to fail—whether that's in a relationship or in some other endeavor—have the least talent for quitting.

That's exactly what a study by Heather C. Lench and Linda J. Levine found. The researchers gave participants three sets of seven anagrams to be solved in a specific amount of time; the first set of seven was unsolvable. Since it was a timed test, you would get better results if you didn't use up the time trying to work on the first one; in addition, since you couldn't skip an anagram or go back, you had to fully disengage in order to move forward.

Just as the researchers hypothesized, people who identified themselves as being motivated by approach goals stopped their efforts on the first set when they realized persistence wouldn't pay off. But those with avoidance goals not only worked longer at this frustrating and hopeless exercise, but also stayed stuck as the approach group moved forward and exhibited more intense and enduring emotional distress.

In a second study, rather than rely on the self-report of the participants, the researchers primed the participants to fall into one of the two categories. The approach group was told the test was "a measure of your strengths in verbal intelligence" and was told to "try to attain success"; the avoidance group was told that the test was a measure of "your weaknesses in verbal intelligence" and was instructed to try to "avoid failure." Dealing with the first unsolvable anagram set, as expected, left all the participants with negative emotions, but those who had been primed for an avoidance approach had more negative emotion; in fact, the angrier the participants got, the greater the level of persistence.

"Ironically," the authors explain, "their focus on avoiding negative outcomes was associated with an inability to recognize that failure was inevitable and proceed to the next anagram." Lench and Levine suggest that people with approach goals have more cognitive flexibility and may generate more alternative strategies for achieving a goal than those focused on simply avoiding a negative outcome: "Counterintuitively, people who focused on the potential failure of goals were less likely to recognize failure."

This avoidant focus—combined with the other biases in thinking we all have, including the sunk-cost fallacy and how a goal becomes more valuable once it's unattainable—makes it clear that sometimes persistence is only the path of least resistance. It's precisely why the art of quitting needs to be mastered. No matter what you've been told, if your impulse is always to stick it out, you're going to need an alternative at hand.

Fear of Failure

Spend a moment thinking about your own upbringing and your way of relating to others—are you securely or insecurely attached?—and the role that fear of failure, or failure itself, has played in your life. Two of America's most cherished cultural tropes are that failure is often a necessary stepping-stone to success and that the lessons imparted by failure are often key to an individual's achievement. Popular thinking often casts fear of failure as a motivator too. It purportedly encourages the student to study those extra hours, the worker to try harder to please the boss, and the athlete to keep pumping iron. These cultural tropes, alas, are largely false and over-simplified at best, as we'll explain. We've already described how fear of failure, rather than being a motivator, is closely tied to choosing avoidance goals as well as to insecure models of attachment.

A fascinating study by Elliot and Thrash investigated the fear of failure; they posited that fear of failure was transmitted from parent to child and that the mediator was the parents' use of love withdrawal in socialization. As the authors point out, it's not "failure per se that is feared and avoided, but the shame that accompanies failure." As an emotion, shame eats away at the whole construct of self, making the person feel unworthy of love and worthless. Fear of failure, the authors write, causes the individual to "experience anxiety prior to and during task engagement and seek to protect the self from failure by escaping the situation physically (quitting) or mentally (withdraw-ing effort) or by pushing hard to succeed (in order to avoid failure)."

The kind of quitting the culture disdains accounts for the first two of the three possible responses to fear of failure. Only the third response, the most unlikely possibility, supports the cultural trope. We'll argue later that it's not failure but the mastery of the art of quitting that paves the way to new and fulfilling goals and achievement.

Elliot and Thrash posited that parents' own fear of failure would lead them to respond to their children's mistakes, omissions, and failures in ways that taught their offspring that failure was to be avoided at all costs. The researchers specifically focused on one parenting practice, that of love withdrawal. The threat of love withdrawal, especially with small children, can be very subtle, communicated by a cold stare or a stony face, physically turning away from the child, removing the child from the room, or threatening to remove him. (If you think about it, the traditional time-out, which is used by countless parents as a form of discipline, could, if handled in a specific way, also feel like love withdrawal to a child.) Notably, the researchers do not believe that most parents adopted love withdrawal as a conscious strategy: "Most who use it are simply responding to their children in a reactive manner out of their own deeply engrained self-evaluative processes."

The authors found that both a mother's fear of failure and her love withdrawal were directly related to her college-age children's fear of failure. Both fathers' and mothers' fear of failure were predictors of the adoption of avoidance goals and, in the case of fathers, predicted that their children wouldn't adopt mastery goals. Can aversive motivation be passed from one generation to another? Elliot and Thrash think it can be. Withdrawing love or threatening that it might be withdrawn may not be the only behavior that inculcates avoidance goals and a fear of failure. Other parenting styles—such as authoritarian or controlling behaviors—also directly affect the ability to disengage, as we'll see in the perspective offered by the work being done on what's called active and state orientations.

So let's take fear of failure off the shelf as a motivation for achievement. If you attribute your persistence to a fear of failure, it's time to reevaluate.

The Cost of Avoidance

While all of us will certainly have, at any given point in our lives, a mixture of approach and avoidance goals, the focus on avoidance affects your sense of well-being (SWB) in literal ways. For example, in a study of patients in therapy, Andrew J. Elliot and Marcy A. Church showed that patients who entered therapy with avoidance goals didn't experience as great an increase in well-being as those with approach goals, and felt that both the therapist and the therapeutic experience were less effective. Keep in mind that the actual goals may be the same, but the way they are framed—in terms of approach and avoidance—makes the difference. Some examples from the study make the difference clear:

- "To understand myself and my feelings" versus "To stop being confused about my feelings"
- "To have closer relationships with my friends" versus "To avoid feeling alone and isolated"
- "To be more stable and happy" versus "To avoid becoming depressed"

Take a moment to think about how you frame your goals when you set them and how you tend to think about them when you decide whether to quit or keep going. Is it your habit to think that "If I do X, Y won't happen"? Or do you usually think "If I do X, Y will happen"?

In real life, what looks to be a persistent stance from the outside may be motivated by avoidance. People who grow up in unstable families with constant friction or fighting, an alcoholic parent, or some other form of dysfunction often adopt avoidant strategies unconsciously to stay out of the fray.

That was certainly the case for Henry, a fifty-eight-year-old lawyer who had, by his own account, never quit anything. Seen from the outside—his twenty-five-year marriage, the steady climb of his career, his twenty-nine-year association with a single law firm—his life seemed to testify to remarkable stability and persistence. He'd grown up in comfortable circumstances, but his childhood had been chaotic; his father was a binge drinker who disappeared without notice and returned as abruptly without any discussion or overt acknowledgment within the family. Nothing was ever talked about, and Henry unconsciously applied this lesson to his life, avoiding confrontation at all costs. But he finally reached a tipping point and came to realize how deeply unhappy he was. How he left his marriage was clumsy and fractious, took years to resolve, and left his relationships with his children in tatters. He now says that he wishes he'd had the tools to deal with things far earlier, because it would have been better for everyone.

Sometimes, an avoidance strategy—adopted by someone with performance goals—can also have an effect on well-being. Quitting in the real world, as opposed to the laboratory, is sometimes a complicated affair, a decision freighted with consequences. That was the case for Sarah, who at the age of twenty-two landed her first post-college job at a large public-relations firm in San Francisco. She was reasonably confident in her abilities since she'd held six internships over the years, and she thought this was a good fit. She had applied for literally dozens of jobs during the summer, had made it to the interview stage for several positions, and was pleased that the process was over. She started work with high hopes and energy, one of several new, entry-level employees. Ironically, she received another offer just weeks after she started work. Her managers practiced a brand of tough-love leadership; she and the other new employees were criticized (scolded, actually) regularly. Her first review, six months later, was daunting: In six or seven pages of written review, there was not one word of praise. For the next six months, Sarah redoubled her efforts, but her boss remained highly critical, even hostile. When Sarah did well, landing significant publicity for one of the company's clients, she was faulted for some other omission. She began to dread going to work.

But she was only one year out of college, in a lousy economy and with rent to pay. She applied for jobs at every opportunity but now had the problem of being "in between" skill levels. Though she was not quite a beginner, she also lacked the skill set for the next promotional level. Desperately wanting to quit, she nevertheless worried about how this would look on her résumé and how she would pay her bills; her parents encouraged her not to quit. She did her best to try to disengage emotionally and adopted an avoidance strategy, engaging her boss as little as possible, and began to focus on finding a new job. But hanging in took a toll on her health. Over the next six months, she developed a series of stress-related health issues. She came close to landing a few jobs, but found it hard to keep up the effort consistently. Her next review—roughly eighteen months after she started—was a clarifier: They were going to let her go if she didn't "improve." The review was full of personal remarks that had little to do with what she had accomplished. At that point, finding a new job became the only goal she had, and three months later, she quit right after receiving a good job offer.

She says now that if she had it to do over, she would have quit the job much sooner than she did, without a safety net: "If it happens again, I'll take bigger risks and figure it out. It just wasn't worth being that unhappy for so long; it literally made me sick. I should have simply left and taken my chances. I think I would have found a new job anyway. It would have just been a matter of time."

Sarah is young and at the very beginning of her working life, but her story still illustrates that once you put goal disengagement in a real-world setting, the question of how to manage it gets more complicated. It's more nuanced and fraught than the diagrams you see in psychological studies, which have a box labeled "goal disengagement" and an arrow pointing to another box marked "new goal/positive outcome," suggest. Sarah was lucky in that she was a performance- and goal-oriented person and could summon up the energy to continue applying for jobs, even though she was mightily discouraged and upset.

If, as Carsten Wrosch and others argue, goal disengagement is part of adaptive self-regulation and helps lower stress and raise the potential for positive outcomes, we also have to acknowledge that in a real-world setting, regulating your emotions takes skill and concerted effort.

Another Perspective on the Talent for Quitting

What's your coping style when life goes south? Or when you're under a great deal of pressure? Do you choke, or does pressure just rev up your engine? How do you react when you realize you've missed a fabulous opportunity? Do you come up with a plan to try to recoup it, or do you drop back five and stew about it? How do you resolve conflicting goals or demands? What would you do if the boss told you that you had to work this weekend, the very weekend that you promised your loved one would be a getaway without distraction? Would you cancel or go? When you have to give up on a goal, do you summon up your vision of your best self and move on? Or do you feel so down that you're unable to act?

Those are the kinds of questions another psychological theory called *personality systems interactions* (PSI) has asked and answered over the last three decades by focusing on two kinds of coping: action-oriented and state-oriented. This theory, another way of looking at goal engagement and disengagement, differs from approach-avoidance theory, although PSI also connects to attachment theory and parenting styles. PSI specifically acknowledges the stress induced by goal implementation and disengagement and thus focuses on coping skills. These orientations, *action* and *state*, are also formed early in life. It's been estimated that roughly half the people in the Western world are action-oriented and the other half predominantly state-oriented. The orientations represent a continuum of behavior, can be specific to a situation or domain, or can be a dominant trait. Under extreme stress, almost everyone becomes state-oriented.

Let's define a few terms. *Action-oriented* is actually what it sounds like, that is, people who, when they are under stress, are capable of regulating negative emotions, can muster up positive and confirming images of self, are decisive, don't rely on external cues, and are effective in the sphere of action, in terms of both goal engagement and goal disengagement. *State-oriented behavior*, on the other hand, refers to the way an individual's emotional state dominates how he or she functions in the world under stressful conditions. When there's stress or conflict—what's called a high-demand or threatening situation—state-oriented people become flooded with negative feelings and can't manage them. When they have to choose a new path under stress, they tend to hesitate. They ruminate, are sensitive to external cues, depend on structure and deadlines, and tend to procrastinate. They have trouble staying focused on their own. They have difficulty disengaging.

While the action-oriented disengage from thoughts of failure when they're pursuing a goal and ignore distractions, the state-oriented become preoccupied with the possibility of failure. Under stress, the action-oriented initiate and the state-oriented hesitate. While the action-oriented focus on tasks, the state-oriented are more volatile. The latter may become unfocused, get sidetracked, or simply give up without letting go on the levels of thought and emotion.

As James M. Diefendorff and others have noted, these differences between action and state orientations may explain "why two individuals who have similar goals, knowledge, ability, and desire to perform well nonetheless fail to achieve the same level of performance."

How these orientations look in the real world may be easiest to see on the playing field. Imagine that two golfers of roughly equal ability are in a competitive match and find themselves tied on the last hole. The hole lies behind a bunker. One golfer is focused on the hole, mentally rehearsing his swing and what he needs to do to make the shot and win the match. He puts the pressure of the tied score and the bunker out of his mind completely, pumping himself up by reminding himself how he has made shots like this dozens of times before. He doesn't see or hear the crowd of spectators; it's all about the shot. The second golfer, who had enjoyed an early lead in the match, is focused only on avoiding the bunker; all he can think about is the tied score, how he blew his early lead and how stupid that was, and how if he hits it into the bunker, he'll surely lose. His rumination is a distraction, and his focus has shifted from the win to avoiding the loss. He's not concentrating on the shot, because he's painfully aware of the moving, murmuring crowd of spectators. This is what action and state orientations look like on the golf course, but the phenomenon of the *clutch player*—the person who's high-functioning under stress—is well known in almost every sport, at the negotiating table, in the courtroom, and in many other endeavors.

PSI posits that goal implementation happens on both a conscious, volitional level and an unconscious one. Similarly, affect is both consciously and unconsciously regulated. An action orientation is distinguished by the ability to take advantage of *intuitive affect regulation*, a largely automatic process that functions outside conscious awareness and takes place quickly and effortlessly, unlike the conscious processing of thought and emotion.

To simplify, if a person can successfully regulate emotion at a time of stress, he will also have access to those intuitive programs which contain his own emotional preferences, his self-representations, and autobiographical experience. That's what the first golfer is doing in our example when he brings his best self to mind under stress. He's using his inner self-portrait—his skills, his history as a golfer, his confidence—to execute that shot. Put another way, action-oriented people are more in touch with themselves and have better access to what motivates them on a purely unconscious level which is then combined with more conscious motivations.

In contrast, state-oriented people behave the way the second golfer did. He's mired in negative thoughts, effectively cutting off access to the good things he knows about himself. He's taking his cues from the environment, which is, from his point of view, primarily defined by a blown lead. This behavior is typical of the state-oriented; under stress, they can't bring their mental images of their best selves to mind, and they lose access to those unconscious and intuitive motivators.

When action and state orientations are measured in a laboratory setting, the questions posed are like the following, which are
drawn from the scale developed by Julius Kuhl in 1994. As you
read, answer the questions for yourself.

1. When I know I have to finish something soon, (a) I have to
   push myself to get started, or (b) I find it easy to get it over and
   done with.
2. When I'm told my work is totally unsatisfactory, (a) I don't let
   it bother me for long, or (b) I feel paralyzed.
3. When I have a lot of things to do and they all must be done at
   once, (a) I often don't know where to begin, or (b) I find it easy
   to make a plan and stick to it.

Question 1 depicts a high-demand situation, and the action-oriented answer is (b). Questions 2 and 3 represent threat situations,
and the action-oriented answers are (a) and (b), respectively.

These orientations appear to be shaped by socialization during
childhood rather than by genetic factors. Children learn how to
self-regulate during infancy and childhood. An infant in distress
turns to his or her mother to be comforted, and with secure and
attuned attachment, the mother helps the baby to self-regulate consistently. In this safe and sustaining environment, the baby eventually learns to self-soothe, thus internalizing the cues the baby has
learned from the mother, using the same neural pathways forged by
those initial maternal behaviors. In that way, the securely attached
individual becomes autonomous in a self-regulatory sense, while
still needing connection. With insecure attachments, if the mother's
comforting and attuned behaviors are inconsistent or absent, the
progress of self-regulation is hampered.

The development of self-regulation continues past infancy,
of course, and in early childhood, parenting styles either facilitate
or hinder a child's ability to manage his or her emotions. Environments that provide structure without being controlling and
attuned parenting styles that set firm boundaries for a child while

encouraging exploration yield people with an ability to self-regulate and who are action-oriented. In contrast, an authoritarian way of parenting, with high demands and an insistence on conformity to parental rules and where the child is made to feel bad about himself or herself for inconsistency or lack of achievement, facilitates a state orientation. So does an environment that ignores a child. It has been theorized that parental divorce may contribute to state orientation as well.

An experiment conducted by researchers in Amsterdam, the results of which were published in an article aptly titled "Getting a Grip on Your Feelings," demonstrated how action- and state-oriented people cope in the same situations. After filling out questionnaires on action or state orientation and self-esteem, half of the participants were asked to visualize a demanding person in their own life and specifically to recall not just incidents dealing with that difficult person but also their feelings at the time. To make the visualization even more vivid, they were also asked to identify that person by his or her initials and to type up some of their experiences. The other half were asked to go through the same exercise, but this time visualizing their experiences with an accepting person in their lives. All of the participants were shown alternating screens of schematized faces showing emotions (happy, sad, or neutral) and tested to see how quickly they could identify a discrepant face—that is, a single happy face in a crowd of angry ones or an angry face among happy faces. Finally, all of the participants were asked to identify or not identify ("me" or "not me") with a series of words pertaining to traits evenly divided between positives (creative, reliable, etc.) and negatives (silent, impulsive, etc.).

Visualizing a demanding relationship caused the action-oriented people to be able to pick out the happy faces in an angry crowd more quickly, which the researchers posited was due to these people's ability to self-regulate their emotions intuitively without conscious process. In addition, visualizing a demanding relationship in detail didn't affect action-oriented moods or their self-evaluations of positive traits. In contrast, the state-oriented participants who recalled a demanding relationship were slow to pick out happy faces in an angry crowd but quick to identify negative traits in themselves; this finding reflected the propensity of state-oriented individuals to internalize negative expectations of others. This seems to be supported by other observations as well. When visualizing an accepting relationship, state-oriented people reported a more positive affect and identified more positive traits as theirs. In contrast, the moods of the action-oriented were unaffected by visualizing an accepting relationship.

Should you find yourself identifying with the list of state-oriented characteristics, don't despair. While these individuals have more trouble functioning under stress, they're just fine under friendlier circumstances, thank you very much. Indeed, although they may be at a disadvantage when it comes to artful quitting, their orientation can stand them in good stead in other circumstances.

State-oriented people can often outperform their action-oriented counterparts. Their hesitation in response to stress may not always be a bad thing, especially if taking action would be premature. Their wait-and-see demeanor can, sometimes, be a plus. (Note that action-oriented people also take more time with a big decision.) In addition, the state-oriented can and do get support from others and often enjoy closer relationships than action-oriented people have. Their lack of self-regulatory skills can be improved by the support of others.

Because state-oriented people rely on external cues (rather than the internal representations of self), they are good at taking direction and relatively tolerant of frustration; they work harder and longer at tasks that require concentration but aren't particularly creative or interesting. They outperform action types on these kinds of tasks and any that require self-discipline. Unfortunately, precisely because they are reliant on external cues, they are vulnerable to the *self-infiltration effect*, which means that they mistake an extrinsic goal for a self-chosen one, even it doesn't fit with their personal needs or preferences—their inner picture of self.

We are all influenced by primes in the environment, the external cues that interact with the automatic processes of the mind. We all adopt goals or strategies that we think are consciously chosen but are really being cued from the outside without our conscious awareness. Because of their sensitivity to cues, a series of experiments by Sander L. Koole and David A. Fockenberg examined whether state-oriented people would be more affected by negative primes than their action-oriented counterparts. After taking an inventory to determine their orientation and performing a timed addition task, participants had to classify words as negative or positive. Before the words appeared on the computer screen, a priming word (which was either positive or negative) flashed on the screen. People usually classify words more quickly and accurately when the target word and the prime are congruent. As the researchers hypothesized, the performance of the state-oriented participants was more affected by negative priming—a function of their general dependence on external cues.

But it was the third experiment that illuminates how state orientation can be bolstered in real life. Half of the participants were asked to visualize a demanding period in their lives, while the other half were asked to visualize a relaxing time. They took another affective priming test, this one with an equal number of positive and negative target words and primes. As expected, negative priming led the action-oriented to reverse the priming effects, again using their ability to override and regulate negative cues from the environment. But—and here is the important part—after visualizing a stress-free and relaxing time in their lives, the state-oriented folks actually were less affected by negative primes than their action-oriented colleagues. Just thinking about a happy time in their lives decreased how responsive they were to negative cues. While this underscores how sensitive the state-oriented are to context and how context influences their feelings and actions, it also shows how they can help themselves by changing their focus in times of stress. Changing the context consciously—thinking of a relaxed or happy moment at a time of stress, or seeking support when it's necessary to regulate negative emotion—may be all that's needed for a state-oriented person to override his or her potential deficits.

When it comes to getting a grip on thoughts and feelings—the first step of artful quitting—the state-oriented are at a disadvantage compared with their action-oriented brethren. So, if you see yourself in the action-oriented profile, congrats! You've got a leg up. But if you don't, keep reading; we'll show you how you can better manage those pesky emotions and thoughts, learn how to set your own deadlines and plans, and listen to that inner voice of yours more carefully.

CHAPTER FIVE

Managing Thoughts and Emotions

Lizabeth's career path has been a long road, full of twists and turns, and out of the ordinary. She's now sixty-two and has been, by turns, an EMT and a specialist in cardiopulmonary resuscitation, a professional Frisbee player, the owner of a holistic health center, a teacher, and, now, a farmer, writer, and beekeeper. She has been successful at all of these endeavors, and so her pattern of moving on has had little to do with failure. What she has always had is an unerring sense of when it's time to move on and quit, a quality she attributes to her parents, especially her father, who, she says, "taught me that it was important to think for myself and to be entrepreneurial. That gave me the ability to decide when I was enjoying my work and when it ceased to be important to me. I've always felt that I had the freedom to do something else without being pressured into continuing with something I no longer enjoyed or felt was worth my time and effort." The eldest of four children in her family, she describes a childhood that was warm and supportive. She felt secure and loved by both her parents and her grandparents, each of whom imbued her with different strengths. Her father was practical, grounded, and self-made; her mother taught her to trust her intuition; and her grandmother was her cheerleader. She emerged from her adolescence into young adulthood not problem-free but trusting in herself and her instincts.

Lizabeth's story makes it clear that her goals have always been intrinsic—that is, adopted from the inside out, rather than coming from an outside source—and have been defined by a larger, over-reaching goal that is more like a philosophy of life than not: "I had this idea that I was meant to grow myself into knowledge throughout life. Moving into new situations, staying as long as I needed, and then moving on was pretty much required to live that idea." She sees quitting as a necessary skill in life: "Each time I quit something, the next door was allowed to open up. Each successive situation I entered into was a better next step in my personal development. I really like who I have become in my life, and I count part of that education as knowing when to step away from a situation that no longer served me. I think quitting takes courage; making a leap isn't always easy. I liked tasking myself with stretching into a new way of being."

Sometimes, when she quit one endeavor, what was next wasn't always immediately apparent. "While I'm not totally fearless, I like to do my best to keep fear and doubt at bay when deciding what to do next. I hope that doesn't come off as arrogant or self-absorbed. I appreciate the body and brain I have and seeing how we move through life in an expansive manner." This doesn't mean that she never ruminates. "I often have an intuition about how to make a decision and take action. If there's something more to the decision, I like to take my time and think about it."

Living fluidly was, she admits, easier because she didn't marry until she was forty. She lost one child and then a later pregnancy that took motherhood off the table. But she says, had she had more personal responsibility, "I would hope I'd have had the courage to leap when I knew leaping was a good idea." Still, she counts the decision to marry her husband as the most important one in her life: "Because I shift so easily, committing to doing something for the rest of my lifetime has been illuminating and wonderful." She and her husband run a biodynamic farm together and have for the last decade.

Her ability to reframe her energies, though, shouldn't be confused with a lack of persistence because, as she sees it, "quitting because you lack the energy to bring something to a productive close is a weakness in character." She sends on an e-mail which is worth sharing: "The alternative to quitting is tenacious resolve to riding that horse where it's most productive to go. Staying the course until (a) you get there; (b) it's no longer right to go there; or (c) you find yourself heading to a better place. Even with resolve, two out of three of those destinations involve quitting what your original intention was. What's not on my list is (d) because it's too hard or (e) because there were too many roadblocks."

Lizabeth's history of secure attachment, along with her ability to manage her emotions and trust her own intuition, encompass many of the characteristics associated with an innate talent for quitting. She's lucky to have been raised with a sense not just of her own capabilities but of her own autonomy, the ability to set goals for herself and, if need be, disengage from them. Those goals, though, were intrinsic, reflecting both her current and long-term needs, and when they became outdated, she was able to quit. She also had the ability to self-soothe and manage her feelings during the anxiety of transition, which sometimes felt more like a free-fall than anything else.

But quitting can be learned and our skills buffed up, as you'll see.

Emotional Intelligence and Self-Knowledge

Another way of looking at the skills, especially self-regulation, that are key to both artful quitting and artful goal setting is in the context of what John D. Mayer and Peter Salovey have called *emotional intelligence*. An early version of their theory was, in part, the basis for Daniel Goleman's enormously popular and culturally influential book of the same name, but they have publicly disavowed the broad-brush approach of the book and its generalizations. For simplicity—since this book is about quitting and the specific skill set it requires—we'll stick to their definition of emotional intelligence: "the ability to perceive emotions, to access and generate emotions so as to assist thought, to understand emotions and emotional knowledge, and to reflectively regulate emotions so as to promote intellectual thought." Mayer and Salovey summarize their description: "This definition combines the idea that emotion makes thinking more intelligent and that one thinks intelligently about emotions."

Being emotionally intelligent not only helps you manage your emotions but also lets you consciously regulate them to improve your ability to think and forecast what will make you happy—something human beings aren't generally very good at, as we've already seen. Cultivating your emotional intelligence can help you navigate not just the thicket of emotions and feelings roused by assessing your goals and aspirations but also the work of dealing with the emotional fallout from giving up something you thought you wanted.

Let's briefly consider how children learn to manage emotions in the first place, most particularly, negative affect. Because all of this happens in early childhood, we offer an example based on the work of Daniel J. Siegel, M.D., and Mary Hartzell, M.Ed., in their book, *Parenting from the Inside Out*. If you're a parent, the scenario will be familiar, but if you're not, you'll understand it because you were a child once. In a section titled "The Accelerator and the Brakes," Siegel and Hartzell use the metaphor of a car to explain how the prefrontal cortex of the brain is shaped by experience. In this metaphor, a parent's *yes* is the accelerator, *no* is the brake, and the child's ability to develop emotional regulation is the clutch. Imagine a child, full of energy and old enough to voice what he or she wants and to initiate action.

The positive affect bestowed by a parental yes communicates enthusiasm and validates the child's excitement and sense of self and gives the child permission to explore. The word *no*, on the other hand, is the braking mechanism, a literal downer, as the child will feel sad and thwarted in the moment. While *yes* induces positive emotion, *no* yields a negative one. Ideally, the parent says no because what the child wants to do is dangerous, unhealthy, or inappropriate; in the best of all worlds, the attuned parent directs the child away from the off-limits activity (climbing the bookshelves, throwing blocks at a sibling), explains why, and then—recognizing the child's need to expend some energy and do something—redirects him or her to some other appropriate activity (e.g., playing ball outside). In this scenario, the child learns how to use his or her emotional clutch.

But alas, that's not the only scenario. There will be the parent who says no simply because he or she can—controlling for the sake of controlling—and who will shame the child for an emotional response, whether it's tears or a tantrum, thus teaching him or her that these feelings aren't worthy of respect or that any response is shameful. (Imagine, from a child's point of view, the impact of a parent's saying, "I'll give you something to cry about.") Siegel and Hartzell describe what happens when a crying boy or girl is confronted by parental anger at the child's tears of frustration as "a toxic situation, like trying to drive a car with both the accelerator and brakes applied." Similarly, children whose parents don't set limits—who ignore the child in that sense or always say yes—also fail to teach emotional regulation.

As a result, the playing field of emotional intelligence isn't precisely level for everyone. Some of us will have family backgrounds that have bequeathed us more emotional intelligence than some of our peers. Others will leave their childhoods and embark on adulthood relatively impoverished in this domain. Nonetheless, understanding precisely which skills constitute emotional intelligence can help each of us pinpoint both our strengths and our weaknesses.

The first and lowest branch of emotional intelligence begins with an infant's ability to recognize positive and negative emotions and includes:

- The ability to identify emotion in oneself
- The ability to identify emotion in others
- The ability to express emotion accurately and to express needs
- The ability to discriminate between honest and dishonest, accurate and inaccurate expressions of emotion

This part of the theory is relatively straightforward. How well developed these abilities are will clearly be reflected in every relationship we have, at home, at work, and in the world at large. Every goal we set that has a social context will be affected by how many of these skills we bring to the table, as well as how well honed they are.

The second branch of emotional intelligence includes the facility of using emotion to inform thought and action:

- Using emotions to prioritize thinking
- Using emotions as aids to judgment, assessment, and memory
- Understanding and managing mood swings (optimism and pessimism) to foster multiple points of view
- Using emotional states to encourage fresh approaches to problems

How finely developed this group of particular abilities is will directly affect how good we are at anticipating our feelings in some future situation. Being able to use emotions to inform our thinking about future events is incredibly useful when we're deciding to pursue a goal or, alternatively, to abandon it. Keep in mind, too, that according to the work done by Daniel Gilbert and others, forecasting isn't, for a number of reasons, humanity's strong suit. The more emotionally intelligent we are, the more closely our choices will mirror what we really want. Understanding our moods—and seeing that emotion is part of thought, not antithetical to it—also serves as a counterbalance to the overoptimism and other biases described earlier. Similarly, having a bead on a negative emotion (recognizing, for example, that it's coming from an external cue) allows us to step back and consider our choices differently. Understanding the link between what we're feeling and what we're thinking is useful to all aspects of goal setting, as well as artful quitting.

The third branch of emotional intelligence is more nuanced and hints at the complex role emotions play in our decision-making process on both conscious and unconscious levels, whether we are deciding to set a goal, persevere in its pursuit, or quit. These processes of understanding and analyzing our emotions, in turn, yield *emotional knowledge* about events, situations, and people in our lives. From the most simple to the most complex, these are the following capabilities:

- The ability to label emotions and recognize the relationship between the words and the feelings
- The ability to interpret emotions
- The ability to understand complex or blended emotions
- The ability to recognize likely transitions between emotions

This part of the theory acknowledges that emotional knowledge very much depends on our ability to know precisely what we're feeling when we're feeling it. Sometimes, we can label an emotion with relative ease because the situation is comparatively simple and the cause and the emotional effect are easy to see. For example, our friend moves away or our cat dies and we are sad; we are afraid that we'll miss the deadline for our project because we're running very late; we're angry because the deal we worked on for months fell apart through no fault of our own.

But sometimes it's hard to identify precisely what we're feeling. Being fired may arouse anger at first but then may segue into shame, embarrassment, or sadness. Fighting with our partner may make us angry and frustrated, but at the same time, we may also feel guilty or sad. Sometimes, waves of different feelings may wash over us at once, making it hard to know exactly what we're feeling and why; this emotional muddle make us unsure of what we may want to do in response.

The theory of emotional intelligence suggests that labeling and knowing what we're feeling is a skill and, in addition, that it's not necessarily part of everyone's tool kit. A study by Lisa Feldman Barrett and others hypothesized that individuals who were able to differentiate among emotions more finely would be better able to regulate negative emotions than people who tended to think about their emotional experiences in a much more rudimentary way. As the researchers write, some people think about their emotions "along a single unpleasant-pleasant dimension"; others, though, make finer distinctions between and among feelings. The ability to recognize an emotion and to correctly name it (distinguishing between embarrassment and shame, for example, and knowing what each feels like) lies at the heart of emotional intelligence, separating those who have a more nuanced and detailed understanding of their feelings from others who don't. The researchers hypothesized that people with a more differentiated sense of their negative emotions would, in fact, be able to regulate negative feelings with more facility and come up with specific strategies to cope with specific feelings.

Participants in Barrett and her colleagues' study kept daily diaries of their most intense emotional experiences, both positive and negative, as well as accounts of their efforts to regulate their negative feelings over two weeks. The hypothesis was borne out: Individuals with a better bead on their feelings were able to regulate their negative emotions with skill and efficiency. This aspect of emotional intelligence is an enormous advantage when it comes to goal engagement, as we've already seen over and over in these pages. The management of negative emotions (as opposed to their suppression) is one of the lynchpins of artful quitting.

The final branch of emotional intelligence, the capacity to regulate emotion and use it for emotional and intellectual growth, is also central to artful quitting:

- The ability to stay open to both unpleasant and pleasant feelings
- The ability to engage or detach from an emotion, depending on whether it's useful or not
- The ability to monitor emotions in relation to oneself and others
- The ability to moderate both positive and negative emotions without either repressing or exaggerating the information they convey

It's here that the intelligence part of the theory really shines through. This last branch involves using your emotions and emotional understanding to inform your vision of yourself, your decisions, and where you find yourself. Openness to emotion is key to the process—even though it may not necessarily be pleasant or painless—and to mastering the art of quitting. This branch of emotional intelligence involves thinking about thinking, and thinking about feeling, and is necessarily a part of the aptitude for quitting as described in this chapter. Since goal disengagement is about disengaging your thoughts and feelings, how much intelligence you can bring to bear on the process is an enormous plus. The fancy name for this is *metacognition*, but it all boils down to being able to know what you're feeling and thinking at any moment in the process. Later in the book, we'll be talking about how to bolster whatever level of emotional intelligence you bring to the table.

The Marshmallow and You

Learning to manage your emotions is closely tied to your ability to regulate impulse or, put another way, to delay immediate gratification in the cause of another goal. This is where the "marshmallow" of our subtitle comes in.

In a famous experiment in the 1960s, Walter Mischel and others put a large number of four-year-olds—the offspring of Stanford University faculty, graduate students, and employees—to the test. The children were put in a room where a researcher told them to stay seated at a desk; a plate with a single marshmallow on it was placed in front of them. They were free to eat the marshmallow, but they were told they could get a second marshmallow if they waited for the researcher to leave and come back. They were to ring a bell if they decided to eat it right away. The researcher was gone for fifteen minutes, an eternity if you are only four and there's something yummy parked right in front of your nose.

There are videos of some of these experiments; it is both hilarious and excruciating at once to watch these very small people struggle with the choice. A number of them simply went for it, forgoing the possible reward immediately, popping the treat into their mouths before the researcher even made it to the door. Others fidgeted, stroked the marshmallow longingly, licked its edges, their faces scrunched up, trying so hard but finally succumbing to the lure. But roughly 30 percent of the children waited it out—fiddling with their hair and clothes, laying their heads on the desk or covering their faces with their hands, trying desperately to distract themselves until the door opened and the researcher came in—and they got the second marshmallow.

What put this experiment into the psychological hall of fame was that Mischel and his colleagues tracked down those four-year-olds much later, when the participants were in late adolescence. Through the reports of parents, SAT scores and grades, psychological profiles, and other evidence, the researchers discovered that the small cadre able to resist that marshmallow and delay gratification had ended up with very different skill sets than their marshmallow-grabbing peers. It turns out that the children who were able to delay in preschool were more likely, as late adolescents, to exhibit self-control when frustrated and were more intelligent and focused, less distracted when they tried to concentrate, and less likely to yield to impulse. They were planners who could think ahead, concentrate, and respond to and use reason, unlike the kids who couldn't delay. The researchers concluded that "the association between preschool delay behavior and adolescent competencies may reflect in part the operation of 'cognitive construction competencies.' In this view, the qualities that underlie the effective self-imposed delay in preschool may be crucial ingredients of an expanded construct of intelligent social behavior that encompasses social as well as intellectual knowledge, coping, and problem-solving competencies."

So, ask your four-year-old self this question (he or she is still in there): Would you have gone for the marshmallow, or would you have waited? Better still, ask your adult self what you're likely to do when faced with a "marshmallow" challenge (you can substitute whatever you want for the candy); are you the type who'll wait for the payoff, or will you simply go for it?

Taking an Inventory

Take a moment and answer the following questions. Just thinking about the answers will, we think, give you a better sense of where to locate yourself in terms of your quitting skills.

- Do I usually focus on the long term, or am I quick to grab the short-term solution when I feel frustrated?
- How do I react when things go badly? Do I find it easy or hard to deal with my emotions?
- Is initiating action easy or difficult for me?
- How good am I at knowing how my thoughts are being influenced by my feelings?
- Do I tend to react more to negatives or positives in my life?
- How often do I second-guess myself?
- Do I seek out support in times of stress, or do I tend to go it alone?
- How good am I at reading situations and what other people are feeling? How good am I at knowing what I'm feeling when I'm feeling it?

Cultivating Your Quitting Aptitude

Quitting artfully has applications beyond just being able to extract yourself from situations or endeavors that no longer serve your needs. While it may seem counterintuitive, being able to quit after you've been fired or laid off from a job or, for that matter, a relationship, is equally important, as the following stories show.

Jack had been fired once before, years ago, when he was in his early thirties, after he got married but before his children were born. He recalled how angry he'd been because his supervisors had essentially told him he had to go for the promotion in corporate relations to show his allegiance to the firm, to make his bones as a would-be player. The truth was, he loved his niche in the company and the day-to-day routine, but he'd been told flatly that he would never last unless he showed the bosses some real ambition. So he did what he was told, and less than a year later, he was fired. All these years later, his face still darkens with anger when he tells the story.

But he had lasted six years, and with his marketable skills, he landed another job. The eldest of five—with three brothers—he'd grown up in an athletically competitive family where persistence was the mantra. He was at his next job for seventeen years, which, given American culture today, seemed like a throwback to another era. There were signs, now and again, that things could change for Jack—the business was no longer growing at the same pace as it had when he had started, there were new competitors and a new management team—but Jack felt reasonably secure. He knew he was good at what he did, and it wasn't in his nature to shake things up, so he stayed put. Then, someone much younger—and who made considerably less money than Jack did—was brought into the department by management. Six months later, without ceremony, Jack was ushered first out of his office, and then out of the building, through the lobby he'd walked into every morning and out of every night for seventeen years.

There was no question in Jack's mind that he'd been fired because he was older and made more money. He seriously considered a lawsuit but hesitated when he was told that the litigation might take up to two years to even get to court. He was angry and resentful and couldn't stop revisiting how he'd been treated, and a lawsuit seemed both appropriate and fair. But, after taking counsel with his family and friends, he realized that pursuing a lawsuit would effectively keep him stuck where he was, leaving his being fired front and center in his life. Did he really want to live that way?

He had never quit anything important in his life, but now, it was clear that he needed to "quit" what had happened.

Jack was lucky, in a sense, he says: "I don't tend to ruminate much, so once I figured out that I had to put this behind me, I did by starting to make other plans for myself. I didn't really know where I was going next, but just the mere fact of going out there and talking to people about possibilities got me going again. I didn't think about it as quitting at the time, but it was, in a real sense. The only way I could get my life back was to leave where I'd been all those years—not because they threw me out but because I decided to leave all of that behind. It sounds like a mind game, but it honestly wasn't." He pauses and adds: "Maybe I've always had a somewhat inflated image of myself, perhaps built on a sterling education and the ego benefits I've derived from several high-profile jobs. But when you fire me, in time I'll more than likely feel that it's your loss, that the company will miss me more than I'll miss the company, that I'll land on my feet in what's probably a better place."

What he's talking about, of course, is affective and cognitive disengagement. His decision not to pursue litigation and recognizing that it would leave him stuck contrasts with the many cases of divorce that effectively leave people stalled in a holding pattern for years and years, because they believe they should persist and "win."

Delia faced a decision too, and it was a difficult one for her. The mother of four had had the good fortune to work long distance for close to twenty years, literally out of her kitchen, as part of a mail-order company that sold organic baby gear. The idea for the company had been a friend's. Delia was an unpaid volunteer at first, but she really believed in the mission; it wasn't long before she was being paid by the hour. As the company grew, so did Delia's involvement. Over time, however, the disparity between what she brought to the enterprise and how she was profiting began to nag at her. The problem was that she had trouble asserting herself and was completely conflicted about making demands: "I didn't know how to put myself in the equation," she says. "I loved the work, the people, the goals—basically everything—but at the same time, I felt I was being taken advantage of. I didn't know how to ask for what was fair or how to say no. I've dealt with most things by being loyal and persistent, staying involved, instead of pulling back and setting boundaries. I really didn't know what to do." It won't come as a surprise that her relationship to her friend and boss became more and more strained.

What ended up happening was that Delia got sick as the stress of unresolved conflict took its toll. Study after study has shown that being sick with worry or stress isn't just a figure of speech but happens on a literal level. In the end, Delia did quit but only because her doctor pretty much insisted on it. She's still sorting out what was lost and gained in this experience but now recognizes that being able to quit has to be part of her skill set in the future.

Being able to quit—even when a circumstance or situation isn't of your own making—is one way of getting control back over your own life.

Faking Out the Ruminator

Rita's story sheds another light on why it's sometimes hard to quit. "I'd gone to work with an old friend to set up a new nonprofit," she explains. "At the beginning, it was really exciting—brainstorming, coming up with a mission statement and plans for both the organization and its functions, laying the groundwork, doing publicity, and getting the word out. I felt terrific because I was finally using all the skills I'd accumulated and honed in two decades of corporate work and putting them to use for a goal bigger than advancing sales. But three years in, I realized I'd become a kind of nonprofit beggar, begging for money from companies that supposedly supported our cause but honestly didn't want to give us much of anything. It didn't help, of course, that all this effort pretty much coincided with a recession and a retrenching of corporate giving."

She describes how her work life just deteriorated. "My friend was my boss, and to be sure, she was bummed and frustrated too, but she was sure that if I only tried harder, I could make it work. She pushed me hard and wouldn't listen to what I reported back from these meetings, where I would pitch and smile and they'd smile and make promises and then no check would be forthcoming. She laid all of that at my feet."

Rita wanted to quit, but she was also hesitant: "Hanging in has always been my stock-in-trade. I felt I owed it to the organization and my boss to keep going. I finally began to run out of gas, but every time I thought about quitting, I was enveloped by worry. Every story of every person who couldn't find a new job after quitting stuck in my head—horror stories about people who'd been looking for work for years. I did the math on what our family finances would be like without my income, and I clutched. I couldn't stop myself from thinking about the worst-case scenarios, not even at night. I was utterly stuck."

There's a difference between reflecting on what's happened in your life—whether it's a setback, a stumbling block, or an outright failure—and ruminating about it. Rumination is passive, creating a closed loop of images, feelings, and thoughts that focus solely on the negatives, effectively preventing you from reframing your vision, coming up with solutions, and taking action. It's a closed room in the mind without windows and doors. At one point or another, most of us have found ourselves, momentarily at least, trapped in that dark night of the soul; for some of us, though, it is a chronic problem.

Studies have shown that women are more likely to ruminate than men, although the reasons aren't entirely clear. It's been suggested, by Susan Nolen-Hoeksema and others, that women's tendency to ruminate may be a reflection of living a more stressful life than men (parenting strains, increased role burdens, and the like), or it may reflect how women are socialized. Studies show that mothers tend to teach their male infants to contain and suppress emotion in infancy, in part because they're often fussier than girl babies. Cultural norms that require males not to show negative affect, especially tearfulness, because it's a sign of weakness doubtless also play

a role. In addition, mothers talk to daughters about emotions generally and sadness specifically earlier and much more frequently than
they do with sons.

Nolen-Hoeksema and Benita Jackson, in a series of studies to
investigate why women were more likely to ruminate than men,
found that several factors contributed. First, compared with men,
women tended to believe that negative emotions (fear, sadness, and
anger) were harder to control, and this belief resulted in their having more trouble controlling those emotions. This belief too may
have been bolstered by the widespread cultural belief that women are
more emotional than men by nature. Second, women are socialized
to feel responsible for the emotional tenor of relationships; this, the
researchers hypothesize, "may make women vigilant to their own
emotional states as barometers of how their relationships are going,
contributing to their rumination." Finally, the cultural belief that
women have less control than men over the important events in their
lives may contribute to increased rumination. Whatever the underly-
ing causes, women should be especially attentive to how rumination
figures in their lives and affects their ability to quit artfully.

Opening the windows and doors on rumination is what's
called for, and getting support can make all the difference if you
are stuck in a pattern. Gather friends whose judgment you trust,
and talk to them about where you find yourself; listen to how they
see your situation, and try redirecting your thoughts. Of course, a
good therapist can also help you get off the ruminative merry-go-
round. Focus on disrupting the ruminative loop with new thoughts,
not just distractions. Remember that telling yourself not to worry
is basically a strategy for inviting your worries to stay for a while.
Consciously focus on positive cues, and push yourself into acting,
even if it's only making a list of what you plan to do to get yourself
out of the loop. As the lab studies make clear, visualizing a happy
and stress-free event that has actually happened in your life can also
help you cope with rumination.

Become conscious of how you're stacking the deck with negatives, and make a list of your worries. Sort them out: Which are
likely to happen, and which aren't? One strategy for dealing with

repetitive and intrusive thoughts is to confront them head-on; confronting your fears has a way of defanging them. Imagine what you would do in the worst-case scenario you keep thinking about. What if you can't make things work and the relationship ends? What if you have to admit that the project you've embarked on will most likely fail? Or that you're not the right person to try to make it work?

Answering that last question—"Am I the person to make this work?"—was what finally gave Rita what she calls permission to quit: "I realized I was making myself responsible for everything that did or didn't happen at work, but when I took a hard look at how my job description had shifted—I was nothing but a fund-raiser—I realized how bad a fit it was for me. I didn't feel comfortable in the role, and it probably showed. Once I understood that, I stopped stewing and took an inventory of my life and what I wanted. And what I had to do was clear. I quit."

Chasing White Bears: Outsmarting Your Shortcomings

Daniel Wegner, the very man who discovered the way white bears work in our thoughts, has offered some suggestions about how to deal with them in a piece called "Setting Free the Bears." Most of the suggestions are eminently practical and worth pursuing, though none of them is, as he readily admits, scientifically proven. First of all, he suggests, recognize that stress and overload decrease the ability to exert self-control, so whatever you can do to lighten your mental load is helpful. Make yourself aware of the memory tasks you're juggling, and let go of the pressure to respond quickly. You can use the technique that's been shown to work for state-oriented people by visualizing a relaxing or happy time in your life, too. Wegner mentions that consciously assigning yourself a worry time—a specific time slot called "thought postponement"—works for some people.

While it may seem counterintuitive, inviting the white bear in may be the best strategy. Making the thought intentional has a way of exposing it. You can say it out loud or simply think about it.

Try meditation or other exercises that inculcate mindfulness. Originally a Buddhist technique, directing the mind intentionally to the present moment—the "now" of experience—has the effect of quieting insistent thoughts or worries that may occupy center stage. Various programs that induce mindfulness may include different elements, among them breathing techniques, yoga, or other exercise, but all serve the same end.

Learning Curve

By her own account, it took Jill thirteen years to quit the practice of law. Like many young people, she'd graduated from college unsure about her future career path. Even though her degree was in science, she knew she didn't want to go to medical school or pursue a Ph.D.; teaching appealed to her, but with student loans to repay, she considered that path too economically challenging. She ended up going to law school pretty much by default, realizing, she says now, "that I wasn't likely to be passionate about law or working as a lawyer."

But she was good at it. She did very well in law school and joined a firm where she focused on litigation. She liked the people she worked with and they liked her. The problem was that she hated the adversarial nature of the work. "I know it sounds crazy, but it was the worst possible career choice for me because I hate arguing. I knew that from the start. But I'd invested so much time becoming a lawyer and then working that it was hard even to think about quitting, and besides, I couldn't envision any alternatives. So I kept going."

Five years in, she moved to a large firm that offered her more money. She seriously considered quitting during her first maternity leave, but she found no support among her family and friends. She was making a large salary and working at a prestigious job, and the consensus was that she should consider herself lucky. She shelved the idea. The day-to-day, though, didn't get any better, and whenever she began to consider getting off the track and finding something she was passionate about, she encountered stiff resistance. Even her husband thought the idea of quitting made no sense; if she hung in there until she made partner, she'd be able to cut down on her travel, work fewer hours, and spend more time at home. Then again, if she put in another ten years, she'd have enough money so she could retire, if she wanted.

"You have to understand that while I hated the hours and the time away from home, the idea of quitting wasn't about getting back on the mommy track, as it is for some women," Jill says quietly. "The truth is that my kids were happy and thriving, and my husband was there when I wasn't. My salary made our life very comfortable. What made it hard was that wanting to quit was about me, my needs, and it felt selfish. The longer I worked, the more I felt obligated to everyone—my husband, my kids, my parents—to keep going. But at the same time, I just hated the work. So I focused on making partner as the interim goal and hoped like anything that it would change how I felt."

Jill was treated for depression during these years and was sometimes put on medication. "Unfortunately," she notes, "it wasn't about a chemical imbalance. I just hated the work I did and how uncomfortable it made me, even though I was successful at it." She made partner and while she was then making even substantially more, nothing really changed. Then, the management made an offer to the partners: They could work part-time, if they chose. Jill jumped at the chance, only to find herself facing stiff opposition. "They retracted the offer," she says. "It was as though I'd crossed a line somehow. They basically told me the work I did had to be done just the way I was doing it."

That moment forced Jill to recognize that she only had two choices: to stay or leave. She decided to give her notice, a full year ahead so that she could fulfill all the obligations she had to clients and colleagues, and immediately felt better. The firm was grateful for how she handled things and treated her well in return.

"I felt I actually got to know myself in this long process of quitting," she says now. "I was finally forced to figure out what I wanted, instead of navigating a course that was defined by what I didn't want." Even though she didn't have a plan B, she gave herself a year to find her footing. She decided to explore a career in education—something she'd been interested in long ago but had rejected as impractical at the time. But now, with her years of earning and saving as a cushion, a career in education seemed possible, and she began to explore it systematically. She volunteered at a school, then observed classes, and taught as a substitute. Convinced that this was the right path, she went back to school to earn a master's degree in education.

Jill is now happy in her work, teaching science, and loves being part of a team, mentoring young people and feeling that she's part of a larger community and serving a higher purpose. She's glad to have the luxury of time with her family, instead of being on the road or stuck in a court case being tried in another city. "A lot of people see the choices I've made only in terms of financial sacrifice, and I've taken some flak," she says. "But there are also some of my former colleagues who say they envy me. It's true that life isn't as financially stable or easy as it once was, but at the same time, it's a blessing to love what you do every day."

Conscious Goal Setting

While we've stressed cognitive and affective disengagement in this chapter, mastering the art of quitting includes the redirection of thoughts, feelings, and energy toward a new goal or goals, as well as strategies for their achievement. In the next chapter, we'll turn to the task of assessing the goals we have and those we will set for ourselves.

Your Quitting Aptitude

This exercise is intended to increase your awareness of how you approach the task of managing your emotions. Read the following statements, and decide whether they belong in the "me" or "not me" category.

1. I consider myself a realist, and I think my optimism gives me a leg up.
2. I consider myself a realist, and thinking about the downside doesn't overwhelm me.
3. The minute I finish one thing, I start worrying about everything else I have to do.
4. If I've done all I can about a situation, I put it out of my mind.
5. At work, I focus on making as few mistakes as possible.
6. I focus on doing the best I can in any situation.
7. When I'm bummed out, it's hard for me to focus on the positive.
8. I deal with stress by thinking of happier times.
9. When I argue with someone, I'm quick to flash and lose my temper.
10. Even when I'm fighting with someone, I try not to become hostile or demeaning.
11. I deal with stressful situations by pulling away consciously so I don't react.
12. I deal with stressful situations by trying to stay open to the other person's point of view.
13. Don't look to me to "kiss and make up." It's not going to happen.
14. I try to come up with constructive solutions to a fight or disagreement.
15. I worry a lot about failing and what people will think if I do.
16. Sooner or later, everyone's bound to fail at something.
17. It's really hard for me to move on from a disappointment.
18. I've been concentrating on letting go of old hurts and disappointments.
19. I hate it when I feel nervous, anxious, or afraid. I do whatever I can to stop feeling what I'm feeling.
20. I listen to my inner voice when I'm upset or afraid.
21. I get hugely pissed off when I've lost an opportunity or an edge. I'm really competitive, and I can't stop thinking about what has happened.
22. When things go wrong, I do my best to remind myself of what I'm good at and that there will be other opportunities.
23. I don't believe in intuition, just clear thinking.
24. I think it's important to listen to my gut and pay attention to my feelings.

25. I get flooded with emotions under stress.
26. I'm able to calm myself down through exercise or talking to my friends.
27. I think showing emotion is a sign of weakness.
28. I focus on what I'm feeling before I act.

The number of even-numbered items you've identified as "me" in this list reflects how much you've already cultivated your aptitude for quitting.

CHAPTER SIX

Taking Stock

Even though you might have assumed you were driving the car that's you when you started reading this book, you probably have come to realize that you're not in as much control of that vehicle as you thought. It's time to help you adjust your brakes, steering, and accelerator—your conscious behaviors —so you can start assessing your goals to see if they're feasible, congruent or conflicted, and, most important, making you happy. But first, we're going to tell you about the invisible gorilla, which may, once again, leave you feeling that you haven't been driving the car after all. The invisible gorilla is important at this point because it proves that for at least half of us, when we focus on a goal with full concentration, we also narrow our focus and make it more likely that we'll miss crucial information that's hiding in plain sight.

How and why our attention to detail doesn't come close to our mental image of it is important to understand as we set about the business of taking stock of the goals we have and considering whether we need to quit some of them.

Did You See the Gorilla?

In the late 1990s, two Harvard researchers, Daniel J. Simons and Christopher F. Chabris decided to follow up on some startling observations about attention first examined in the 1970s by Ulric Neisser. They videotaped two teams of students, one group dressed in black and the other in white, who were passing an orange basketball to one another. In the middle of the videotape, though, for a period of roughly nine seconds (the whole video was roughly a minute), a woman wearing a gorilla suit walked amid the players, faced the camera, thumped on her chest, and exited. Simons and Chabris showed the video to students in a lab setting, divided them into two teams, and had them count the number of passes made by the white team or the black team. The investigators ran a number of variations of the experiment, with students either counting just passes or combinations of passes and bounces. Then they asked the participants if they'd noticed anything unusual about the video, which finally led up to the last question: "Did you see the gorilla?" Most amazingly, roughly half of the participants missed the gorilla entirely; in fact, they were utterly shocked that there *was* a gorilla. (You can watch this video on YouTube or on the Web site connected to Simons and Chabris's book of the same name, www.theinvisiblegorilla.com. Of course, you'll see the gorilla because you already know it's there.)

We've already seen how much of what we "see" and judge is, in fact, governed by automatic processes or by the brain's relatively limited ability to take in the huge amount of stimuli and outside information offered up by our senses. The technical term for what makes half the people miss the gorilla is *intentional blindness*. The bottom line is that half the participants were so focused on counting the passes and bounces that they were blind to the gorilla hidden in plain sight; their missing the gorilla is only surprising to us because humans tend to overestimate the amount of detail we can pay attention to at any time. So much for multitasking. Intentional blindness accounts for why eyewitness accounts are hugely unreliable (we completely overestimate our ability to take in detail) and why memories of events and situations are often faulty.

One of the researchers, Simons, and his colleagues wondered whether missing the gorilla had to do with the passivity of watching a video. Was seeing something in two dimensions making people blind in a way that they wouldn't be in a real-world, three-dimensional setting? Their experiment, which involved an experimenter posing as a lost visitor on a college campus, holding a map in his hand, and asking directions from random pedestrians, is astonishing. As the experimenter and the helpful pedestrian are talking, two men carry a door between them, momentarily hiding the experimenter from view as they pass; behind the door, another experimenter takes the first experimenter's place, armed with an identical map in hand, and continues the conversation. The helpful pedestrians, by the way, ranged from age twenty to sixty-five.

Again, only half of the people noticed the switch! Interestingly enough, all of the people who noticed the switch were roughly the same age as the experimenters; all of the older people missed it. The researchers hypothesized that noticing the switch has to do with belonging to the same social group (someone close enough in age to be a student) and thus paying more attention to individual features. In other words, the older people simply automatically categorized the experimenter as "other" (young) and looked no further. Again, keep in mind that human beings are wired to assess situations (dangerous or not, friendly or not) without being consciously aware of the process.

To test that hypothesis, they ran the experiment again, this time dressing the experimenters as construction workers who would, of course, be "other" in terms of the population on a college campus and thus outsiders to their social group. But these men were visually readily distinguishable, even though they were similarly dressed; one had a construction hat with lettering and wore a tool belt and a light blue shirt while the other wore a hat without a logo, no tool belt, and a black shirt. This time, all the pedestrians who were stopped were young. And this time, only one-third of the pedestrians noticed the switch—even fewer than the first time!

If you're shaking your head, thinking that this had to be an extraordinarily oblivious group of pedestrians and that you would notice the switch for sure (just the way you know you'd have seen the gorilla), then you've got plenty of company. In fact, in a follow-up experiment by Daniel T. Levin and others, change-detection scenes were either described or shown in the form of still photos to participants in the experiments. A whopping 83 percent of them said with confidence that they would have noticed the switch—a rather larger number than the 11 percent who did notice when they participated in the actual experiment. When it came to the pedestrian asking directions in the door-switch experiment, almost 98 percent were sure they would have noticed the switch.

Knowing about intentional blindness and change blindness is useful, especially as it pertains to goal pursuit; when we're focused on one goal, we may not be seeing what's actually in plain view. In fact, the invisible gorilla may be most valuable as a metaphor for what *can* happen when you're single-mindedly in hot pursuit of a goal and completely focused. Substitute what you will for the word *gorilla*— the tensions in your marriage you're ignoring, the signs that you are no closer to achieving your goals despite all your efforts, how your focus is shortchanging you and others, or even the more accessible goal that might yield more life satisfaction—and you'll have a glimpse of the possible cost of not seeing that gorilla. In the same way, your overconfidence in your ability to spot detail and assess a situation accurately may blind you to other aspects of goal seeking. Knowing that the gorilla might be there, even if you can't see it, or that you might be missing the forest for the trees in a very literal way—not noticing that the person you were talking to has been replaced by someone else, for example—is a first step in self-correction.

If you're thinking to yourself that there's no doubt that you're part of the 50 percent who saw the gorilla, we'd still like you to keep the gorilla in mind. And that goes for the almost 98 percent of you who are positive you notice every change in your immediate environment. Keep in mind that both how you set goals and how you pursue them are also influenced by all the unconscious and automatic processes described in the first chapter and elsewhere. When you're rating how successful your efforts are, you're likely to be paying more attention to hits than misses, and it's likely that you'll be qualifying some of those misses as near misses, too. After all, you're only human.

Because much of what passes for popular wisdom about goals, goal setting, and motivation, alas, is wrongheaded at worst and simplistic at best, it's likely you're not thinking about your goals in the way you need to. Let's take a look at some of it and see what applications there are to the task at hand.

"Goals Gone Wild": You As Your Own Manager

No, that's not a typo (we got your attention, though); it's supposed to be *goals*, not *girls*. "Goals Gone Wild" is actually the title of a Harvard School of Business white paper that challenges some of the wisdom cultivated in the last twenty-five years of research and advice about goal setting in the work environment. Some of what they have to say is pretty counterintuitive and has more than a little application to the task of assessing your own goals, as well as analyzing how the company you work for uses motivation. If you're thinking of establishing a start-up, working on something entrepreneurial, or going into partnership with someone, these observations are valuable; they can equally be applied to relationships. The point here is to get you thinking about goals consciously, and what better place to study goals than in the business world?

Let's begin with what theorists have proposed first, as discussed in an important summary by Edwin A. Locke and Gary P. Latham:

"Specific, high (hard) goals lead to a higher level of task performance than do easy goals or vague, abstract goals such as the exhortation to 'do one's best.'" This statement basically repeats the mantra of "the higher the bar, the better the jump," but it has an important qualifier: The person has to be committed to the goal, has to have the ability or skill to achieve it, and must not have any conflicting goals. The question about conflicting goals is especially important because while it may be possible in a work environment to rule out conflicting goals—particularly since a third-party is determining them—in the larger setting of life, it's often difficult. Congruency matters. The mantra assumes that the harder goal will inspire not just more motivation but also greater feelings of personal success and satisfaction than an easy goal.

But the virtue of the high goal is, in part, contradicted by certain important caveats that apply to the goals you set for yourself as well. These too demand attention.

Learning goals *aren't* enhanced by raising the bar in this way. This is a point everyone, especially parents, should keep in mind. Focusing on a learning goal only in terms of performance can lead to tunnel vision—worrying about the grade instead of the acquisition of skills. One study, for example, showed that MBAs who embraced broader learning goals beyond just getting good grades (focusing on mastering specific material, working on networking, etc.) actually ended up with higher GPAs than the students who focused on GPA alone. (This may go a long way toward explaining why the emphasis on test scores and grades in high school and college has resulted in not just lower levels of skill acquisition but a pandemic of cheating.)

It's important to frame the goal correctly. In light of the discussion about both framing and avoidance and approach goals in the previous chapters, this caveat addresses how various carrot and stick approaches work in real-life situations. There's wisdom here that needs to be applied both to the goals you set for yourself—making sure that the bar isn't set too high—as well as to the goals set for you by others, both in relationships and at work. It's another reason to let go of the notion that failure is a learning experience from which success will, inevitably, come; most people don't learn from their failures. In addition, goals presented as challenges lead to higher performance than those that include the threat of failure.

Numerous studies, including one by Anat Drach-Zahavy and Miriam Erez, have shown how framing affects performance directly. Their study, which had participants predict stock performance on the basis of business data, showed the difference between a task presented as a challenge, which promoted strategizing and produced better results, and the same task presented as a threat, which focused only on immediate performance and the possibility of failure. In the experiment, they framed the task as a challenge by telling participants to provide their names and phones numbers so that the *best* performers could be contacted; the researchers also told the participants that only 15 percent of the students who had previously performed these tasks had succeeded. In contrast, in the threat framing, participants were asked to provide their names and numbers so that the five *worst* performers could be contacted, and the investigators added that 85 percent of the students who had performed the task earlier had failed. Finally, the participants were asked either to (1) do their best (easy, vague goal); (2) meet the goal of 80 correct predictions (challenging, performance-based goal); or (3) spend the first twenty minutes of the hour-long test finding the best strategies for completing the tasks successfully (challenging, broader goal). Not only did the challenge participants outperform the threat group significantly, but those who were focused on strategy over performance did the best of all.

How you frame your goals is essential.

Remember the Pinto

So, is setting the bar high for yourself a good strategy? According to Ordóñez and the other folks who wrote the deliciously titled "Goals Gone Wild," not necessarily.

Perhaps "Remember the Pinto" doesn't quite have the staying power of "Remember the Maine" as a call to arms, but it's one of the best examples that Ordóñez and her coauthors present. (Their paper predates the financial meltdown of 2008–2009, so they didn't have the skinny on the subprime mortgage debacle and the goals set by banks to draw on, but they do mention a precursor, the collapse of the Continental Illinois Bank.)

Anyway, the short and long of the Pinto story is this: In the late 1960s, Lee Iacocca, the legendary and flamboyant best-selling author, president of Ford, and marketing guru, was concerned by foreign competition. He announced that the company would produce a new car that would cost less than $2,000 and weigh under two thousand pounds and, moreover, that the Pinto would be ready for the market pronto. The company went into overdrive (forgive the pun) to deliver on its promise. Alas, the pressures of both the goal and its timing essentially forced managers to take shortcuts to get the car out there. Among the things cut were safety checks, and it turned out that these shortcuts yielded a not-so-tiny problem: The Pinto had a tendency to catch fire in an accident. But the executives didn't stop and redesign; with Iacocca's goal still firmly in mind, they did the math and figured that whatever it might cost to settle lawsuits about the car's deficiencies would be outweighed by the number of cars they could sell and, of course, the achievement of the goal Iacocca had set.

The Pinto is only one of several examples that lead the authors to caution against the "high bar" goal. The narrowness of focus induced by a single difficult goal not only encourages people to take shortcuts like those Ford's executives took but also facilitates lying and cheating, all in the name of achieving the goal. Interestingly, one of the article's examples is the disastrous and tragic failed Mount Everest expedition, which became the subject matter of Jon Krakauer's book *Into Thin Air*. In that case, the team leaders, who were the experienced climbers, so identified with their clients' goal to reach the summit that like the Ford executives, their focus overrode their caution and judgment.

How the setting of a time limit for achievement affects human behavior is amplified by other examples beyond the Pinto; similarly, goals that are simply too challenging also encourage unacceptable amounts of risk taking, as does setting too many goals at once. Finally, stringent goal setting undermines intrinsic motivation in a business setting. These are, the authors assert, the very predictable consequences of setting high performance goals. In fairness, we must add that the rejoinder to "Goals Gone Wild" was published by Edwin A. Locke and Gary P. Latham, who criticized the authors' use of anecdote.

What are the takeaways for the rest of us, trying to manage our own goals? Here are some suggestions, none of them vetted by science but entirely in keeping with what research has suggested.

Setting a performance goal isn't necessarily a good thing. Thinking about what you want to achieve as a learning goal—one that requires the mastery of certain skills or the formulation of strategies to achieve your end goal—may be more helpful than simply setting a performance goal. The cultural wisdom about persistence, of course, tends to emphasize performance, and as a result, people tend to think about their goals in those terms. In the arena of work, it might be making $150,000 a year; becoming a vice president of the corporation or making partner in five years; hitting X amount of dollars in sales. But focusing on how you are going to get there—and being flexible about your strategies—is more likely to increase your chances of success than is focusing on performance alone.

That's also true of goals we set in the area of relationships—smoothing out problems, improving communication, becoming closer, making new friends—which may be better served by thinking about what you need to do to achieve that end, rather than thinking about the end itself. This requires a mental shift: instead of thinking about finding the right partner for yourself, think instead about what you can do to make yourself more open and more communicative when you meet someone you might consider as a partner. In the next chapter, we'll tackle how mental contrasting may help you achieve more in every area of goal pursuit.

Framing may be the key to successful goal setting. Understanding how you personally respond to challenges in your life is a necessary first step before you begin to assess your own goals and how they connect to your own happiness. As discussed, your propensity for seeing things in terms of either approach or avoidance will influence both the goals you set for yourself and how you respond to the work of achieving them. In addition to articulating your goals consciously, you'll need to become fully aware of how you frame them or, for extrinsic goals, how other people are framing them for you. Imagine that you are assigned a task and are told that 85 percent of the people who attempted the task failed; are you more likely to identify yourself with the 15 percent who succeeded? Does the stress of a challenge energize you, or does it stop you in your tracks? (That's a sneaky way of asking whether you are action or state oriented.)

If you're having difficulty in a relationship—it could be with a spouse, a friend, a relative, or a colleague at work—do you tend to frame the difficulty in terms of a challenge ("We could be so much closer if we learned not to argue over the small stuff"), or do you often frame it as a threat ("I'm not seeing how we're going to stay together if we don't stop bickering over every little thing")? How would you respond to those two ways of framing? In any kind of partnership—whether it's in the arena of work or love—it's important to pay attention to how the other person is framing not just his or her goals but also your mutual goals. The kind of conscious appraisal of goals we're advocating relies on being aware of framing as a process.

Single-mindedness isn't reliably helpful. Along with rugged individualism, our cultural mythologies extol keeping your eye on the prize, but as the examples of the invisible gorilla and the Pinto demonstrate, that's not necessarily the best approach. In fact, single-mindedness is, in many ways, the very opposite of the mental contrasting that you need to learn to function at your best. A narrow focus, too, makes you much more vulnerable to other kinds of cognitive distortion—making us more vulnerable to counting hits rather than misses, intermittent reinforcement, the sunk-cost fallacy, and a brand-new one based on an article written by B. F. Skinner, called "The Superstitious Pigeon."

What Skinner did—and we apologize ahead of time to animal lovers and advocates, but this all took place over sixty years ago—was to put a very, very hungry and deliberately starved pigeon in a cage. A food dish swung into the cage at random intervals. Skinner discovered that three-quarters of the pigeons attributed causality to their actions and the appearance of the food. How did Skinner deduce this? By the repeated behaviors of the pigeons themselves. Whatever they happened to be doing—which, of course, was totally unrelated to the delivery of food—when the food appeared was what they would do to "make" it appear again. These behaviors were very distinct and obvious—one bird would twirl around, stretching its neck, while another would hop from side to side, and so forth.

Skinner drew an analogy between the pigeon's behavior and the superstitious rituals people engage in, such as wearing a lucky shirt or hat. Skinner focuses on the bowler who, having already released the ball, continues to motion with his or her arms and shoulders to keep the ball out of the gutter and on line to strike the pins. This behavior will certainly be familiar to anyone who has ever set foot in a bowling alley or who has watched someone try to sink a putt.

Think of the bowler as a metaphor, and ask yourself whether you're like the bowler when you're pursuing a goal single-mindedly. Are you likely to assume a causality every time you think you're making progress? Is your focus letting your brain go on automatic— the kind of fast thinking that has people drawing inferences where there are none—or are you paying attention to strategy? The single-minded approach, alas, is more likely to make you the bowler gesturing at the ball than not, no matter what the "keep your eye on the prize" myth says.

Perhaps even more importantly, the narrow focus encourages you to look at a single goal out of context, without looking at its relationship to other important goals in your life.

Are your goals in sync? As we'll see, much of our happiness, in fact, depends not on achieving a single goal but how close we come to achieving all the various goals we have at any moment. For most of us, this is a grab bag of short- and long-term aspirations, personal and professional goals, and learning and performance goals that may be approach or avoidance oriented. The kind of reductionist thinking that comes out of focusing on one goal animates many of the cultural discussions about having it all.

Seen from the point of view of goal theory, whether we can have it all has a great deal to do with the amount of conflict or congruence between important goals. A good example is the article published in the *Atlantic* in 2012 by Anne-Marie Slaughter. Titled "Why Women Still Can't Have It All," the piece ignited a firestorm of comment, pro and con, and garnered a lucrative book deal for its author. Slaughter, a Princeton professor, was at the time working for the US government, which required her to work in Washington, D.C., and to travel frequently; she was also the mother of two sons, who stayed in Princeton with their father, a professor, during her two-year tenure. A crisis with one of her children forced her to give up her government job—hence the "not having it all" gist of the piece.

From our point of view, the real question is why she didn't anticipate, as her children neared adolescence, a possible conflict between her goal of holding down a high-level job in the government and that of being a mother. Why was it surprising that goals that appeared to be manageable, if not really congruent by definition, came into conflict, and that she was required to make a choice? It seems that if we are hell-bent on having it all, each of us needs to take a look at our goals in relation to each other, not as single, unrelated items on a wish or to-do list. Changing our focus to a broader view in this way may be the only way to get close to having it all—whatever *all* might be.

Thinking about our goals as interrelated instead of singular aspirations—as pieces of an interlocking design—helps us weigh our decisions about whether it's actually possible to achieve several goals at once and whether we should hang in or bail with greater intelligence. If what we want for ourselves consists of goals that are nearly congruent, then we're in good shape, but we'll still have to keep in mind that at some point, there might be a conflict. (This is exactly what Slaughter should have been able to imagine.) We also have to be prepared for the likelihood that, sometimes, goals we've achieved will stop making us happy.

That was the case for Robert, a property lawyer, whose main priorities included both a good salary and a challenging work environment, and for years, he achieved both. But after years of his practice, he found himself increasingly dissatisfied and bored; additionally, in a job that involves a tremendous amount of attention to detail, the more bored he got, the more he worried about making a mistake. His anxiety left him sleepless—reviewing details in his mind in the middle of the night—and only made him unhappier with his work. He realized that rather than manage the deals for his clients, what he wanted to do was be a part of the transaction itself. He found a partner for his venture, a designer, and bought his first property, which he intended to refurbish and put up for sale. Like most shifts in life, this change required him to redefine other goals as well and manage new stresses, one of which was the risk of failure. The pace of his new business required patience and vision, something else he had to come to terms with, along with the loss of the steady income stream he had been used to for many years. His faith in himself, too, was newly tested, but still, he was happy with the shift he'd made in his life.

Sometimes, a goal needs to be adjusted to accommodate other priorities. Getting married when she was a resident in pediatrics forced Diana to rethink both her specialty and the arc of her career. An only child, she'd always wanted children—her love for children drew her to pediatrics in the first place—but when she married Martin, whose specialty was international finance and who traveled widely, she realized she wanted a specialty that would be less demanding of her time. She basically started over, switching to radiology. It's a choice she has never regretted, she says: "In my case, the overarching goal was to live a life that balanced work and family. I knew that from the start. Is radiology as soul-satisfying as a pediatrics practice might have been? Perhaps not. But my choice was very deliberate, and I would have had to sacrifice a lot as a mother if I hadn't switched."

Too many of us find ourselves living with perpetual conflict because we haven't consciously made a choice about which goals are our absolute priorities.

Goals and Identity

The boy looks to be about six or seven and is wearing a Batman outfit. He and his father are waiting for their lunch to be brought to the table. The child is smiling broadly, holding a Batman action figure in his hand, gesturing as he speaks: "I know what I want to be when I grow up. I want to be Batman." The father smiles and says, "Jake, you can't be Batman, because Batman isn't real. He's a character in a story." There's a pause, and then the little boy says, "Well, I still want to be him. Getting the bad guys."

The father answers, "Well, you could be a policeman. Or a detective." "No," the little boy says firmly, "I don't want to be a policeman. I want to be Batman." This seems to take the father aback, but he answers anyway: "You could be a doctor like me, Jake. I decided to be a doctor when I was about your age, but you have lots of time to decide what you want to do." "Nope," says the little boy. "I want to be Batman, not a stupid doctor." The father looks up to see if the server is anywhere nearby, as if her presence might rescue him. "Jake," the man says, "Batman isn't real. You can't be Batman." The young woman puts their plates down just as the little boy answers, "You're wrong. I can be Batman. Just wait and see."

As children, we fantasize about what we'll be when we grow up—a veterinarian or an equestrian, a ballerina or an astronaut, a bus driver or pilot, a mommy or daddy, a professor or policeman, or perhaps Ariel the Little Mermaid—or even Batman. For a few of us, the trajectory will be the one the culture loves the best—the goal set early, the progress sure and steady, the rise respectable or meteoric. (This is the Steven Spielberg script: He knew that he wanted to be a filmmaker when he was a kid, set his plans accordingly, had early success, and kept going.) The myths of persistence have us imagining an upward trajectory, with a best-case scenario that's somewhere between very successful (for work) and happily ever after (for relationships) and that continues this way throughout life. But these stories of finding a passion early and achieving success without setbacks are the exceptions to the rule.

Many of us will choose a different path, trying on a number of things for size—different jobs, different relationships—to find out what will make us happy. Others of us will find work we like but may discover that it doesn't satisfy other important needs and goals at the time. Because our identity is fluid at different points in our lives, our goals may change in relation to each other. That was certainly the case for Daniel, now in his late fifties, who'd been happy teaching at a private school in his twenties, but became dissatisfied with the pay and how the role defined him. "I wasn't seeing myself in twenty years, wearing a frayed tweed jacket, still lecturing to sixteen-year-olds about Shakespeare," he says. "I just wasn't. So I retooled myself, first as a newspaper writer, and then, through a friend, I got a job at an advertising agency. I frankly wanted some prestige—it was important to me that I felt as worldly and accomplished as my friends—and how much money I made absolutely mattered. But with my kids grown, my sights began to shift. The truth was that teaching fed my soul in ways that my other work didn't; advertising was fun, competitive, and lucrative, but I still wanted something else." With his kids grown, Daniel was able, not without difficulty, to get back into teaching, which is what he's doing today.

Distractions, competing or interim goals, or even pressures of day-to-day life may complicate or disrupt our ability to reach an intended goal. That was certainly the case for Carolyn, now fifty-three, who decided to quit graduate school when she was twenty-four—a decision that, she says, is now "the bane" of her existence. "I loved my classes, and I was only twelve credits away from my degree—I had twenty-four out of the thirty-six—but I was also frazzled and clueless about what I wanted. I was going to school, holding down a job, trying desperately to sort myself out, and going through all the turmoil that twenty-somethings go through when they don't know what they want. Anyway, I quit graduate school." She ultimately got married, took some counseling classes, and then had a series of jobs she loved, doing prevention work and counseling for teens. After augmenting her education with graduate classes and then working as a drug counselor, she then quit to stay home with her three children. "It seemed like the right thing to do at the time, both economically and emotionally, but I was miserable," she says. "I felt like a useless lump, and when I got a call about a possible job, I jumped. I quit full-time motherhood without a single regret." She spent the next ten years doing drug and other counseling in a public school system until budget cuts made the job disappear.

This is the part of the story where that early decision—almost thirty years ago—comes in. Carolyn hasn't been able to find work as a counselor, a position she's held for two decades, because she doesn't have a master's degree in social work or another advanced degree. Nevertheless, it's clear that her overarching goal—wanting to work with people and counsel them—has stayed remarkably consistent over the years, even though she lost sight of it at the beginning and at other points in her life. Like many of us, she made her decisions caught up in the day-to-day, distracted by other interim goals, without being fully aware of her larger goal.

The truth is that Carolyn is not all that unusual. What she says now, though, reflects what she's learned: "I think the most important thing you can do for yourself is find out what's important to you before you find out what's important to everyone else. When I quit graduate school, I had no idea of what I really wanted, and no long-term vision. I didn't know how to pay attention to myself or my instincts, and that's been a struggle for me over the years. I've gone back to school and have gotten sidetracked because we needed money or other issues. Now, with my youngest child about to graduate from high school, I know both what I want to do and what I need to do to get it."

All of us juggle priorities and goals in the day-to-day, which is all the more reason we need to work on being clear about our aspirations. As Daniel Gilbert asserts, we don't just stumble into happiness, but also stumble into jobs, relationships, and all manner of other situations. Life is a lot messier than the laboratories in which experiments take place and theories are tested. That's why consciously appraising our goals is necessary, as Lynne's story of what is now known as a starter marriage demonstrates.

"I married a man my parents had introduced to me at the age of twenty-two," she says. "He was six years older than I, which was a substantial age difference—he was working and stable, and I was just out of college—and I had my doubts but somehow was swept into the energy of it all. He proposed to me in front of thirty people—what could I say, after all?—and though I thought about not going through with the wedding, I don't think I was sure enough of myself to do anything. But once we were married, I felt utterly stifled, boxed in. It was clear that he and I had different goals for ourselves, different ways of looking at the world, different priorities. I lasted two years, trying to see if I could make it work, and then I fled, literally fled. It is the first and only time I quit anything important; I married again at the age of twenty-eight, and I've been married for thirty-one years. I still wish I had handled it differently—talked to my ex-husband directly instead of being a runaway bride—but I wasn't able to at the time. I felt lonely and terrible afterward but not nearly as lonely as I did during the two years I was married."

Now, all these years later, with a satisfying career that she was able to balance with raising three children, she says, "What I did realize from this experience is that I needed a relationship that gave me more autonomy than that first relationship. That became one of my goals, and it's stood me in good stead."

Becoming as conscious as we can be of what we really want takes time, effort, and more than a little strategizing.

The Cost of Shifting Identity

Considering and evaluating our goals consciously, and perhaps even going a step further and actually disengaging from them, may also involve a true and sometimes painful shift in how we think of ourselves. Remember the story of Deidre, the young woman who was defined through her childhood, adolescence, and early young adulthood by her competitive swimming and who asked the question "Who am I if I'm not swimming?" Her question reflects the emotional and psychological cost of transition that may keep us from reevaluating our goals and disengaging from them.

That's the point William Bridges makes in his classic book, *Transitions,* which was inspired by his abandonment of his career path as a professor of literature. Bridges describes this "disidentification process" as "the inner side of the disengagement process. . . . The impact of such losses can be much greater than one imagines it will be." In his own experience, he was sure that he'd be fine with not being able to call himself a professor of literature anymore—the shorthand each of us uses as we sum ourselves up to strangers we meet as well as people we know—until his daughter came home one day and asked, "What are you, Daddy?" It turned out that the reason behind her question was benign—a discussion at school about what the children's fathers did for a living—but Bridges was utterly discomfited by not having a noun or two to describe himself, like "a college professor," as he had in the past. Instead, he had what he calls a "participial" identity, defined only by words ending in -*ing*: He was a man who was writing, consulting, lecturing. His realization that what his daughter wanted to take back to school wasn't a bunch of participles but something normal and concrete was painful.

This potential loss is what stops many of us from cataloging our goals and deciding whether to keep moving forward. The potential pain of disengagement is averted, as is the loss of those everyday definitions of self—whether it's "real estate lawyer," "Peter's wife or girlfriend," "artist," "stockbroker," or something else. It's significantly harder to lose the comfort of that label when it happens without volition—when we've been fired, laid off, or left by a lover or a spouse. The ability to disengage from the loss of self-definition is as much a part of the art of quitting as is managing regret.

Whenever we have to quit one goal and commit ourselves to something new, each of us moves from the safety of terra firma to the shaky and sometimes scary terra incognita. It's usually a bumpy ride.

Another Inventory

Because so much of human life is lived on automatic, taking an inventory of all of your conscious goals—figuratively going through your cupboard of aspirations—is a helpful first step toward becoming the best possible manager of your life. We recognize that the whole idea of these automatic processes is a bit unsettling—it's much more comforting to think that you're driving the car that's you. But acknowledging automatic processes will, in the end, give you more control. Your conscious goals will be thrown into high relief, and at the same time, help you see how your moods, emotions, and attitudes toward your goals are shaped by forces you're not even aware of.

Evidence of automatic processes is pretty much everywhere. One day, you'll consciously choose to drive a longer route to work so that you'll have more time to think about the upcoming day, but on another, you might not even know why you decided to take Main Street when St. Paul's is less clogged with traffic. What made you think that Jack was a nice guy and Philip a loser when you first met them? What makes you instantly comfortable in one environment, while being in another puts you in a lousy mood? Why is it that, on Tuesday, you're flying high and your goal looks good to go, but by Thursday, all you can think of is how totally doomed all your efforts are? Why can't you stop worrying about tomorrow some nights, no matter how hard you work at clearing your mind?

We already know that the answer to all of these questions is automatic process, and how the brain/mind is always "prospecting" for ways of getting goals, even unconscious ones, moving along. How that might work was demonstrated in a study that took on the question of why it's so hard to clear your mind of intrusive thoughts when all you really want to do is sleep. The researchers' hypothesis was that while these thoughts seem random or out of the blue, in fact they're triggered by future tasks that could (in the mind's opinion, at least) benefit from forethought. In other words, the mind or brain is actually jostling you to think, when consciously all you want to do is sleep. The researchers devised an experiment that tested whether anticipating a future task in which performance would be boosted by forethought would actually trigger more automatic intrusive thoughts than a task that was unlikely to be improved by forethought. The task they chose for participants was a geography quiz.

One group of participants was told that following an exercise in concentration, they'd be given a quiz in which they'd have to name as many U.S. states as they could. In truth, the researchers had no intention of actually giving them this quiz. The concentration exercise involved listening to an eight-minute audiotape on meditation and breathing. Because of the ironic-processing effect described by Daniel Wegner—telling people not to think about white bears makes them think of them—the subjects weren't instructed to clear their minds or ignore distracting thoughts. They were asked to focus on the breathing exercises but were told to write down any intrusive thoughts they had. The audiotape, of course, mentioned only breathing, not geography.

There were two control groups. One was given the same instructions as the test group but then was told there wouldn't be a geography quiz, just the concentration exercise. The second control group, though, was told they'd be given a speed counting test of the names of states at some point (as in "New York has seven letters"). Since forethought wouldn't actually improve one's ability to speed count, the researchers hypothesized that this second control group, like those who knew that they wouldn't be tested on the states' names, wouldn't have intrusive thoughts.

And that's exactly what happened. Only the first group—the ones who thought they were going to have to name states—actually experienced intrusive thoughts, as many as six pertaining to geography during the playing of the tape. Moreover, the intrusions weren't deliberate rehearsals but had the same random nature of out-of-the-blue thoughts. What's really remarkable, as the researchers note, is that given the short length of the concentration test, during which they were reminded again and again to focus only on breathing, the participants experienced any intrusive thoughts at all, "let alone those that were predicted to intrude into consciousness." (The audiotape was a scant eight minutes long!) The findings testify to the persistent nature of the mind's automatic processes.

You can't, of course, change how the mind functions, but by increasing your awareness of how and why you make the decisions to pursue one goal but not another, you can make yourself less vulnerable to automatic process. When your thoughts keep you up, you should look at whether they're really random or whether the mind is trying to plan for you. Substituting a conscious plan will help quiet your mind down, as will deliberately refocusing your thought process. Similarly, by becoming more conscious of not only what you're feeling but also why you're feeling it, you will also strengthen your command of your objectives. Research has shown that mood—separate and distinct from emotions—influences the goals you set for yourself and your pursuit of them.

To that end, before we catalogue our goals, we need to take a close look at "mystery" moods.

Moods and Emotions

We've already seen how the management of emotion and honing our ability to use our emotions to bolster our thought processes are key to both goal setting and goal disengagement. Examining how mood—another affective state—influences goal pursuit and appraisal adds another level of understanding.

What is mood, anyway? We've all experienced moods—the good, the bad, and the downright ugly—but how do they differ from emotions? We all know from experience that moods affect our judgment and our ability to regulate emotion and they challenge our objectivity. Moods, good and bad, shape how you perform at work, how much fun you have at that party, how quickly you're likely to lose your temper when your kid acts out, how you react when there's stress or a problem to be solved. What, if anything, can we learn from what science knows about moods, especially mystery moods?

In contrast to moods, emotions are consciously experienced and stem from an identifiable source: you feel happy because you've been praised or your beloved looks at you tenderly; you're blue because you've let your friend down or your dog has died. Moods are different; they are more diffuse, and while you may be aware of the mood you're in, sometimes you might not be. That is a *mystery mood*. How many of us have had a friend or spouse ask why we're in such a good or bad mood, only to answer—either defensively or indignantly—"No, I'm not!" Once you've had your mood pointed out, you may become aware of it, but you still might not know why you're feeling that way. The "nonconscious" nature of the mystery mood operates on two dimensions: the person's lack of awareness of the mood itself and his or her lack of conscious awareness of its origins.

When you know you're in a bad mood—or a good one, for that matter—and you know why you are (your boss screamed at you for no reason, or your long-awaited promotion came through), you are conscious of how your mood is affecting not just your general outlook on life but how you're processing information and thinking. That's not true of the mystery mood, though, and in that case, you'll be taking out your rose-colored glasses (or your doom-and-gloom ones) as you survey not just the general landscape but your goals and make decisions. Of course, just because you may be unaware of your mystery mood and its source doesn't mean something isn't causing it. One possible cause is what Tanya Chartrand and her colleagues call a "nonconscious" goal. What, precisely, is that?

It could be a goal that you've pursued for so long—chatting up and flattering your boss, trying to be more outgoing—that it's become automatic or a goal you haven't thought about consciously. The example Chartrand and her colleagues use is that of a guy named John, a perennial partygoer who, once upon a time, consciously cultivated his behavior to gain social acceptance. Since then, he has been to so many parties that he shifts into party mode without even being aware of what he's doing. But even though he's no longer conscious of that goal he set so long ago, the goal of being well-liked and appreciated is still present and is activated by simply being at a party. One night, though, no one smiles at him appreciatively or laughs at his jokes, and his mood darkens. But he can't really pinpoint why this party is leaving him feeling so dispirited.

Mystery moods can also be triggered by the environment—by objects, people, or situations that act as primes—or may be caused by the other people's nonverbal social behavior. Psychologists call this *social contagion*. You've probably experienced this yourself when you've realized that your blue funk is a result of spending too much time with a friend or friends who are down.

Mystery moods affect us both emotionally and cognitively. Because we don't know why we're feeling the way we are, we're likely to attribute those feelings to something random—another variation on Skinner's superstitious pigeon—rather than its true cause. Our mood, whether it's good or bad, affects how we process information and hence the tenor of our thoughts as well as our judgment about our goals. In line with the other evidence of the effects of overoptimism, positive mystery moods "lead to less effortful processing than negative moods," leading us to put a spin on our efforts to reach a goal that may not have any basis in reality. Mystery moods can convince us to keep pursuing a goal or can cue us to disengage. Even more important, trying to regulate our feelings and get out of the mood we're in may lead us to formulate new goals.

You can deal with mystery moods by countering them with conscious self-awareness, by making yourself focus on the possible cues that might have triggered your mood and then actively working to regulate that feeling. It's another step in the process of learning when you need to disengage from a goal and reengage your efforts in another direction.

Next, we'll turn to mapping our goals—surveying the territory of our wants, needs, and aspirations.

CHAPTER SEVEN

Mapping Your Goals

For years, many books and talks famously included a reference to a supposedly renowned and definitive study—variously attributed to the Harvard MBA class of 1954 or the Yale class of 1979—that explained why 3 percent of the class had made ten times more money than the other 97 percent within ten years after graduation. The answer was deliciously simple and very cool: The 3 percent had written their goals down. It's not hard to see why this supposed study made a fabulous sound bite—easy-to-remember numbers, marquee schools, and an easy way to guarantee success.

Not an Urban Legend, After All

Alas, no such study was ever conducted. But like the alligators in the New York City sewers, this urban legend deserves to be true. As it happens, a study done in 2011 at McGill and Toronto Universities shows that writing down goals is beneficial and that elaborating and reflecting on personal goals actually improves the performance of struggling students. Putting your goals in writing can enhance your ability to evaluate whether your efforts to reach a goal are working and whether attaining it is feasible; it helps clarify whether you should continue to pursue a goal or disengage from it. Mapping also allows you to see your goals in relation to each other, which is invaluable.

We mean *goal mapping* in a rather literal sense, with pen and paper or a computer screen at hand. (We suppose that if you're fabulously good at visualizing, you might even be able to do it in your head.) For most of us, though, writing about something clarifies our thought processes in important ways and forces us to be more articulate and concrete about our wants and aspirations. You can read through the pages of this chapter first without mapping your goals on paper or screen, if you like, and then double back, or you can map them, step-by-step, as you read.

Listing Your Goals

Use the following categories to organize your goals. Make two columns, one for short-term goals and the other for long-term ones. You can, if you wish, personalize the categories further; they are meant only as a starting point. Feel free to include any goals you think are pertinent. How you define *short term* and *long term* is up to you; a short-term goal can be defined in months or years as you wish.

Life Goals (Personal Strivings)

Your life goals include personal aspirations that pertain to the growth of the self (becoming a better leader, being less impulsive, feeling better about your choices, making peace with your limitations, for example). They can be broad or abstract (becoming a better listener, being more mindful, cultivating gratitude, being more responsive to others) or concrete (reading more books, wasting less time online, spending less money, working to resolve disputes, mastering a new language). They should include both approach goals—such as having children, being financially stable, owning a home, traveling the world, or doing anything else important to you—and goals focused on avoidance.

Career or Work Goals

The goals you have for your job or career can be as various as becoming a novelist or hedge-fund manager, finding a more interesting job, going back to school to switch careers, making more money, or working for a more sympathetic boss. You can also make the goal more specific, going beyond the mere description of the work or career and adding what you hope your work will add to your life, such as meaningfulness, a sense of community and belonging, daily satisfaction, and intellectual challenge. In the same way, you should add your avoidance goals, if you have any (such as staying out of fractious or demanding environments).

Relationship Goals

For relationship goals, list your aspirations for connection and affiliation (such a establishing an intimate and satisfying relationship, getting married, expanding your social circle, deepening your friendships, or improving family communications); add in concrete steps that will help you reach your more abstract goals (such as socializing more, doing volunteer work, joining a sports team, starting a book club, mentoring a child). Avoidance goals (e.g., staying out of family fights) may also be part of your list.

Learning and Achievement Goals

Your learning and achievement goals should be more concrete and reflect the other three categories; if a personal goal is financial stability, getting a higher-paying job or paying off student debt or incurring no new debt might be interim goals. If you're contemplating a career change, going back to school or networking could be one of your short-term goals.

In this first iteration, write down your goals in no particular order. If you'd like to see samples of what a goal map might look like, see Sample Goal Maps 1 and 2, at the end of this chapter on pages 171–172.

Intrinsic or Extrinsic?

Review your list of goals, and begin by asking whether each goal is extrinsic or intrinsic. As described by psychologists Richard M.

Ryan and his colleagues, extrinsic goals aren't just those imposed by third parties (e.g., your father, mother, mentor, or spouse wants you to be a lawyer, or your coach wants you to continue swimming) but are those that depend on the reaction or approbation of third parties. Extrinsic goals also tend to be the means to other ends, rather than ends in themselves. Our culture is, of course, obsessed with definitions of success that depend on extrinsic goals—namely, money, fame, and image.

In a study called "Further Examining the American Dream," Tim Kasser and Ryan asked adults and college students to self-report on four intrinsic aspirations and three extrinsic ones and denote which goals or principles were most central to their lives. The four intrinsic domains were self-acceptance (achieving psychological growth, autonomy, and self-regard); affiliation (having satisfying relationships with family and friends); community feeling (improving the world through activism or generosity); and physical fitness (feeling healthy and free of illness). The three extrinsic principles were financial success (being wealthy and materially successful); social recognition (being famous or well-known, and admired); appealing appearance (looking attractive in terms of body, clothing, and fashion). People who focused on more intrinsic goals reported greater well-being, less anxiety and depression, and fewer physical ailments than those who were directed toward extrinsic goals.

This doesn't mean that extrinsic goals are inherently bad or that striving for them necessarily dooms you to a life of unhappiness. Have no fear: You can safely keep lusting after a closet full of Louboutin shoes or a fully loaded Porsche. What does appear to matter is whether, first, you are pursuing extrinsic goals with autonomy and, second, how central to your sense of self the extrinsic goals are. Extrinsic goals, unfortunately, don't feed the soul; as the researchers write, "their allure usually lies in the presumed admiration that attends them or in the power and sense of worth that can be derived from attaining them." It turns out that just as the Beatles had it right when they sang, "Money can't buy you love," fame, money, and even beauty don't appear to guarantee happiness or life satisfaction, either, no matter what you see on television or in the pages of celebrity magazines. The happiest and healthiest people are those whose goals are preponderantly intrinsic, and contribute actively to their sense of self.

Write an *I* for "intrinsic" or an *E* for "extrinsic" next to each of your goals. Keep in mind, though, that even intrinsic goals may become shopworn over time; even a long-held intrinsic goal can stop making you happy, because both your sense of self and needs are fluid over time. While that is a good thing for personal growth, it does complicate life and may require you to make sometimes painful changes and abandon your goals.

That was certainly the case for Marie, who, after over twenty years as an artist, knew she had to quit. She'd known she wanted to be an artist from a very young age—three or four—and had the requisite talent, drive, and perfectionism. She went to a prestigious art college, launched her career as a commercial artist at the age of twenty-two, and married shortly after. She enjoyed success and moved from doing one-shot illustration to creating four-color books, which yielded a steady royalty stream; she then branched out into cards and calendars. Marie had wanted a career that gave her autonomy, permitted her to do what she loved in solitude, and let her make her own hours, but over the years, the very things she'd wanted for herself at the beginning began to make her increasingly unhappy. Because she had trouble managing her time, each project was chronically late and she felt trapped in her studio, cut off from the world.

Looking back, she says, "The way I worked was self-sabotaging and exhausting—physically, emotionally, artistically. My work was spectacular, but it was also eating me alive. I missed weddings, funerals, christenings, family holidays. At the same time, the marketplace shifted as the demand for gift books dried up. I was getting paid less and less for the work I did." She began slowly to reimagine her goals and to take steps that would propel her into a life with very different aspirations. More than anything, she wanted to be out in the world, connected to other people, away from her solitary working life as an artist.

Sometimes, a goal that appears to be intrinsic will turn out, in the end, to be only extrinsically rewarding. David was a child of divorce himself, and choosing family law as his specialty was conscious and deliberate; his goal was to work with couples to try to mitigate the strain and anguish experienced by families going through divorce. But some ten years into his practice, he began to understand that his own efforts on his clients' behalf often prolonged the divorce process and, from time to time, even amped up the damage inflicted on the family. The realization threw him into crisis; he quit his practice as a partner in a law firm and retrained as a mediator. It took him two years to decide to quit and another three to establish his solo mediation practice, but what he does for a living is now intrinsically motivated. His work reflects and is a part of his sense of self.

Articulating and mapping your goals and anticipating changes you might have to make in the future are effective strategies.

Conflict or Congruence?

The next step in the process is to review both your short- and long-term goals for conflict or congruence between them. Ask yourself if any of your short-term goals are related to your long-term goals or can be seen as stepping-stones to larger goals. In the best-case scenario, your short-term goals will facilitate your chances of succeeding at some of your long-term goals. In the worst, you will find that some of your goals—personal or professional—are in conflict.

As we've already discussed, conflicting goals are a reliable source of unhappiness and stress. Of course, the achievement of certain long-range goals—making partner in a large institution, building a business from the ground up, going to medical school and becoming a specialist—that require a tremendous investment of time and energy will, inevitably, be in conflict with other goals that draw on the same limited amounts of time and energy allotted to each of us. The conflicts between the demands of making enough money and the desire for an intrinsically rewarding and satisfying job are well known, as are the often conflicting demands of being an available and hands-on parent and pursuing a job or career that requires an outsize amount of time, effort, and diligence. Similarly, you're not likely to have the time to cultivate your other interests— whether that's playing golf or studying bookbinding or carpentry— no matter how personally rewarding they are, if you are devoting yourself to your career. Only you can answer the question of which of two conflicting goals is more important to you; there is no hard-and-fast rule that can be applied generally.

Rick grew up poor in Wisconsin, the only child of a mother whose husband had abandoned her. He attended college on a football scholarship and then earned an MBA from an Ivy League institution. His goals, set early in his twenties, were financial success, emotional stability and security, and the ability to work on his own terms with some autonomy. Strong-willed and very persistent, he married right out of college, eager to have the kind of family he hadn't had himself. After business school, he got a job at a prestigious consulting firm, working sixty to seventy hours a week, outflanking his peers and consistently racking up a series of promotions and pay raises. He was both praised and valued by his bosses. But the long hours he put in took a toll on his marriage, and he chafed at the total lack of autonomy he had in a traditional corporate setting; his job was to please both his bosses and his clients. Still, he kept on going until the day his wife walked out on him and he realized something had to give.

This moment, which might have been a turning point for him, wasn't. Most of his friends worked the same long hours he did, and their wives, their eyes on the long-term prize of big houses and expensive cars, didn't complain. As a result, Rick settled on the idea that what was wrong was his wife's attitude. He married again some three years later, and this time, the union lasted less than a year. He finally hit a wall at the age of thirty-five with a big bank account but little else. It took him close to two years to find a start-up opportunity he believed in, and he began soliciting investors. He succeeded in getting the venture off the ground and then settled into a forty-hour work week, which permitted him to start and pay attention to a new relationship. He finally managed to find a way of making his career and personal goals work without sacrificing one for the other.

If you have discovered potentially conflicting goals, start a new column and list those goals side by side under the heading "Conflict." If your goals are congruent, leave your lists as they are.

Approach and Avoidance

With your goals mapped out in front of you, think about how you tend to frame your goals. Are you in the habit of seeing your goals in terms of avoidance or approach? Is there a balance of each, or is there a preponderance of one or the other? Paying attention to how you frame your aspirations will help you get a better bead on whether you should continue heading in the same direction or whether you need to change your course, if only partly.

A Question of Priorities

To deepen your understanding of your goals, follow the steps described in the next few paragraphs. This expansion of the mapping exercise has three distinct parts. The first is creative and was inspired by the Toronto and McGill study.

Step 1: Write a description of what your future would be like under ideal circumstances. Imagine this as fully as you can, with as much detail as you can bring to it. You should include a description of the ideal you—with all of your personal strivings met. Include qualities of character and deportment as well as learning and mastery goals you would like to claim as yours.

Be as specific as you can be about your real-world goals. Imagine your personal and working life, where and how you're living, and how you spend your time and energy. Think about what goals you've already met, the balance between your leisure and work activities, and the amount of personal satisfaction you experience. Imagine your social circumstances, your circle of family and friends. Your financial circumstances should be part of your imagined scenario as well.

Step 2: Go back to your list of goals, and rewrite them in order of importance, giving each a number. If you have a list of conflicting goals, list them in order of priority too. Leave enough space so that you can write a few sentences or phrases beneath each of them. Drop from your list any goals that you feel, on reflection, aren't worthy of inclusion, and add any you think you have missed. Be as precise as you can about prioritizing; if two goals are too close to be easily distinguished, please number and label them as (a) and (b).

Step 3: Under each goal, write a sentence or two explaining why the goal is important to you and how achieving it will contribute to your sense of well-being, happiness, or success. If you have conflicting goals, write a sentence or two about the one you think you would have to give up and how disengaging from it would affect your life. Similarly, write a sentence or two about the goal you intend to continue pursuing and how achieving it would enrich or otherwise change your life.

With these three steps completed, reread what you've written about your ideal future, and then review your goals in order. Ask yourself the following questions:

- Do my goals reflect my vision of an ideal future?
- Are my short-term goals contributing to my long-term goals? Are they bringing me closer to achieving those goals?
- How many of my goals are abstract rather than concrete? Do I have the concrete steps in mind to be able to achieve them?
- Will my strategies be effective in achieving my goals? If not, do I have alternatives?
- If there are conflicts between different goals, which of them am I considering abandoning? What criteria am I using to make the choice?

- If I intend to disengage from a goal, what will be my game plan? Do I have a replacement goal in mind?
- Is there a balance between my intrinsically motivated goals and those that are largely extrinsic?
- Of all my goals and aspirations, which are the most likely to make me happier in the future than I am today?

This last question may be the most difficult for some of us to answer. To that end, we'll look at our goals in terms of how we feel when we achieve them.

Using Flow to Assess Your Goals

We've remarked more than once that human beings aren't very good at knowing what will make them happy. While there isn't a one-size-fits-all, how-to recipe for individual happiness, some principles can bring greater understanding to how to identify sources of happiness. One such principle is that of *flow*, as set forth by Mihaly Csikszentmihalyi; it's also one we can use to great effect while mapping our goals, assessing them, and deciding which we should pursue or discard.

The idea of flow is easiest to explain by example. Recall a moment when you were utterly absorbed in an activity, so completely focused on what you were doing that everything around you seemed to disappear. Your concentration was complete, without distraction. This activity could be any task, as long you felt happy or even serene doing it, so immersed in it that you lost the sense of time. Along with a feeling of oneness with the activity, you also felt a deep sense of satisfaction, of meaningfulness in what you were doing. This moment endowed you with a sense of mastery, as well as freedom from the ordinary worries and hesitations that accompany most of us throughout the day. This is what Csikszentmihalyi calls *flow*. As he explains it, the feeling of flow is a universal experience that knows no cultural boundaries and isn't limited by age or gender.

Athletes often describe how they feel playing their sport in terms of being in the flow; on these pages, you may remember Deidre the swimmer describing racing as "an incomparable feeling of exhaustion, of exhilaration, of feeling alive" while James the rower talked about becoming "completely engrossed in a single task with full mindfulness." These are descriptions of flow. Writers speak of characters "writing themselves," whereas musicians talk about being "in" the music; a weaver describes the lightness of being she feels as she works, how she gets lost in the process. Flow is probably what the poet William Butler Yeats had in mind when he wrote, "How can we know the dancer from the dance?"

But the experience of flow isn't limited to activities that are, by their nature, creative. Nor do you need to be an artist or athlete. Ordinary people experience flow at moments doing their jobs, as well as during activities like knitting and gardening. You can experience flow in a great conversation with friends or while spending time with children.

The experience of flow does require certain conditions, which Csikszentmihalyi outlines, beginning with what he calls the "autotelic experience." This term is derived from Greek (*auto* meaning "self" and *telos* meaning "goal") and refers to the activity that lies at the heart of the flow experience. It is an activity that is, in his words, "an end to itself" and that, moreover, "even if initially undertaken for other reasons, the activity becomes intrinsically rewarding." His understanding of an intrinsically valuable and rewarding goal dovetails with other theories we've already reviewed about goals. But among Csikszentmihalyi's unique contributions is his assertion that first, most activities are neither "purely autotelic" nor "purely exotelic" (the word he uses to describe activities done solely for external reasons) but a combination of the two. His understanding makes it possible to see how goals, originally pursued largely for extrinsic reasons, can become intrinsic in meaning and value, and how they can put us in a state of flow.

Among the examples he uses is that of someone who trains to be a surgeon for "exotelic" reasons, including helping people,

making money, and achieving prestige. But, he says, "if they are
lucky, after a while they will begin to enjoy their work and their
surgery becomes to a large extent also autotelic." Flow lifts us above
the everyday, transforming how we feel, because we are deeply connected to our actions.

A trial lawyer explains his experience of flow: "It has happened
to me when I'm addressing a jury and I suddenly realize that I've got
command of the courtroom. Every person on the panel is looking at
me, watching, listening and paying attention to my every word. In
that moment, time seems to slow down and I feel no hesitancy at all.
I have the opportunity to choose my words carefully, to pick precisely
the right word, to craft my argument and every phrase with forethought because my mind is ahead of the words. I am fully caught
up in the moment but in command nonetheless. I know that sounds
strange—how can a person be both 'in command' and 'caught up in
the moment' at once?'—but that's exactly what it feels like."

A woman describes her experience of flow when she taught literature to college students: "It didn't happen every class, of course,
but it happened with some regularity, when the discussion of the
poem or novel suddenly shifted and my students were all drawn in
and paying full attention, and I knew that in the moment, they had
simply gotten it. I could see the wonder in their faces—that they'd
understood something about the words and their meaning, or the
characters and their emotions in a firsthand and direct way that was
a revelation—and when the bell went off signaling the end of class,
they looked surprised, just as I did. They sat for a moment and then,
with some reluctance, got up. It was as though a spell had been broken." That, too, is a description of the experience of flow.

The optimal experience of flow depends on other factors than
the "autotelic" nature of the activity. Among them are these:

- That the goal be clear, free of contradictory demands. What
  we need to do should be obvious.
- That the challenges of the goal and our skills be in balance,
  unlike ordinary life, where a too-demanding situation may produce frustration or anxiety or an unchallenging task boredom.

- That there be immediate feedback. We know immediately how well we're doing and are secure in the knowledge that what we're doing is right.
- That we are totally concentrated on the activity without distraction.
- That we are fully immersed in the activity, unaware of everything that lies outside of it.
- That there's no thought or concern about failing.
- That we experience a falling away of self-consciousness in a literal way; we're not thinking about how other people see or judge us, nor do we worry about impressing or influencing others.
- That we experience a distortion of time.

The work you do, the activities and interests you pursue for self-fulfillment and pleasure, the relationships you're in—in short, many of the goals you've just mapped—can be evaluated in terms of flow. One of the important lessons to take away from Csikszent-mihalyi's work is the balance between the challenges of the goal and your skills. Understanding that flow emanates from balance runs counter to the cultural view of what makes people successful and happy. It's another potent argument for letting go of the folk wisdom of "The higher the bar, the higher the jump."

Think about the activities you engage in as well as the goals you've set for yourself in terms of flow. What revisions can you make to your life so that you experience flow more frequently? Just on the basis of flow, are there goals you should be pursuing more aggressively? What changes can you make to the way you do your work or the work you do?

One woman, now in her midforties, describes how she revised her goals: "I'd ended up in marketing pretty much by accident; being an assistant was the first job I landed right after college, and then I climbed up the corporate ladder without thinking much about what I did and didn't love about my job. I was happy enough, you see, and making enough money and being able to travel too, which was great. But then the company changed hands, and I was fired and I finally had to sit down and ask myself, 'What's next?' There weren't a lot of jobs around I was actually interested in, and I started thinking about starting my own business. I realized that what I really liked was the planning and troubleshooting more than actually implementing the marketing plans, and that's how I got into the consulting business, working one-on-one with small companies. It's the brainstorming that gets me jazzed."

The woman is not using the word *flow*, but she could have. Many of the other stories we've told, especially that of Jill the lawyer, who left her job as a litigator to become a teacher, have to do with flow and the individual need to experience satisfaction and a deep sense of connection to work and other activities.

In addition to viewing your goals, realized and unrealized, in terms of flow, it's important to see whether attaining them is possible. That, too, pertains to the question of balance.

Mastering Mental Contrasting

With the first part of goal mapping completed, it's time to review your goals to see if they are attainable. Keep in mind that a range of factors determines whether a goal can be reached: having the necessary time, energy, and other resources; having the right level of skill and appropriate strategies to attain it; and whether it's in conflict with other important goals. The skill we should rely on to determine whether we should set and try to implement a goal or disengage from it is, as we've mentioned, called *mental contrasting*.

Mental contrasting requires that you have your desired future in mind while you focus on the real-life factors that may impede its realization. It's a mental exercise that requires you to hold your vision of the future in your mind at the same time that you realistically appraise the present. The balance of future and present is absent from the two other possible ways of thinking about a goal: positively about the future alone (indulging) or focusing solely on the negatives in the present reality (dwelling). According to the research by Gabriele Oettingen and colleagues, both indulging and dwelling yield only moderate goal commitment, even if there's a good chance of succeeding. Similarly, indulging in the future alone or dwelling on present obstacles actually keeps people committed to a goal that has scant chances for success; they can disengage from this goal only through mental contrasting. In addition, mental contrasting facilitates realism about both short-term and long-term goals and their possible implementation.

A short-term goal might be knocking it out of the park on that forty-minute presentation your boss has asked you to give at the corporate sales meeting; he's given you the opportunity to decline or accept the invitation to present. The conventional way of dealing with this challenge might be to give yourself a pep talk ("You can do it, Dan!"), reminding yourself of other times you've successfully met other challenges, or simply imagining the enthusiastic applause and your boss's smiling face when you're done talking. That indulging approach, of course, glosses over any of your habits of mind or propensities that might stand in the way of resounding success. On the other hand, you might be filled with dread and find yourself unable to summon up anything other than the vision of a tongued-tied you standing in front of graphs and a PowerPoint chart, looking out over a sea of bored faces; this is dwelling.

Using mental contrasting, you'd focus on the goal of giving a dynamic presentation in combination with the things that potentially stand in the way of that end: your anxiety about public speaking; your tendency to fidget when you're stressed; your habit of procrastinating; your way of speaking too quickly and swallowing your words when you're stressed; your tendency to say "um" almost every sentence.

Thinking about potential pitfalls in concrete terms permits you to consider both whether these obstacles can be overcome and the potential gains of giving the speech (winning the boss's approval, bringing yourself to the attention of the president and other high-level executives, perhaps paving the way to future promotions). Your thinking about the upside is grounded in realism, forcing you to turn your attention to what needs to be done to succeed. You realize that preparing ahead may ease your speaking anxiety, which, in turn, will allow you to develop and rehearse your speech so that you feel more at ease. You decide that exercising before you practice your speech will relax you and allow you to really focus. You take notes, write your speech, and then pare it down to talking points and recruit a buddy to coach you in your efforts. Mental contrasting permits you to go forward with the goal on all levels: cognitive (thinking and planning); affective (feeling responsible and in command of the task); motivational (feeling energized by the potential benefits); and behavioral (investing time and effort).

Mental contrasting can be used to assess and facilitate any goal in any realm. These goals could be as various as establishing a community garden (the obstacles might be researching zoning laws, getting municipal approval, raising funds, getting publicity, finding volunteers, finding a source for mulch, etc.) or switching careers (researching the necessary credentials, planning how to attain them, getting the requisite experience, networking and getting recommendations, finding employment). In every realm, mental contrasting promotes if-then thinking, such as "If X happens, then I will react by doing Y," or "If X doesn't happen, then I will do Y," or "If he or she acts in X way, then I will respond by saying Y" and planning ways to get past the impediments to your goal. It promotes action, rather than stasis, or being stuck in old patterns. The process clarifies the possibilities, including the realization that persistence may be futile.

In contrast, both indulging—putting on those rose-colored glasses and dreaming that your ideal future will happen as if by magic—or dwelling—focusing on the negatives and sinking beneath the weight of them—are completely self-referential. They particularly limit your choices in the area of relationship. The if-then thinking that comes out of mental contrasting helps you plan your reactions to situations ahead of time, using what you know to anticipate problems.

Imagine, for a moment, that your goal is to stop arguing with your spouse or partner about money. While an indulging point of view might have you imagining a life without disagreement and with limitless funds, and a dwelling one might have you focus on the fights you've had over the years and what a spendthrift or tight-wad he is, mental contrasting has you thinking about how you'll react to the various cues that you know have triggered fights in the past. Focusing on the present reality in terms of problem solving—what you can say to defuse the situation and make the conversation more productive—will, in fact, make you a more attentive listener as well. If-then thinking allows you to reframe any situation in terms of action and response.

Just as emotional intelligence helps us manage our emotions and use them to inform our thought processes, so too mental contrasting can help us become more motivationally and behaviorally intelligent. It can provide a balance to how we're wired to persist no matter how low the chances of our eventual success, can free us to formulate plans of action with greater authority, or can give us the energy and incentive to disengage if need be.

Mental Contrasting from the Inside Out

Studies that measured brain activity have shown that mental contrasting isn't simply a theoretical construct but is an activity that is different from either indulging, dwelling, or resting. The research also suggests that mental contrasting can only be mastered under certain conditions; our brains should come with a label that reads, "Warning: Capacity Limited." These findings are in line with what Roy Baumeister and others have noted about ego depletion and other capabilities.

Using brain imaging, researchers have found that mental contrasting and indulging were two separate activities and that mental contrasting resulted in heightened activity of the regions of the brain associated with working memory and the formation of intention. Interestingly, there was also heightened brain activity in the areas responsible for episodic memory and vivid mental imagery, "suggesting that mental contrasting is rooted in the retrieval of past personal events, as well as the processing of complex stimuli such as reexperiencing past incidents."

According to the researchers, these findings suggest that since mental contrasting taxes working memory, it needs to be done at times when there isn't great cognitive demand; it should be done as a stand-alone activity, not in combination with other tasks or when the person is stressed or tired.

With your goals mapped for clarity, mental contrasting becomes an empowering tool that can help you decide whether to stay engaged, redefine your goals, or disengage. No matter what your ultimate intention, there's another tool left to add to your arsenal.

Forgetting the Little Engine

We apologize in advance for battering some of your fondest child-hood memories, but when it comes to psyching ourselves up to achieve our goals, it turns out that the cheerleader-type declaratives we've all been told really work—whether it's "You *can* do it!" or even "I think I can"—actually don't. In a study of self-talk, Ibrahim Senay and his team hypothesized that the interrogative form ("Will I") would produce greater motivation to pursue a goal than the declarative "I will," because the format would inspire thoughts about the intrinsic reasons about its pursuit and thus engender better task performance. And that is exactly what they found.

Participants who were asked to think about "whether" they would solve anagrams performed better than those who simply thought they "would" definitely solve anagrams. In a second experiment, the participants were primed by writing "Will I," "I will," "I," or "Will" twenty times and then given ten anagrams to solve. Only the "Will I" prime produced better performance. In the third experiment, first the participants were asked to write down a sequence of twenty-four numbers that the investigators read aloud and that were either random or patterned; they were told that this exercise would clear their minds for the handwriting test (in this case, writing only two primes, "Will I" or "I will"). They were then asked to report on their plans for physical exercise in the next week and the hours they planned to devote. The researchers thought that writing a random sequence would weaken the effect of writing "Will I" repeatedly, and that was shown to be true. The prime "Will I" worked best with the patterned numbers. The fourth and final experiment asked the participants about their plans either to continue exercising regularly or to start doing so, after being primed with "Will I" or "I will." They then rated how twelve reasons for exercising reflected their thinking. Six of the reasons given were intrinsic (such as "Because I want to take responsibility for my health"), and six were extrinsic ("Because I would feel guilty or ashamed of myself if I didn't"). The prime "Will I" had no effect on extrinsic goals but facilitated intrinsic reasons for exercising.

So if you are going to engage in self-talk to motivate yourself, don't phrase it as "I can" or "I will"; instead, motivate yourself by the question only you can answer: "Will I?" That will kick in all the intrinsic reasons you have for pursuing the goal and bolster your sense of autonomy.

A Leap of Faith

Let's go back to the story of Marie, the artist who, after twenty years as an independent, realized that her original goals were no longer making her happy. At first, unable to think of what she could possibly do next—she had no practical job experience other than being an artist—she cobbled together temporary solutions to the dual demands of making a living and being happy. She continued to take on assignments, but started new projects that got her out of her studio and into the world. She became an artists' advocate and was certified as a mediator; she began giving workshops and advising artists on how to resolve their disputes with clients, negotiate rights, and understand the intricacies of copyright law. Still, while her new work had her out in the world, connecting to people and helping them, which she'd realized was one of her primary goals, she didn't want to spend all of her time on the road. At the same time, she was still making art and wasn't ready to stop being an artist, not yet at least.

Marie's dilemma is typical of what happens when a major goal that closely defines the self isn't working, and quitting isn't yet a real consideration. When persistence isn't balanced by the ability to disengage, there is no chance of imagining a different future.

In Marie's case, the impetus to act came from the outside—the horrific events of 9/11 and its loss of life. As a born and bred New Yorker, that event inspired a new sense of urgency to give her life both meaning and stability. She stopped making art and turned her focus on pursuing a new career in retail in which she could use both her design sense and her ability to deal with people. In time, she became a successful store manager. That experience, in turn, led her to a job that really fulfilled the sense of purpose she'd been looking for—a job in the nonprofit world working with disadvantaged youth. It has now been ten years since she last called herself an artist, and she doesn't miss drawing or painting. She has digitalized all of her work over two decades and occasionally finds ways of licensing those images. Being an artist is no longer her primary way of defining herself, and she has no regrets.

Unfortunately, that's not always the case for everyone, especially if the goal has been intrinsic and central to oneself. It's at these moments that mastering the art of quitting is absolutely essential, and even more so if the loss of self-definition isn't chosen, as it is when someone is laid off or fired from a job, or left by a spouse. Managing feelings of loss, regret, and inadequacy may be part of the work required to fully disengage and to come out the other side, ready to reengage and set a new goal. Troubleshooting the path with self-knowledge and conscious strategies is where we'll turn next.

Sample Goal Map 1

This goal map was filled out by a twenty-five-year-old single woman who is a college graduate and has worked in public relations and social media. This is the first iteration of her goal list without ordering or numbering.

	Short Term	**Long Term**
Life Goals	Try to be true to self	Live an authentic life based on true values
	Be more understanding of others	Feel comfortable with my choices
	Not to be so hard on myself about past decisions	To accept that the past is past
		To realize we learn from mistakes
Career/Work	Develop and hone skill set	Work in the nonprofit world
	Work on writing and media contacts	Focus on helping others
	Network with those in not for profit	Wake up feeling good about my career
	Find a job in a supportive environment	
	Become fully self-supporting	
	Feel challenged and as if I am working hard	
Relationships	Make effort to date more	Establish and maintain an intimate, trusting marriage
	Deepen existing friendships	Have children
	Be proactive at problem solving	
	Edit friendships for superficiality, and end with a small true group	
Learning/ Achievement	Explore volunteering more	Travel the world
	Graduate degree in art history	Learn another language
	Be more proactive about the things I am interested in learning about	Try living in another city

Sample Goal Map 2

This goal map was filled out by a married thirty-eight-year-old male who has an infant son, is a college graduate, and works as a journalist and an editor. It is his first version, without numbering or prioritizing.

	Short Term	Long Term
Life Goals	Financial stability; save to move to a larger home	Save for family's health and future education
	Make sure daily tasks and stress don't detract from being a better listener	Continue to exercise
	Focus on enjoying the moment	Run a half-marathon
Career/Work	Perform at a high level	Constantly improve my professional knowledge and skills to remain relevant and vital in my industry
	Secure raises, promotion, bonuses	
	Balance work hours and family time	
	Be an effective mentor to younger team members	
Relationships	Let my wife know I love and appreciate her every day	Be the kind of father who makes it to his son's ball games
	Travel on at least one great adventure a year	Be a present and positive influence in my son's life
Learning/ Achievement	Find time to read as many books as possible	Write a novel
		Learn a language, perhaps Portuguese

CHAPTER EIGHT

How to Quit Well

Sometimes our ability to galvanize ourselves into action and quit has less to do with personality, character, or innate habits of mind than it does with our personal histories. The words *personal histories* refer to the events of our childhood years and the tenor and quality of the attachments we had to our parents and caregivers. Those early attachments are tied to broad patterns of behavior which affect our ability to regulate emotion, whether we take an avoidance or approach stance in life, and our attitudes toward success and failure. People who were securely attached in childhood tend to gravitate toward healthy and nurturing situations—echoing their childhood emotions—but also have a better bead on potentially uncomfortable or toxic situations. Insecurely attached people may find themselves attracted to people and situations that echo the past but make them actively unhappy.

There's something else to consider as well: bad events have a more lasting impact on people than do good ones. This isn't terribly positive, we know, but it's realistic and confirmed by lots of scientific inquiry. As Roy Baumeister and his colleagues write in "Bad Is Stronger than Good," "bad emotions, bad parents, and bad feedback have more impact than good ones, and bad information is processed more thoroughly than good."

These events aren't always consciously remembered or even realized, but they affect our conscious actions and our decision making nonetheless. We may not always recognize why we're acting a certain way or making certain choices, not because of the brain's automatic processes but because of past patterns that lie beyond our conscious awareness.

These patterns may get in the way of both goal engagement *and* disengagement, stopping us from going after what we need or want or keeping us in a holding pattern when we really need to quit. As with all unconscious processes, the solution is to become aware and conscious of these patterns.

The story of Carolyn, an aspiring photographer, demonstrates one way in which these old patterns may influence both your thinking and your goals. Carolyn was from the Midwest but moved to New York City after college with high ambitions, as so many young people do. She landed what looked like the opportunity of a lifetime as the receptionist in the studio of a renowned photographer. It was the bottom of the ladder, but after two years of diligence, she became one of the photographer's assistants. The staff of the studio was always in flux, with people coming and going; the photographer was brilliant, but she was also testy, brusque, and a perfectionist. She'd lose her temper in a flash, berating the person closest at hand, and most of her assistants just gave up and quit. But Carolyn hung in, even though the photographer was likely to rail at her to take more initiative and then to excoriate her for "violating boundaries" when Carolyn did.

In this no-win situation, Carolyn's sense of self took a beating. Her friends and even her colleagues counseled her to quit and move on, but she was determined to try to weather the days at work. She thought that staying put was what she needed to do, that it was the best avenue to further her dream of becoming a photographer and having her own studio. She hoped that what she was learning about her craft would ultimately outweigh how miserable and upset she was, day after day, week after week. Another year passed and things were no better.

She hung in until the day her sister came in from California and tagged along on a shoot. Her sister was there when the photographer unloaded on Carolyn for not setting the lights up correctly, even though she had personally instructed Carolyn on their placement. Carolyn apologized profusely, even though she'd done nothing wrong. Afterward, her sister commented on how abusive the photographer was and how the tirade reminded her of their hypercritical father's rants when they were young and how Carolyn used to apologize to him just to stop him from belittling her.

Carolyn was shaken and surprised by her sister's observation but, with a sudden burst of clarity, understood why she was still in her job and had been so hesitant to quit. Her boss was treating her just as her father had, and Carolyn was placating the photographer just the way she had her father when she was young. It was at that moment that she understood that she had to get out, that it wasn't healthy or productive for her to stay. She set a new goal for herself—moving on—and put the word out that she'd be amenable to a change. A few months later, a rival photographer offered her a job, and she jumped ship.

Carolyn was lucky to have an astute and observant older sister who'd done her own work dealing with the fallout from her childhood. Luckier still, Carolyn was able to recognize the pattern once it was pointed out. For most of us, the path to understanding will be a bit rockier, and it will take time and effort to figure out why we're persisting at something that is actually either no longer satisfying or even making us unhappy.

That was certainly the case for Bill, who felt stuck and dissatisfied in his job in the banking industry, where he'd started at the age of twenty-two. There wasn't really room to grow in the department, but despite his lobbying, he hadn't been tapped to move within the organization. Despite his frustration, he still couldn't get himself to start looking for a job outside the bank and to quit. After six years, he was comfortable in his work, he liked his colleagues, and he felt both responsible and loyal to them, as well as to the company that had given him a start. Loyalty was important to him as a first-generation American and the eldest of four. He'd been his parents' right hand growing up, doing what needed to be done for his siblings; he was the first to attend high school and then college, and he valued and appreciated his parents' support. Bill wasn't able to separate his own feelings of loyalty for his work "family" from his own need for growth and autonomy in his work without feeling conflicted. Working with a therapist helped him sort out those issues, and he was finally able to begin to look for a new job more suited to his needs and quit his old job.

Companies and corporations aren't families, of course, but not surprisingly, many of us will unconsciously transfer feelings about our original families—good, bad, and indifferent—onto the workplace setting, most usually in the relationships we have with coworkers and even bosses, as the stories of Jill and Bill demonstrate. What we learn during our formative years about adapting to the situations we find ourselves in—dealing with a critical parent or a fractious sibling and the broader patterns of how we express ourselves—can be triggered by events at work. These "comfortable" patterns—which don't really offer comfort except that they are familiar to us—explain why we sometimes sabotage ourselves unwittingly, participating in our own unhappiness by staying put or persisting when we need to leave.

These patterns, though, assert themselves most often in the area of personal relationships, especially romantic alliances and friendships, and often it's the pattern, not just the specific relationship itself, that really needs to be given up, artfully and consciously.

Elizabeth had grown up with an often distant, highly critical mother, the kind of attachment described as insecure. Like all children, Elizabeth desperately wanted and needed her mother's love and approval and did what she could to please her, to no avail; the pattern persisted throughout her childhood and into her young adulthood. While Elizabeth appeared, on the surface at least, to be functioning successfully in the world—she had gone to Ivy League schools, had a fulfilling career in finance, enjoyed close friends, and was interested in lots of things—she foundered over and over again in intimate relationships. Unknowingly, she was most attracted to men who treated her as her mother did; inevitably, they treated her in ways that made her miserable, but she always stayed anyway and rarely, if ever, initiated a breakup. When she reached her late twenties, she understood that she had to deal with why she was choosing the men she was, and started working with a therapist. It was with his help that, in time, she stopped re-creating the emotional circumstances of her childhood. She left her last critical and demanding boyfriend and set herself the goal of finding a partner in life who treated her differently.

These comfort patterns can get in the way in the office, at home, and even among friends, as Dawn realized in her mid-thirties. Dawn could never turn down a request for help, no matter how inconvenient it was for her. She was the go-to person in the office when a project ran late, because she was the only one without children; that was true as well when it came to helping her aging parents, even though she was one of three children. Being helpful was how she'd managed in her childhood as the go-between for two bickering parents; her helpfulness had been the basis for many of her friendships during college and after. She was the impromptu picker-upper of everyone's slack, which she didn't mind because being there for people made her feel good about herself. But when she married Rick, he resented having their plans and sometimes even their needs put on hold or scotched because someone needed her to pitch in. Even though she understood Rick's complaints, it was nonetheless hard for her to break these patterns until she and Rick consulted a therapist and she realized that she had to set boundaries. Even so, it remains, even now, something she has to work on and be conscious of.

Thousands of years ago, when the ancient Greeks went to the Oracle at Delphi to get counsel about their decisions, whether to follow one course or to leave another, what they saw first were the words "Know thyself." That wisdom remains just as valuable today as it was then. Use mental contrasting to ask yourself whether persisting is what you need to do, or whether you need to work harder at being able to quit. Ask yourself questions about how the situation in which you find yourself fits into your own patterns of behavior. What follows is a series of questions you might want to begin with as you explore your own interior reasons for staying put or leaving.

- Does the situation I find myself in feel familiar? In what ways?
- What benefits would I derive from continuing on this path? How do these benefits measure up against the possible benefits of changing course?
- How much of my behavior is motivated by avoidance? Can I articulate what I'm trying to avoid?
- Do I see myself responding to people or situations in ways that I've responded in the past? How does responding this way make me feel?
- How much of my persistence is fueled by my fear of the unknown—of what might or might not happen next?
- Am I persisting to gain control of the situation? Is it even possible to get control?
- Am I using the right strategies to manage my emotions? Do I feel flooded with feelings? Am I beset by intrusive thoughts?
- How motivated am I by fear of regret? Of making a mistake by quitting too soon or by quitting altogether?

Considering possible regret in relation to action or inaction is closely tied to the other persistent habits of mind we've already discussed, including the sunk-cost fallacy and the escalation of commitment. But these are ways of thinking. While regret involves thinking (comparing what you did and where you ended up with what might have been, setting reality against an imagined construct), it is an emotion, one that flits in uninvited and insinuates itself into your decision making, including the setting of goals as well as disengaging from them.

Managing Regret

Of all emotions, perhaps regret is one of the most complicated, which is why it has been studied by theorists in the fields of psychology, including consumerism, and economics. All of us have felt regret at one point or another in our lives—an emotion falling somewhere on the spectrum from Édith Piaf's "Non, je ne regrette rien" ("No, I regret nothing") to the line written by Arthur Miller for one of his characters: "Maybe all one can do is end up with the right regrets."

Regret comes in all sizes and shapes, from the tiny (wishing you'd gone to that party on Friday night instead of staying home, or bought that dress when they still had it in your size) to medium (if only you'd taken that job offer instead of the one you did, or invested in that stock your buddy touted) to enormous (you should have broken up with your girlfriend instead of marrying her, or held on to your inheritance instead of gambling it away). We can feel twinges of regret about things that will end up being insignificant in the long run as well as deep regret over decisions that cast a long shadow over our days and are truly life-changing. Regret can be closely tied to blame, self-recrimination, and remorse.

As Dutch psychologists Marcel Zeelenberg and Rik Pieters point out, unlike more basic emotions such as happiness, fear, or sadness—all of which babies feel—regret isn't accompanied by a facial expression and is acquired later in life. One study found that while seven-year-olds were capable of regret because they could contrast what was with what might have been, five-year-olds were not. The technical term for this process of comparison is *counterfactual thinking*.

Understanding how big a role avoiding regret plays in your life facilitates artful quitting and helps elucidate the reasons behind your patterns of persistence.

One of the first theories about regret was proposed by the Nobel Prize winners Daniel Kahneman and Amos Tversky as a result of a study that asked students to consider which of two hypothetical situations would yield a greater sense of regret. The respondents were asked to picture two investors, one of whom owns stock in Company A, considers selling it and buying stock in Company B, but decides against it; the investor learns that he would have made $1,200 if he'd gone ahead and bought the Company B stock. The second investor owns shares in Company B and sells them in order to buy stock in Company A; he too learns that he would have been $1,200 richer if he'd stayed with Company B. Which of these two investors feels more regret?

Answer that question for yourself, and then consider what Kahneman and Tversky found: A whopping 92 percent of respondents thought that the guy who acted—by selling his Company B stock—would feel more regret than the man who lost the same $1,200 opportunity by inaction (not buying Company B stock).

The result is, of course, strangely counterintuitive since both investors found themselves in precisely the same place—missing out on the same potential $1,200 gain—so why should anyone assume that one investor would feel more regret than the other? In his book *Thinking, Fast and Slow,* Kahneman explains that "people expect to have stronger emotions (including regret) to an outcome that is produced by action than to the same outcome when it's produced by inaction." He asserts that the asymmetry is as strong for losses as gains and that it applies to blame as well as regret. He offers an explanation for why: "The key is not the difference between commission and omission but the distinction between default options and actions that deviate from the default. When you deviate from the default, you can easily imagine the norm—and if the default is associated with bad consequences, the discrepancy between the two can be the source of painful emotion." Among the examples he cites are the players of a computer blackjack game. Taking action— whether it was choosing to hit or stand by saying yes—produced more regret than saying no and doing nothing. Loss aversion ties into regret in his view: "The asymmetry in the risk of regret favors conventional risk-averse choices."

But this theory was challenged by a series of later studies by Thomas Gilovic and Victoria Husted Medvec. These studies countered that while Kahneman and Tversky's results were powerful, they didn't really jibe with common observations about regret, namely, that "when people are asked about their biggest regrets in life, it seems they tend to focus on the things they *failed* to do." To paraphrase Robert Frost, which do we regret more: the road taken or the one *not* taken? (The disagreement between Kahneman and Gilovic and Medvec was later addressed in a paper the three of them published.)

Gilovic and Medvec's findings are fascinating and illuminate how many of the processes of mind already discussed in these pages affect and mediate feelings of regret. They hypothesized that the passage of time affects how we experience regret over actions we've taken and those we haven't; they argued that while people are initially more upset by what they've done, the failure to act induces more regret over time. A broad survey they took confirmed exactly this observation, as well as another interesting one: Twice as many people regretted failures to act, rather than actions they took. Since a very small percentage of regrets focused on circumstances beyond a person's control, the researchers also concluded that a sense of personal responsibility was central to the experience of regret. For example, you would deeply regret that you didn't heed your financial advisor's advice in 2007 to sell off your stock portfolio before the market crashed; conversely, if you had no prior information, you might regret the amount of money you lost, but you wouldn't feel personally responsible.

Gilovic and Medvec conducted experiments to determine the difference between short-term and long-term regrets, offering subjects the following scenario. Two young men, Dave and Jim, both attend the same university, although they're not acquainted. Neither of them is happy, and they both consider transferring to some other prestigious school. They both agonize over the decision, but ultimately, Dave decides to stay and Jim transfers. It turns out that neither is happy with his choice; Dave wishes he'd transferred while Jim wishes he'd stayed put.

Answer the questions respondents were asked as you read: (1) Who would regret his choice the most in the short term? (2) Who would regret his choice the most in the long term?

The answers validated the researchers' hypothesis: 76 percent thought that Jim, who had acted by transferring, would have more short-term regret. But the majority (63 percent) thought that Dave, who did nothing, would regret it more for longer. Most pertinent to our discussion, though, is the framework Gilovic and Medvec propose for understanding why regret shifts over time. Many of their observations dovetail with ideas already encountered in these pages, but are worth reviewing because they help explain how regret works in life and can interfere with disengagement.

Regrettable actions become less painful because people take compensatory action to help "fix" the past mistake they've made and find "silver linings" that justify the action. People point to the lessons learned from mistakes and failures as part of this process. Similarly, your realization that you married the wrong person might have you file for divorce, but you might nonetheless bring up memories of your courtship and how charming he or she was back then to justify marrying in the first place. Or you offer the ultimate silver lining: "If I hadn't married this person, I wouldn't have had the wonderful kids I have." Reframing what happened in terms of positives—rationalizing them—is what Daniel Gilbert has, in another context, called the *psychological immune system*.

While inaction can be reframed in ways that reduce the pain of regret, it's neither effective nor consistent. For one thing, regrettable inactions are much harder to reframe because, in retrospect, it usually seems eminently clear that the reasons you had for not doing whatever it was (not going to that university across country, because you'd lose touch with your old friends; not asking that girl out for a date, because she was bound to reject you; not marrying your college sweetheart, because of your different political beliefs) don't seem to hold water over time. Most of us will dismiss what we once saw as the key and deciding factors that justified what we didn't do with what Gilovic and Medvec call "retrospective confidence": you could have figured out a way to get home now and again from California; you can't think of a reason she wouldn't have gone out with you; you and your sweetheart would have worked it out because your love was so strong. Over time, you're more likely to have trouble grasping exactly what your reasons were for not acting at the time, rather than nodding your head in agreement.

While the regret caused by action is finite and mitigated by the retrospective spin, the open-ended nature of inaction—the cinematic quality of "What Might Have Been" and "If Only"—has infinite possibilities, as F. Scott Fitzgerald's novel *The Great Gatsby* makes abundantly clear. The Zeigarnik effect—the way the mind hangs on to uncompleted tasks, nudging us to go finish them—also makes it harder to tamp down the regret caused by inaction.

Regret is a complicated emotion precisely because of its origin in a comparison, which makes it possible to feel regret even when your actions don't result in a bad outcome. That observation has led Terry Connolly and Marcel Zeelenberg to propose their *decision justification theory*, which posits that regret has two sources, one connected to the comparative evaluation of the outcomes and the other with the self-blame for having made a poor choice. The "poor" choice would be one you find inconsistent with your own standards of behavior and intentions. The point is that you can blame yourself for your choice and feel regret, even in the absence of a bad outcome. The example they give is of someone who drives home from a party having had too much to drink. Nothing happens—you make it home without incident—but you still regret what you did, because it's not like you to do something that risky and stupid. Decision justification theory suggests that the feeling that your action or inaction was inconsistent will lead to greater regret than decisions that are inherently consistent with how you think and behave. All of this makes eminent sense. If you are normally a cautious person, an impromptu decision that turns out badly will be regretted more, with a healthy dose of self-blame, than one on which you did your usual due diligence but tanked nonetheless.

Because regret is considered an aversive emotion (it doesn't feel good), human beings are presumed to be motivated to try to regulate it. As you might expect, then, researchers Todd McElroy and Keith Dows found that action-oriented individuals—who are better at regulating their emotions and thus are more skilled at goal disengagement—don't suffer as much regret as their state-oriented brethren. They also found that state-oriented people reported high levels of regret whether the situation involved action or inaction. This observation shouldn't come as a surprise, either, since the state-oriented have trouble managing negative emotion generally, and regret wouldn't be an exception. The action-oriented, in contrast, had low levels of regret, except when they didn't act. That finding underscores how inconsistent behavior factors into regret, while consistent behavior does not.

If you've already identified yourself as either action-oriented or state-oriented, you'll be able to gauge your own ability (or inability) to manage regret and how the anticipation of regret affects both your decision making generally and your ability to quit.

Learning from Regret

While most of the psychological literature assumes that feelings of regret are negative and hence to be avoided, Colleen Saffrey and her colleagues took a counterintuitive stance, exploring whether the experience of regret had any psychological benefits and whether ordinary people recognized those benefits. They wondered whether regret could help trigger or guide future behavior toward desirable outcomes. Did the feeling of regret help people make sense of negative experiences in positive ways? Did people view regret as potentially beneficial, aversive, or a combination of the two?

Their first study examined whether individuals valued the experience of regret and whether their seeing a value in that experience was in line with seeing the "bright side" of other negative emotional experiences. The investigators had the participants complete a survey of nine negative emotions (regret, anger, anxiety, boredom, disappointment, fear, guilt, jealousy, and sadness), in addition to four positive emotions (joy, love, pride, and relaxed). Not surprisingly, the four positive emotions were universally viewed as favorable and beneficial, but in addition, there was a general positivity associated with even negative emotions. The notable exceptions were anxiety, boredom, and jealousy, the last of which was considered unambiguously unfavorable. Both regret and disappointment, however, scored much more favorably than anger, guilt, or sadness, surpassing even pride, a positive emotion—showing that individuals do see a value in regret.

Saffrey and colleagues' second study examined whether the experience of regret might help individuals make sense of situations and guide them to pursue desired outcomes or avoid the status quo. In addition, the researchers looked at whether a negative emotion might impel an individual toward self-examination or other insight, as well as whether a negative emotion might bring him or her closer to other people. (They did not test whether negative emotions actually accomplished these ends, but only tested whether people believed that they did.) Finally, the researchers wondered whether, given that individuals tended to see regret in a positive light, the participants would assess themselves as experiencing more regret than others. This sounds wildly counterintuitive—why would anyone want to believe he or she experienced more regret?—but since, as we've already seen, people tend to see themselves as not only above average but also possessing more positive traits than others, might people exhibit the same self-bias when it came to regret, if they saw regret as a positive, even enlightening experience?

The participants were administered a regret scale composed of a series of statements. They were told to agree or disagree with each statement, first as they might answer it themselves, and then as a friend might. The statements are interesting in and of themselves and are listed below, so that you can consider them as well. (The statements were originally developed by Barry Schwartz and Andrew Ward and others for another study.)

    1. When I make a choice, I'm curious about what would have happened if I had chosen differently.

2. Whenever I make a choice, I try to get information about how other alternatives turned out.

3. If I make a choice and it turns out well, I still feel like something of a failure if I find out another choice would have turned out better.

4. When I think about how I'm doing in life, I often assess possibilities I have passed up.

5. Once I make a decision, I don't look back.

You can see the nuances here; there's a lot of territory between the first statement (being curious) and the fifth (never looking back). If you can, try to locate your own stance somewhere on this list.

The participants were then asked to focus on twelve negative emotions (regret, anger, anxiety, boredom, disappointment, disgust, fear, frustration, guilt, jealousy, sadness, and shame) and had to agree or disagree with two statements about each emotion, rating them in terms of five positive functions: making sense of a situation; informing or motivating an approach to future action; avoiding making the same mistake; personal insight; and improving relationships with, or understanding of, other people.

The researchers discovered that people thought that regret performed all five of these functions, which confirmed the findings of the first study more specifically, that regret is thought to have positive benefits. (It won't surprise you that among the other negative emotions rated, three others—guilt, shame, and disappointment—were also seen as having positive effects on behavior.) Finally, the participants *did* think that they had experienced more regret than a friend. So, perhaps Édith Piaf wasn't in a good place after all when she sang that she had nothing to regret. Sorry, little sparrow.

As Saffrey and her colleagues note, believing that regret is positive may well be just a coping mechanism, part of what Daniel Gilbert calls the *psychological immune system*. Still, it's worth looking at counterfactual thinking—the very basis for regret—and how it can advance or deter our efforts in mastering the art of quitting.

About Counterfactual Thinking

Just as we've seen that using mental contrasting—holding the desired future in mind at the same time as the present reality that impedes it—initiates action and the implementation of a goal, so too it's been suggested that counterfactual thinking may play an important part in goal seeking and setting. Counterfactual thinking is different in that it uses a revision of past events to inform the future. These thoughts can focus on better alternatives to what happened (*upward counterfactual thinking*, which fosters regret) or worse alternatives (*downward counterfactual thinking*, which may help people manage moods).

For example, you are up for a promotion and pay raise at work but are disappointed when you are passed over. Upward counterfactual thinking has you feeling regret, but you begin thinking about what you might have done differently to get another outcome. That, in turn, spurs you on to frame new ideas, which lead to new behavior, which might, in the future, lead to success. On the other hand, you also know that two people in your department were let go. With downward counterfactual thinking, you reflect on being passed over but observe that it could have been worse—you might have been one of the people fired.

Kai Epstude and Neal J. Roese posit that counterfactual thinking can be a useful part of regulating behavior since it's activated by a failed goal and has the person focus on what might have been done to achieve that goal ("If I'd done X, then Y would have happened"), which in turn yields a directive ("Next time, I will do X so that Y will happen") and changed behavior. Counterfactual thinking opens the door to modifying future behavior by focusing on a revision of the past. As the passed-over worker, you might come to realize that you didn't do enough to make your superiors aware of your contributions to the department and might focus on bringing the quality of your work to their attention in the future. Alternatively, you might conclude that your mistakes were getting in the way of promotion and you might focus on making fewer of them.

Optimally, counterfactual thinking permits you to formulate new strategies by envisioning what actions you might have taken to secure the goal in the first place. To be successful, this demands a certain amount of realism—a steering away from wishful thinking. In the example of being passed over, if your counterfactual thinking only focused on the shortcomings of your superiors and you imagined a scenario where their collective stupidity didn't get in the way of your promotion, the counterfactual thinking would generate no productive or useful action. Of course, not all counterfactual thinking is productive; focusing on an action that can't be changed ("If only I hadn't married him," "If only I had gone to dental school when I was in my twenties," "If only my bosses were different and smarter") is likely to put you in a dead-end loop. Combined with a ruminative style, counterfactual thinking is probably not the way to go.

You and Regret

Only you can answer how regret has worked in your life. Do you see your regret as part of a genuine learning experience, or do you tend to think that looking for the silver lining ("What doesn't kill you makes you stronger") is just a form of self-massage and rationalization? Is the way you handle regret working for you or against you, keeping you focused on ways to succeed next time or keeping you focused just on avoidance? Has regret enhanced your ability to use counterfactual thinking to push yourself forward into action?

In an interesting meta-analysis reported in "What We Regret Most . . . And Why," Neal J. Roese and Amy Summerville (the same folks who offered up the positive vision of regret) came up with a ranked list of the top things Americans regretted the most. You may want to think about where you fit in as you read.

The six biggest regrets fell into the following domains, in descending order: education, career, romance, parenting, self-improvement, and leisure. (If you're curious, the next six were finance, family, health, friends, spirituality, and community.) It's a bit surprising that education was the number one regret, but the authors argue this point: "Opportunity breeds regret. Feelings of dissatisfaction and disappointment are strongest where the chances for corrective reaction are clearest." Seen from that point of view—with the broad expanse of educational opportunities at many levels across the United States—it's not surprising that regretting educational choices (not finishing high school or not going to college, dropping out, not acquiring a skill that might have helped you in other avenues) is at the very top of the list. These observations, of course, bolster the notion that the deepest sources of regret are those roads not taken.

Think about your own regrets, the life domains they fit into, and how they relate to the goals you want to pursue and those you wish to drop. Marcel Zeelenberg and Rik Pieters have cataloged coping strategies pertaining to regret—some beneficial and others not—that individuals use to manage and regulate regret. See if you can locate your own strategies among them. Since some regret seems to be built into the human condition (we're all going to make some bad choices or mistakes), the first strategy is to hone your ability to make decisions and to factor the possibility of regret into your risk taking. Less suitable strategies for managing regret, while common, are increasing your justification of your decision, delaying or avoiding decisions, or transferring responsibility for your decision. ("My investment advisors were lousy. It wasn't my fault.")

Focus on alternatives, either by enlarging or restricting the number of your choices or by ensuring that you can, if you need to, reverse your decision. Similarly, you can consciously avoid feedback about the road you didn't take; it may not be helpful to continue discussing what you didn't do with friends, loved ones, and even acquaintances. In this sense, the old adage is true: There's no use in crying over spilled milk. Remember the story of Tim, the lawyer who wanted to shift careers but kept referring to how he'd screwed up by going to law school in the first place when he went on interviews? That's regret and self-blame—the undigested variety—doing the talking. That was true too of Roberta who, ten years after her divorce, still visited the same regrets daily, as if thinking about them would give her a do-over. Instead, her habit of ruminating on her regrets stopped her from remaking her life in myriad ways.

If you are prone to getting mired in feelings of regret, perhaps the best strategy is to anticipate them. Recognize that some of the choices you're making may entail regrets in the future, and prepare yourself for managing those feelings as best as you can.

Dealing with Stalled Quitting

There's no question that quitting sometimes requires a huge leap of faith—imagining an as-yet unrealized future—and a willingness to take on the possibility of failure, along with the emotional fall-out that accompanies it. Since persistence and staying put are the default settings for human behavior, successful goal disengagement can stall on the affective, cognitive, motivational, and behavioral fronts. Some of the strategies we've suggested throughout this book are worth reviewing.

Managing Rumination

Dwelling on what has or hasn't happened—actions or inactions—isn't just the wellspring of regret but is the basis for rumination. Rumination stymies action, using the same capacities of the mind you need to implement new goals; it keeps you tied to your unmet goals and stops you from imagining future ones. (Yes, that's the Zeigarnik effect again.) You can assign yourself a worry time, as we've suggested before, or confront your thoughts by writing them down and bringing them into consciousness. You can also train yourself to focus on distractors. Leslie, for example, manages her worries by bringing to mind images of flowers. She focuses on each detail in the flower—the stem, the petal, the stamen, the pistil—for as long as it takes to control her thoughts.

A study on rumination conducted by Annette van Randenborgh and others found that participants who were given random distractors that bore no relation to themselves ("Think about the outlines of a cello," "Think about the parts that make up a car") were better able to disengage from unsolvable anagrams than participants who were asked to ruminate before the task ("Think about why you turned out this way," "Think about the expectations your family and friends have for you").

Focusing on Task Implementation

Breaking down the things you need to do into smaller steps, or setting interim goals for yourself, may be helpful. Remember that the common wisdom about a hard-to-reach goal being inspirational simply isn't true. As we've seen, concrete plans are key to most achievement. Writing steps down will allow you to judge whether your strategies are realistic. Since strong mental representations of a desired future provide an impetus for goal setting, visualizing what your life will be like in detail will also spur you on.

Inculcating Realism

Is the new goal you're setting for yourself realistic? Are your talents and abilities sufficient to bring it to fruition? Remember that humans are overly optimistic by nature (and tend to overestimate their abilities and skill sets), so try to assess your goal as objectively as you can. Use mental contrasting to evaluate your abilities, the goal, and the strategies you've set. If you've fallen into patterns of counterfactual thinking, make sure they are reality based. If you're not sure that the goal you've set is actually attainable, set some interim deadlines for yourself so that you can monitor your progress.

Keeping Flow in Mind

Motivate yourself by taking stock of those instances where you've experienced flow, and imagine how achieving your goals will enhance flow in your life. Be your own cheerleader by asking yourself questions ("Will I do X?") as opposed to making plain statements ("I will do X"). Keep in mind that both letting go of a goal and setting a new one are essentially creative activities that demand that you be flexible in your approach.

Getting Support

If you need help disengaging from a goal, managing your thoughts or emotions, or finding a new direction, you should seek advice. There's no virtue in going it alone—no matter what the cultural mythology says. This is especially true if you've struggled because you have been fired from your job or had a reversal of fortune in either your personal life or your career.

Knowing You Have to Put Down the Duckie

The reference here is to the song from *Sesame Street*, which, if you grew up in the 1980s or later or if you had children who watched, you'll doubtless remember. Ernie is trying to play the saxophone and complains to Hoot the Owl that all he gets as music is a squeak. The squeak, in fact, is coming from the rubber duck Ernie is holding on to, which prevents him from playing the sax. Metaphorically, we've all got to put down the duckie—the habits of the past, the comfort zones, the goals that are unmet, the efforts that have failed—if we're going to move into the future.

Mastering the art of quitting requires that you put that duckie down.

CHAPTER NINE

Resetting Your Inner Compass

Real-world compasses can't be reset, of course—the directional points are fixed—but since our "inner compass" is a metaphor for the complex interaction between cognition, motivation, behavior, and the self, this compass can be. The goals we set for ourselves are reflections of both who we are and who we want to be. While earlier chapters have focused on the impediments to true goal disengagement, the process of disengagement isn't complete until there is engagement with a new goal. The forward movement of choosing a new goal spurs renewed motivation that, in turn, leads to new behavior. Reengagement, combined with the lessons learned from quitting, makes us grow psychologically and behaviorally and allows us to re-create aspects of ourselves in the process. The new goal we set reflects both our current self and the future self we envision.

As Charles S. Carver and Michael F. Scheier note, while one key life skill is knowing when to persist and when to quit, they add that "another important skill would be the ability to give up completely—*really* let go—on occasions when giving up proves necessary. The combination of these two skills yields flexibility, permitting the person to recognize and step out of intractable situations while maximizing efforts in situations that are amenable to change."

Directing your energies to your new goal is the first step.

Thinking About What's Next

How do people move from a stymied path to an open road full of possibility? It's a question psychology has asked and answered in various ways. We've already seen how intrinsic goals—motivated from the inside out—yield a greater sense of well-being and satisfaction than extrinsic goals, which are either externally imposed or depend on external validation, such as the admiration of others. Similarly, approach goals, objectives that are positive in and of themselves, deliver more satisfaction than those based on avoiding bad outcomes.

While humans are by nature goal-oriented, how happy we feel—what psychologists call *subjective well-being*—very much depends on our goals' having coherence so that they represent the true self as we each understand it. What does this mean precisely? As Robert A. Emmons explains, human beings don't experience a subjective sense of well-being simply because they are setting and progressing toward important life goals; that's one of the things that distinguishes us from other goal-oriented creatures like earthworms, squirrels, or the dog or cat that might be lying at your feet.

The answer to whether you feel happy at this moment isn't just answered by your goals or the progress you've made toward achieving them but is answered by something else. If reaching our goals doesn't make us happy, what does? It's whether our goals reflect the self. As Emmons writes, "people are more than just collections of personal goals. What's missing is an overall organizing principle that brings together and integrates separate goal strivings into a coherent structure. . . . This is the job of identity or the self, creating an overall life purpose. This organizing principle—be it identity, the self, or a similar structure—is that which links individual goals together and to future states and desired outcomes." He concludes that the principle ultimately is "the search for meaningfulness in one's life. Meaning comes from personally fulfilling goals, the integration of these goals into a broader self-system, and the integration of these goals into a broader social system."

Some of the stories we've told about quitting make it clear that sometimes the search for coherence, for meaning, is paramount and that for each of us, the self isn't static but a work in progress. Robert, the environmentalist whose story we told, wanted work that reflected and integrated what he cared about and that would contribute to a greater good. Deidre the swimmer faced the challenge of giving up a goal that had been her primary definition of self and finding other domains that would define her.

The story of Jill is a good example since she was a skilled lawyer who was extremely well-compensated and had, by many people's lights, an enviable career. Her unhappiness and dissatisfaction stemmed from the fact that her work didn't give her life meaning and actually conflicted with her deepest definitions of self. Teaching children, as she now does, offers her the sense of connectedness and purposefulness she understood as central to herself. When Marie the artist outgrew the definitions of self that had sustained her through more than twenty years, she had to redefine her goals accordingly.

Seeking coherence and meaning isn't just limited to the 1 percent of Americans who have the luxury of thinking about more than a paycheck. Flow can be achieved in almost any activity or line of work, as Mihaly Csikszentmihalyi has shown. In his book *Flow*, Csikszentmihalyi cites one study he conducted that relied on the self-reports of over one hundred men and women who worked full-time in a variety of occupations. When prompted by a pager, the people recorded how they felt generally, how challenged they were, and how many skills they were using at that exact time. They were beeped eight times a day at random intervals. Of the forty-eight hundred responses the researchers collected, one-third were determined to be "in flow." That percentage was even higher—a full 54 percent—when people were actually working and concentrating (as opposed to daydreaming, gossiping, or attending to personal business during work hours). Csikszentmihalyi notes that this percentage of flow experience is much higher than what people report when they're engaged in leisure activities like reading, watching television, having friends over, or going out to eat; in those situations, only 18 percent reported being in flow.

Not unexpectedly, he also found that people who had higher-level jobs—managers and supervisors—were in flow 64 percent of the time, as opposed to clerical workers (57 percent) and blue-collar workers (47 percent). But perhaps surprisingly, while the differences are significant, they're not overwhelming. Flow, or connection, may not be as rare as people think. Remarkably, Csikszentmihalyi found that for leisure activities, blue-collar workers reported being in flow 20 percent of the time, compared with 16 percent for clerical workers and 15 percent for managers. But as he notes, even assembly-line workers reported being in flow twice as much during work time than leisure, 44 percent to 20 percent.

Flow results from coherence, the alignment of the self with action or activity. There's no one-size-fits-all strategy for getting in flow since we define ourselves in singular ways; how we think about and define ourselves is closely connected to how easily we'll be able to reengage after quitting.

The Self and Resilience

Certain cognitive and affective strengths and weaknesses make some of us better at knowing when and how to quit; similarly, some of us will be better equipped at starting over, setting and pursuing a new goal in place of a failed or unattainable one. It's been suggested that this advantage has much to do with the basic conception of the self and whether it is "simple" or "complex" in nature. Why is a setback—a divorce, for example—a life-defining moment from which one person never fully recovers, yet for another person, the setback, while bruising and painful, yields new paths and experiences over time? Psychologist Patricia Linville has posited that the complexity of our mental representations of self directly affects our ability to cope with not just the day-to-day stresses of life but also the major emotional shifts when we fail to attain a goal or stop pursuing an important one. The more complex our self-representation, the more buffered we are from negative affect and emotional fallout; conversely, the simpler the self-representation, the more vulnerable we are to emotional spillover. The subtitle of her article, by the way, is "Don't Put All Your Eggs in One Cognitive Basket."

According to Linville, our self-representation includes specific events and behaviors ("Picked up the kids from school on time," "Worked on a new case for six hours") as well as generalizations about traits (shy, outgoing, enthusiastic), roles (lawyer, husband, father, brother), category membership (male, Jewish, Libertarian), physical features (fit, tall, myopic), behavior (card player, sailor, jazz enthusiast), preferences (urban living), goals (financial success), autobiographical recollections (summers at grandparents' cottage), and relationships (colleague, friend, supporter).

Linville hypothesizes that each of these domains is associated with specific feelings about the self as well as appraisals; each self-representation may evoke either a positive or a negative feeling. We may be proud of ourselves in one domain (e.g., work or athletics), but not in another (e.g., social graces, language ability). Most important, Linville assumes that some people's self-representations are more complex than others'. The fewer domains the self-representation relies on and the more linked the domains, the greater the emotional impact of a failed or thwarted goal. Conversely, when the representations are numerous and independent of each other, the more buffered the individual will be. Imagine a man who defines himself primarily in terms of his career success, his role as the family breadwinner, his luxurious standard of living, and the admiration of others. Say he is passed over very publically for a promotion or is let go. His disappointment will spill over into his definitions of self as a husband, a father, a friend, and an acquaintance; he'll likely lack a domain in which he can feel good about himself to counter the negative affect.

In contrast, imagine a man with the same prestigious and high-paying job but who defines himself in broader ways—by his intimate relationships, his work in the community, by his love of playing guitar. This person can suffer the same setbacks but can continue to feel good about himself in other domains. It's this second person who will be able to reengage with a new goal with greater ease. How many aspects of the self are directly tied into the loss or failure of a goal will also determine the emotional impact.

In another study, which looks at self-complexity as a cognitive buffer, Linville uses the example of two women going through a divorce and offers an answer to the question we posed earlier—why is a setback a momentary blip in one person's life and a catastrophe from which there's no recovery in another's? The first woman has a relatively simple self-representation as a wife and a lawyer. In her case, these two aspects of self are closely intertwined since her about-to-be ex-husband is also an attorney and they worked together often. Linville writes that "the negative affect and self-appraisal associated with her divorce will be massive because it will spill over to affect her thoughts and feelings about both important aspects of self." Another woman going through a divorce defines herself with greater complexity—as a wife, a lawyer, a tennis player, and a friend. Because her husband isn't a lawyer, her professional self-definition is safe from negative fallout, as are her other defining roles. She'll weather the storm of the divorce more easily.

The narrowly defined self may have trouble reengaging after disengagement from a goal, whether it is willingly given up or not. That was true for Lacie, who followed her husband Steven to France when his company transferred him. In the process, she gave up her job and her circle of friends, but she took on the challenge of living abroad, learned to speak French fluently, and, after their children were born, learned to embrace both the culture and the society as an American expatriate. Then Steven fell in love with a colleague and filed for divorce. Lacie went back to the United States, her two children in tow, emotionally devastated. She applied for jobs with little success, even though she was more than qualified; despondent, she consulted a therapist. It soon became clear that since she'd defined herself primarily as a wife for all of those years, her negative thoughts were spilling over into every domain. Prospective employers were put off by her lack of self-confidence, her self-deprecating tone when she talked about her skills, and her hesitancy. It took work, but eventually she was able to recover some of the good feelings she had about herself and began to formulate new goals that were aligned with her own needs and wants. In time, she started her own consulting company to work with and advise American families who were moving abroad for extended periods.

Lacie's story demonstrates that you can, with effort, reframe your self-representations to make them more complex and that it's sage advice not "to put all your eggs in one cognitive basket." If you're still bruised and ruminating after a setback, spend some time thinking about your other definitions of self, and make it an interim goal to take pride and pleasure in them.

In their classic book on self-regulation, Charles S. Carver and Michael F. Scheier note that the ability to pursue an attainable goal after quitting an unreachable one engages the individual in forward movement. This is especially important when what they call the "blocked path" concerns a central value of the self or, to use Linville's term, a central self-representation. They point out the advantage of being able to see the goal in relatively abstract terms, looking beyond the specifics of the goal lost and appreciating its meaningfulness. So, someone who has lost a spouse but prized the closeness of connection, "who understands that the core desire is to *experience closeness* can more readily recognize that there are many ways to do this than can someone who's less clear about the nature of the higher-level goal."

Both complex self-representation and the ability to think abstractly about a goal endow the individual with the flexibility he or she needs to move forward to pursue a new goal creatively through different pathways. If you are having trouble moving forward—reengaging—troubleshoot your efforts by thinking about the domains of the self that endow your life with meaning and that make you feel good about yourself, instead of focusing on the goal that has eluded you. Try thinking about your goal in abstract terms so that you can figure out whether there are different ways of approaching it or otherwise getting what you need in your life.

Take the example of a young woman who was utterly stymied in her efforts to get a job in the nonprofit world; it was clear that budget cuts had made it well-nigh impossible for her to find work that paid enough to cover her rent and bills. Ultimately, she chose to do volunteer work on the weekends in addition to her full-time job, for the pleasure of it, to keep her connected, and to keep her goal in focus. She believes that her volunteerism may well be the path that ultimately gets her where she wants to be.

Understanding your goal in abstract terms may also make it easier for you see opportunities in interim goals. Your ultimate goal may be to remarry after the loss of a close relationship, but it may be easier and more realistic for you to focus on deepening the ties you have in existing relationships in the interim.

Anything that helps you be cognitively and emotionally flexible will serve you well as you move forward. But the closer to your central self-definition the relinquished goal is, the greater the emotional impact. Seek support if you need to; emotional recovery is part of the process.

Optimism and Reengagement

We've talked about optimism in these pages, most often in terms of overoptimism, which often contributes to people's holding on to unattainable goals and encourages their lack of realistic appraisal about both the goal and the skills or opportunity necessary to attain it. Generally, optimism is a cognitive bias that doesn't serve us when we need to disengage. But Carsten Wrosch and Michael Scheier have argued that optimism—which they define as "a relatively stable, generalized expectation that good outcomes will occur across important life domains"—is, nonetheless, an important ingredient in reengagement. In this research, optimism isn't the opposite of pessimism as it is in common parlance ("Are you a person who sees a half-full or a half-empty glass?") but is a spectrum of expectation. By "stable," Wrosch and Scheier mean that optimism, like personality traits, tends to be stable across the life span. They measure optimism and pessimism with a six-item scale called the Life Orientation Test. It's only used in research and not as a clinical tool, but you might as well locate yourself on the scale as you read the questions below.

1. In uncertain times, I usually expect the best.
2. It's easy for me to relax.
3. If something can go wrong for me, it will.
4. I'm always optimistic about my future.
5. I enjoy my friends a lot.
6. It's important for me to keep busy.
7. I hardly ever expect things to go my way.
8. I don't get upset too easily.
9. I rarely count on good things happening to me.
10. Overall, I expect more good things to happen to me than bad.

Items 2, 5, 6, and 8 are fillers and don't get scored. For items 1, 4, and 10, score 4 points for "I strongly agree"; 3 points for "I agree"; 2 points for "I'm neutral"; 1 point for "I disagree"; and 0 points for "I strongly disagree." Reverse-score items 3, 7, and 9 (0 points = strongly agree, 1 = agree, 2 = neutral, 3 = disagree, and 4 = strongly disagree). Add up all your answers. The higher the number, the more optimistic you are; high values imply optimism.

Wrosch and Scheier assert that optimism provides the necessary fuel for reengagement; in addition, they write that optimistic people use a more active style of coping and engage in more problem-solving when a goal has been blocked. Remember that goal disengagement requires both a reduction of effort (ceasing activities in pursuit of the goal) and a relinquishment of commitment. As we've already seen, people who are unable to let go of the commitment end up stuck and unable to set new goals. Wrosch and Scheier argue that being optimistic about your chances of achieving a new goal facilitates the process.

How optimism needs to be balanced by realism is further explained by examining the mind-sets necessary for achieving the goals you set for yourself.

The Question of Mind-Set

Because this book focuses on mastering the art of quitting, we haven't really addressed what contributes to successful goal achievement in detail. Since reengagement demands that we understand not just how to set the right goals for ourselves but how to achieve them, we'll turn our attention there. A highly influential argument by Peter M. Gollwitzer proposes that planning is a key element. Gollwitzer divides goal pursuit into four separate but related stages. The first is what he calls the *predecisional stage*, in which a person considers wishes and desires in terms of feasibility and desirability, pushing some desires to the side and focusing on others that appear to be reachable with effort. That predecisional stage yields to the *preactional* stage, during which the person begins to plan actions that will move him or her closer to the goal. This process focuses on when, where, how, and how long to act. During the third stage, the *actional* stage, the person responds to opportunities for goal advancement and to redouble efforts if there's an impediment. The fourth stage, the *postactional stage*, is more like the predecisional stage in that it's evaluative. The person evaluates not only his or her own performance but also the outcome, asking, among other things, whether the goal has delivered the expected promise. Looking back to the original moment of choosing and setting the goal, the person reevaluates it in terms of both feasibility and desirability and looks ahead by comparing it to other possible goals that may be more feasible or desirable, or both. Goal disengagement, if it is to happen, occurs in the postactional stage.

Gollwitzer further posits that there are two different mind-sets—separate cognitive orientations—that distinguish these phases. The *deliberative* mind-set—utilized in both the predecisional and the postactional stages—is distinct from the *implemental* mind-set, which accompanies the preactional and actional stages. The deliberative mind-set is open-minded, since the individual is still weighing options and deciding which goal to pursue; this mind-set is inquisitive and open to all kinds of information. In contrast, the implemental mind-set is focused, selective, and "close-minded" in comparison. The deliberative mind-set is more accurate and realistic in terms of gauging feasibility, while the implemental mind-set tends toward optimism and self-serving analysis because it is focused on continuing action.

Although you can readily see the usefulness of the implemental mind-set when you're pursuing the right goal that's actually attainable—full steam ahead!—the deliberative mind-set is also invaluable if you must adjust your commitment to the goal or if the goal itself isn't delivering on its promise. The illusion of control, as we've seen elsewhere, is increased by the implemental mind-set.

A number of experiments that induced these mind-sets in participants led Gollwitzer to suggest that these mind-sets have practical application outside the laboratory and in ordinary life. By focusing, people can actually orient their thoughts in a deliberative or implemental direction, depending on the situation at hand. Being able to match your mind-set to the problem at hand is an effective strategy for goal engagement.

If you're having trouble setting a new goal for yourself, try to pinpoint what's standing in your way. Is the failure or obstruction of the goal you've quit preventing you from focusing on new avenues of pursuit? If the answer is yes, the open-ended nature of the deliberative mind-set can be of use to you. If need be, write the possible alternative goals down, and think about which are desirable first, and then consider which are the most feasible. Allow yourself the freedom to imagine where you might go next. On the other hand, if the disappointment associated with quitting is stopping you from acting, an implemental mind-set is in order. Making plans will strengthen your commitment to both the goal and the active behaviors; it's called *implementation intention*.

The Benefit of Planning

The decision to pursue a goal is a conscious declaration of intention ("I will do X"). The single decision to go after a goal opens up to a series of other decisions on how precisely to achieve the goals.

These are what Peter Gollwitzer calls *implementation intentions*, or thoughts and plans about what to do if a specific situation arises. The formulation here is "If X happens, then I will do Y"; basically, you are reframing your goal in terms of specific actions you will take. How does the formation of these intentions connect to goal setting and achievement? Is some way of proceeding more effective at moving a person from the mere contemplation of a goal to action? That is the question Gollwitzer and his colleagues looked at in a paper titled "From Weighing to Willing."

The researchers had participants name two personal problems that were either unresolved or undecided; one had to be relatively simple (e.g., "Should I subscribe to the newspaper?" or "Should I go skiing on vacation?") and the other more complicated (e.g., "Should I break up with my boyfriend?" "Should I start my master's thesis?" "Should I move out of my parents' house?"). The researchers ascertained that all of the participants were, in fact, far removed from actually making a decision about these personal matters. The subjects were divided into three groups and a control group. The first group was asked to imagine and fantasize about the positive expectations they would have, should they move ahead with a decision. The second group was asked to come up with different ways they might achieve their goal without committing themselves to a single plan. The third group, however, was instructed to decide on a single path of action. The control group was distracted from thinking about their personal situation by doing math problems. When the researchers followed up three weeks later, they found that only the subjects in the group instructed to think about and commit themselves to a specific path of action actually moved forward to the goal of resolving the problem.

The lesson here is that implementation intentions facilitate overcoming procrastination and other obstacles to beginning goal pursuit, as well as heightening a person's attention to possible opportunities for action. Gollwitzer asserts that forming an intention to act makes you sensitive to situational cues; furthermore, he says, the linking of a behavior to a chosen critical situation will lead to the "automatization" of the behavior. In other words, the behavior won't be conscious and it will take advantage of the automaticity described by John A. Bargh and others and discussed in Chapter 1. In this case, though, you are choosing the situational cues you'll be responding to.

Thinking about the future in concrete terms—the implemental mind-set—combined with intention or commitment can help you pull out of stalled situations caused by rumination or distraction. Both the deliberative and the implemental mind-sets are extremely valuable tools that can be used consciously as you set goals for yourself and act on them. The deliberative mind-set allows you to reevaluate your efforts along the way and recalibrate or redefine your goal, if need be. Plans or implementation intentions gear your thinking to troubleshoot and problem-solve along the way; they are the engine for the enterprise.

If your goal is to resolve a conflict or misunderstanding with another person, making that intention conscious will help you shape how to respond in actions and words. For example, you would think, "If he's open, I'll respond by making a suggestion about how to mend fences" or "If she says she dislikes my manner, I'll ask her for details in a quiet, nonconfrontational way." Forming the intention will focus you on the cues in the person's behavior—is he or she signaling a willingness to end the friction?—thus allowing you to figure out what you can do to facilitate that willingness and achieve your goal.

Implementation intentions can be used in any domain; they take you out of the vague realm of setting a goal (becoming a nicer or more responsive person) and into a proactive frame of mind ("If my spouse asks me to run an errand, I'll do it without complaint" or "If my neighbor asks me to help with a yard sale, I will"). Implementation intentions don't just turn abstract goals (being a nicer person, getting into shape, becoming more well-read about a subject) into actions, but are also effective strategies for self-regulatory behavior. Suppose, for example, that you've received a pretty mixed evaluation at your job. The report praises you but also singles out your unresponsiveness to criticism as a weakness. Rather than tell yourself that you will be more responsive in the future, instead you formulate a plan for action: "If I'm criticized, I'll immediately ask my supervisor what I should have done, and do what I can to fix things."

Most importantly, implementation intentions can become automatic and thus take advantage of the "nonconscious" thinking that sometimes gets in the way of conscious goal setting, Gollwitzer says, "By forming implementation intentions, people can strategically switch from conscious effortful control of their behaviors . . . to being automatically controlled by situational cues." (That is, "I'll do X when Y happens.") Implementation intentions also help prevent distractions, keep you on track, and strengthen commitment to the goal. As Gollwitzer, Ute C. Bayer, and Kathleen C. Molloch note, "it is important to recognize that all these maneuvers focus on changing the self so that the self becomes a better executive."

Getting to "Happy"

It turns out that the road to happiness—not hell, as the adage has it—is paved with intentions, at least according to a study by Sonja Lyubomirsky, Kennon M. Sheldon, and David Schkade. They posit that there are three factors that affect whether an individual considers himself or herself happy: the happiness set point, life circumstances, and intentional activity. The terms demand explanation, and even though you're probably inured to the idea that what you considered your free will isn't nearly as free as you thought—and that you're not completely in charge of the "car" that's you—this last salvo has a bit of good news.

The *happiness set point* is the factor responsible for roughly half of your potential happiness. The set point, like the personality traits that are a part of it, is stable over time and pretty much genetically determined.

Next up are the *life circumstances*, which, surprisingly, only account for 10 percent of your happiness; these life circumstances include both positive and negative events (a happy, stable childhood or a traumatic one; winning academic awards or failing miserably at school), as well as marital status, occupation, job security, income, health, and religiosity. The researchers note that people who make more money are indeed relatively happier; that married people are happier than single, divorced, or widowed people; that religious people tend to describe themselves as happier than those who aren't religious; and that healthy people self-report more happiness than their sick counterparts. But Lyubomirsky and her colleagues also point out that all of these various circumstances combined only account for 8 to 15 percent variation in happiness levels: "These relatively weak associations have been deemed surprising and paradoxical, given well-being researchers' initial expectations that circumstantial factors such as income and physical heath would be strongly related to happiness."

Daniel Gilbert's work on happiness explains this surprisingly low figure in terms of both the impact bias and the human ability to adapt rapidly to new circumstances. (That's why the bliss you expected when you got that promotion doesn't last, but then again, neither does the emotional devastation of being dumped by your lover.) As Lyubomirsky and her colleagues note, "the hedonic adaptation tends to shuttle people back to their starting point following any positive circumstantial change." So much for the likelihood that your winning the lottery will make you a whole lot happier.

The good news is that while the happiness set point and life circumstance account for 60 percent of what determines how happy you feel, a full 40 percent comes from intentional activity, and that puts you in charge of that piece of the happiness pie. *Intentional activity* is, as you might imagine, a huge grab bag of all the things people do, including behavioral activity (taking a walk in the woods or getting together with a close friend), cognitive activity (reframing situations to feel more positive), and volitional activity (striving for personal goals).

Remarkably, unlike circumstantial changes to happiness, which are relatively ephemeral because of adaptation, intentional activity has long-term effects. Sheldon and Lyubomirsky tested this hypothesis in a series of experiments that compared the longevity of the effect of an improvement in circumstances on happiness with that of intentional activity. In their first study, they had participants self-select into groups with a positive change in circumstances and those who had a positive change in activity. The researchers found that circumstantial change gave less of a boost over time than did continued activity. Their second study took measures over twelve weeks and found that intentional activity boosted happiness over time, though not incrementally; instead, the initial bump in happiness was sustained at the same level by the activity. Their third study measured changes in psychological well-being and found the same pattern.

There's one caveat, though; circumstantial change can have a more lasting impact on happiness if the initial circumstances weren't meeting the individual's basic needs. In other words, moving from a three-bedroom house to a larger one won't sustain happiness—you'll simply get used to the bigger space—but moving from a dangerous neighborhood to one where you feel safe will. It partly depends on what the original circumstances were. In addition, how you deal with circumstantial change in your life also affects whether you will adapt to the change and find yourself back at your happiness set point. Circumstantial change can make you happy for longer, as the researchers write, "only to the extent that one takes action to keep the new circumstances 'fresh'—i.e., by remembering to appreciate or feel gratitude for them, or by making the effort to take advantage of the opportunities for positive experiences that they afford. In other words, this is feasible when one engages in intentional activity with respect to the circumstances in one's life— that is, when one *acts* upon one's circumstances."

Not surprisingly, many of the points about how to judge whether to quit a goal also apply to the choosing of new goals and activities that will deliver happiness or subjective well-being. First, Lyubomirsky and her colleague assert that the goodness of fit between the person and the activity is important; we've seen this observation made elsewhere in different contexts. Second, they underscore the importance of beginning with effort and maintaining that effort. It's easier to maintain effort if the activity is self-sustaining and intrinsic or puts you in flow.

The bottom line is that while we may be lousy at figuring out what will make us happy now or in the future, have a happiness set point that is based on who we are and is stable over time, and may be prone to adapt to or ignore changes in circumstances that should make us happy, there's still lots of wiggle room.

The Big Takeaway

The research we've looked at in this chapter points to the efficacy of conscious behavior and how it can help you drive the car that's you. These theoretical concepts can all be translated into motivated behaviors that can help you choose goals that are congruent, satisfying, and attainable. You can use these cognitive strategies—of mind-set and implementation intentions—to engage in new goals. Similarly, the research on happiness suggests that while there are aspects of happiness you can't influence, there are enough aspects that you can. How you think about what makes you happy—deciding to count your blessings, for example—turns it into intentional activity. Both conscious thinking and acting consciously will feed your sense of self and make you feel empowered. Similarly, while the Mercedes in your driveway or the Guccis in your closets won't sustain your happiness, how you think about them—the work you did in order to pay for them and how that work made you feel—may.

Resetting your compass after disengagement is an act of faith and bravery, but it is also full of possibility. The self that emerges from this transition won't be the same self that began the process. It's our hope that what you've learned from this book will give you permission to take your leave and wave good-bye when you need to, no matter what the culture or onlookers say, and that you'll do it consciously, gracefully, and intelligently. We hope too that the period of not knowing what's next after you've quit will yield to a time when you feel confident. And ultimately, you will take full advantage of that piece of the happiness pie that's yours alone.

The Wisdom of Quitting

One of the interesting things about writing this book was listening to women and men from different generations talk about what they'd learned about persistence during their childhoods. The baby boomers grew up hearing stories of persistence from parents and grandparents who'd lived through both the Great Depression and World War II. The theme of persistence was closely bound up with heroism and echoed in books, movies, and school lessons. Yet this generation's rejection of the sunk-cost thinking that prolonged the Vietnam War changed how the group thought about persistence. In that context, the virtue of persistence became conflated with conservatism, a lack of realism, and a fondness for lost causes. Many young people "quit" their parents' cultural expectations, for a time at least, and a number of them did, as Timothy Leary exhorted, "turn on, tune in, drop out."

Consequently, the boomer's children—those now in their twenties, thirties, and forties—appear to have had more leeway in terms of being able to change their minds about their commitments as children. Nevertheless, these young people also report that even if their parents hadn't touted persistence as a virtue, the parents often modeled it.

The questionnaire for this book—not a scientific survey but a call for stories—revealed how ambivalent most people still feel about admitting to having quit something important, even if, in the end, quitting was the right thing to do. The cultural portrait of the quitter—that never-will-amount-to-anything person who lacks staying power—still looms large. While the parents of the baby boomers tended not to let their children quit anything they signed up for—if you begged for a saxophone, you would be forced to practice it—the boomers themselves appear to have tried to navigate the difficult shoals of teaching a child the value of exertion and sustained effort, on the one hand, and giving that child the freedom to explore an activity and to abandon it when it turned out not to be a good fit, on the other.

"It's hard figuring out why your kid wants to quit," one mother said. "Fear of failure is always a bad reason to quit, and I never let my children abandon an activity if I thought that was what was really afoot. On the other hand, there's nothing to be gained by forcing a child to persist at something he hates." Another mother took the opposite point of view, writing that there was something to be learned by finishing what you started. She said that life was full of situations that required you to persist when all you really wanted to do was quit. That's true enough.

Quitting a team sport presents the thorniest problem for most parents, balancing individual desires against the commitment made to others. One father of a thirty-three-year-old recalled his decision to allow his son to quit ice hockey, even after investing in all the expensive paraphernalia for the sport: "I wonder whether I was okay with it because the sport wasn't important to me. Would I have reacted differently if it'd been golf, a sport I have played all of my life? I wonder."

Both the enormous popularity of Amy Chua's *Battle Hymn of the Tiger Mother* and the brouhaha that accompanied its vision of disciplinarian, persistence-fueled parenting to maximize a child's achievements make it clear that most people still aren't sure whether quitting deserves a place on their agenda.

This book doesn't promote quitting as a stand-alone answer. If quitting isn't accompanied by engagement with new goals, it's not an answer at all. In a celebrity-obsessed culture that focuses on extrinsic goals—chiefly, money and fame—perhaps our job as people, parents, and mentors is to focus less on the value of persistence and more on the nature of the goals we set for ourselves and encourage in others.

We now know that persistence is hardwired in the human species; what needs to be learned is discernment, knowing which goals are worthy of effort and meaningful enough to provide happiness or satisfaction. As technology continues to shape children's and adolescents' definitions of self—where worth means popularity and attention, as judged by the number of followers on YouTube and Twitter, text messages, and "friends" on Facebook—it seems more important than ever to focus on goals that are intrinsic to, and coherent with, the self, rather than extrinsic. In a world where distraction is ubiquitous—cell phones by the pillow, multiple screens open all the time—making sure that children are encouraged to focus on goals that mirror themselves and supported in that effort should be a priority. In a quick-fix culture where the end is too often valued over the means, children need to be taught that goal seeking is a valuable journey in and of itself and that it's not just the end—the achievement—that matters.

For all that culture disparages it, quitting is, inevitably, part of the life cycle, easier at some stages and harder at others. Managing our thoughts, feelings, and actions lies at the heart of both quitting with mastery and living with satisfaction.

Quitting consciously and thoughtfully affords us a different view of decisions, whether they are our own or those of others. As one young man, thirty, wrote of his own experience dropping out of college twice and then becoming a college teacher, "It has changed my views because quitting something is often an attempt to affirm something larger that we can't yet grasp. And while I find it frustratingly negative to hear people phrase their decisions in terms of quitting, I now try to listen instead to the positive move they are struggling to make that they don't yet have the words to express."

Amen to that.

Acknowledgments

The endnotes and bibliography tell all, but this book wouldn't exist without the amazing work of psychologists, economists, and other social scientists who have explored why people do what they do, arriving at new findings on the processes of thinking, automaticity and the unconscious, self-regulation, and goal setting. New discoveries in the workings of the brain continue to enlighten and excite. While these researchers aren't responsible for how these ideas are used or expressed, without them and the body of work they created, this book would have been merely an interesting concept and would have ended up in whatever Elysian fields exist for unsupported but nifty ideas.

On a personal note, the intellectual journey of discovery fueled by exploring this body of work has been exciting and discomfiting at times; I'm still getting used to the idea of consciousness as an illusion.

Many thanks to Elizabeth Kaplan, my agent, for not quitting, and to Dan Ambrosio for seeing the book through and for his enthusiasm. Thanks to Carolyn Sobczak for listening to me bemoan the death of the blue pencil and for being so patient.

Friends and strangers rallied to send e-mails exhorting folks to admit to quitting and to talk about letting go, failure, and regret as well as the joys of starting over and reinventing the self. In alphabetical order, thanks to Jacqueline Freeman, Leslie Garisto, Ray Healey, Ed Mickens, Patti Pitcher, Claudia Karabaic Sargent, and Lori Stein. Thanks, too, to all of those who shared their stories but preferred not to be named; you know who you are and I appreciate your help. A special thanks to Karyl McBride for her morning e-mails.

On the home front, a huge merci to Alexandra Israel and Craig Weatherly, who lived with a distracted writer and piles of articles. Craig deserves special kudos for his newly acquired mastery of JSTOR and other databases in the elusive hunt for scholarly articles I couldn't find on the Internet.

—Peg Streep

I would like to thank—above all—the individuals and groups with whom I've worked over the years. Their courage and tenacity to finding their way and pursuing their dreams has helped me value quitting as an art form.

Professionally, I will group Dr. George Weinberg, Dr. Louis Ornont, and Dr. Larry Epstein together, though each man is distinctive and has created a swath of therapists who have benefited from their unique talents. Each has enlarged my sense of the possibilities in the human spirit and my technical ability to be a therapeutic presence in people's lives.

Finally, my work with Dick Bolles, author of *What Color Is Your Parachute?* encouraged me to see career change as a metaphor for spiritual opportunity. No one has contributed more to enabling people in transition to envisage their future as a process of discovery than Dick.

—Alan Bernstein

Notes

Chapter One: The Psychology of Persistence

10 It's pretty hard to overstate: Carston Wrosch et al., "The Importance of Goal Disengagement in Adaptive Self-Regulation: When Giving Up Is Beneficial," *Self and Identity* 2 (2003): 1–20.

12 One, called *intuition*: Daniel Kahneman, "A Perspective on Judgment and Choice: Mapping Bounded Rationality," *American Psychologist* 85, no. 9 (September 2003): 692–720. See also Daniel Kahneman, *Thinking, Fast and Slow* (New York: Farrar, Straus and Giroux, 2011), 20 ff.

14 The human brain is wired to respond to the near win: R. L. Reid, "The Psychology of the Near Miss," *Journal of Gambling Behavior* 2, no. 1 (1986): 32–39.

14 A British study on gambling: Henry Chase and Luke Clark, "Gambling Severity Predicts Midbrain Response to Near-Miss Outcomes," *Journal of Neuroscience* 30, no. 18 (2010): 6,180–6,187.

15 *availability heuristic*, is another mental proclivity: Amos Tversky and Daniel Kahneman, "Availability: A Heuristic for Judging Frequency and Probability," *Cognitive Psychology* 4 (1973): 207–232.

16 psychologist Scott Plous: *Psychology of Judgment and Decision-Making* (New York: McGraw-Hill, 1993), 121.

19 escalation of commitment: Barry M. Staw, "The Escalation of Commitment to a Course of Action," *Academy of Management Review* 6, no. 4 (October 1981): 577–587.

20 The *above-average effect*: Emily Pronin, Daniel Y. Lin, and Lee Ross, "The Bias Blind Spot: Perceptions of Bias in Self versus Others," *Personality and Social Psychology Bulletin* 28, no. 3 (March 2002): 369–381; Justin Kruger, "Lake Wobegon Be Gone! The 'Below-Average Effect' and the Egocentric Nature of Comparative

Ability Judgments," *Journal of Personality and Social Psychology* 77, no. 2 (1999): 221–232.

21 **We tend to be overconfident:** David Dunning, Dale W. Griffin, James D. Mikojkovic, and Lee Toss, "The Overconfidence Effect in Social Prediction," *Journal of Personality and Social Psychology* 58, no. 4 (1990): 568–581; Robert P. Vallone, Dale W. Griffin, Sabrina Lin, and Lee Ross, "Overconfident Prediction of Future Actions and Outcomes by Self and Others," *Journal of Personality and Social Psychology* 58, no. 4 (1990): 582–591.

21 **Writing in the *Harvard Business Review*:** Dan Lovallo and Daniel Kahneman, "Delusions of Success: How Optimism Undermines Executives' Decisions," *Harvard Business Review* (July 2003), 56–63.

22 **Studies show that a manager:** William Samuelson and Richard Zeckhauser, "The Status Quo Bias in Decision-Making," *Journal of Risk and Uncertainty* 1 (1988): 7–59.

22 **The fancy name for that is the *sunk-cost fallacy*:** Ibid., 37.

24 **As Nobel Prize winners Daniel Kahneman and Amos Tversky:** Daniel Kahneman and Amos Tversky, "Prospect Theory: An Analysis of Decision Under Risk," *Econometrica* 47, no. 2 (March 1979): 263–291.

24 **How sensitive people are to losses:** Daniel Gilbert, *Stumbling on Happiness* (New York: Vintage Books, 2007), 51–52. His example is based on George F. Loewenstein and Drazen Prelec, "Preferences for Sequences of Outcomes," *Psychological Review* 100, no. 1 (1993): 91–108.

26 **Researchers have found that when problems:** Nils B. Jostmann and Sander L. Koole, "When Persistence Is Futile," in *The Psychology of Goals*, ed. Gordon B. Moskowitz and Heidi Grant (New York: Guilford Press, 2009), 337–361.

27 **"The slowness of consciousness suggests":** Daniel M. Wegner, *The Illusion of Conscious Will* (Cambridge, MA: MIT Press, 2002), 57.

28 **There's the influence of *priming*:** Tanya L. Chartrand and John A. Bargh, "The Chameleon Effect: The Perception-Behavior Link and Social Interaction," *Journal of Personality and Social Psychology* 76, no. 6 (1999): 893–910.

28 Other experiments, especially those conducted by John A. Bargh: John A. Bargh and Tanya L. Chartrand, "The Unbearable Automaticity of Being," *American Psychologist* 54, no. 7 (July 1999): 462–479.

28 For example, in one experiment: John A. Bargh, Mark Chen, and Lara Burrows, "Automaticity of Social Behavior: Direct Effects of Trait Construct and Stereotype Activation on Actions," *Journal of Personality and Social Psychology* 71, no. 2 (1996): 230–244.

28 Bargh and his colleagues: Aaron C. Kay, S. Christian Wheeler, John A. Bargh, and Lee Ross, "Material Priming: The Influence of Mundane Physical Objects on Situational Construal and Competitive Behavior Choice," *Organizational Behavior and Human Decision Process* 93 (2004): 83–96.

29 the "ultimatum game": Ibid., 88.

29 Similar experiments, as well as brain scans: John A. Bargh et al., "The Automated Will: Nonconscious Activation and Pursuit of Behavior Goals," *Journal of Personality and Social Psychology* 81, no. 6 (2001): 1,014–1,027; John A. Bargh and Ezequiel Morsella, "The Unconscious Mind," *Perspectives on Psychological Science* 3, no. 1 (2003): 73–79; John A. Bargh and Julie Y. Huang, "The Selfish Goal," in *The Psychology of Goals*, ed. Gordon B. Moskowitz and Heidi Grant (New York: Guilford Press, 2009), 127–150.

29 "once they are put into motion": John A. Bargh and Tanya L. Chartrand, "The Unbearable Automaticity of Being," *American Psychologist* 54, no. 7 (July 1999): 473.

30 "ironic processes of mental control": Daniel M. Wegner, "Ironic Processes of Mental Control," *Psychological Review* 101, no. 1 (1994): 34–51.

30 "The mind actually appears to search": Wegner, *The Illusion of Will*, 141.

30 Wegner and others initially showed: The original experiment reported in Daniel M. Wegner, David J. Schneider, Samuel R. Carter III, and Teri L. White, "Paradoxical Effects of Thought Suppression," *Journal of Personality and Social Psychology* 53, no. 1 (1987): 5–13; Daniel M. Wegner, "You Can't Always Think What You Want: Problems in the Suppression of Unwanted Thoughts," *Advances in Experimental Psychology* 25 (1992): 193–225.

Chapter Two: Unsuccessful Quitting

45 **Richard M. Ryan and Edward L. Deci:** Richard M. Ryan and Edward L. Deci," Intrinsic and Extrinsic Motivations: Classic Definitions and New Directions," *Contemporary Educational Psychology* 25 (2000): 54–67.

45 **"The most basic distinction is between intrinsic motivation":** Ibid., 55.

46 **"Extrinsic motivation has typically":** Ibid.

47 **As John A. Bargh and his colleagues':** John A. Bargh and Ezequiel Morsella, "The Unconscious Mind," *Perspectives on Psychological Science* 3, no. 1 (2003): 73–79.

47 **Andrew J. Elliot and Todd M. Thrash:** Andrew J. Elliot and Todd M. Thrash, "Approach-Avoidance Motivation in Personality: Approach and Avoidance Temperaments and Goals," *Journal of Personality and Social Psychology* 82, no. 5 (2002): 804–818; Andrew J. Elliot and Todd M. Thrash, "Approach and Avoidance Temperament As Basic Dimensions of Personality," *Journal of Personality* 78, no. 3 (June 2010): 865–906.

48 **The distinction between these two motivations:** Andrew J. Elliot, "A Hierarchical Model of Approach-Avoidance Motivation," *Motivation and Emotion* 29 (2006): 111–116.

48 **"avoidance motivation is limited":** Ibid., 115.

48 **"avoidance motivation is designed to facilitate":** Ibid.

49 **Psychologists Robert Emmons and Laura King:** Robert A. Emmons and Laura King, "Conflict Among Personal Stirrings: Immediate and Long-Term Implications for Psychological and Physical Well-Being," *Journal of Personality and Social Psychology* 54, no. 6 (1988): 1,040–1,048.

Chapter Three: Quitting As an Art

53 **Goal disengagement takes place:** Here and elsewhere, the definition of the components of disengagement are derived from Nils B. Jostmann and Sander L. Koole, "When Persistence Is Futile: A Functional Analysis of Action Orientation and Goal Disengagement," in *The Psychology of Goals*, ed. Gordon B. Moskowitz and Heidi Grant (New York and London: Guilford Press, 2009), 337–361. Especially helpful is their table 13.2, p. 347.

54 Daniel Wegner explains: Daniel M. Wegner, *The Illusion of Conscious Will* (Cambridge, MA: MIT Press, 2002), 141.

54 Wegner and his colleagues: Daniel Wegner, *White Bears and Other Unwanted Thoughts: Suppression, Obsession, and the Psychology of Mental Control* (New York and London: Guilford Press, 1994), 65–69.

54 "If we wish to suppress a thought": Ibid., 70.

55 *Ego depletion* is the term: Roy F. Baumeister, Ellen Bratslavsky, Mark Muraven, and Dianne M. Tice, "Ego Depletion: Is the Active Self a Limited Resource?" *Journal of Personality and Social Psychology* 74, no. 5 (1998): 1,253–1,265.

56 "acts of choice draw on the same limited resource": Ibid., 1,257. For another possible model of ego depletion, see Michael Inzlicht and Brandon J. Schmeichel, "What Is Ego Depletion? Toward a Mechanistic Revision of the Resource Model of Self-Control," *Perspectives on Psychological Science* 7, no. 5 (2012): 450–463.

56 Other experiments showed: Ibid., 1,258–1,259. See also Mark Muraven, Dianne M. Tice, and Roy M. Baumeister, "Self-Control As Limited Resource: Regulatory Depletion Patterns," *Journal of Personality and Social Psychology* 74, no. 3 (1998): 774–789.

57 Dylan D. Wagner and Todd F. Heatherton: Dylan Wagner and Todd F. Heatherton, "Self-Regulatory Depletion Increases Emotional Reactivity in the Amygdala," *Social, Cognitive and Affective Neuroscience* (August 27, 2012). DOI:10/ 1093scan/nss082.

57 the *Zeigarnik effect*: Roy F. Baumeister and John Tierney, *Willpower: Rediscovering the Greatest Human Strength* (New York: Penguin Books, 2011), 80–81.

57 the recent work of E. J. Masicampo and Roy Baumeister: E. J. Masicampo and Roy F. Baumeister, "Consider It Done! Plan Making Can Eliminate the Cognitive Effects of Unfulfilled Goals," *Journal of Personality and Social Psychology* (June 2, 2011), advance online publication. DOI:10.1037/ 90024192.

59 In his seminal 1975 article, Eric Klinger: Eric Klinger, "Consequences of Commitment to and Disengagement from Incentives," *Psychological Review* 82, no. 2 (1975): 1–25.

60 Dylan D. Wagner and Todd F. Heatherton: Dylan Wagner and Todd F. Heatherton, "Self-Regulatory Depletion," *Social, Cognitive* *and Affective Neuroscience* (August 27, 2012). DOI:10/ 1093scan/ nss082.

60 **experiments conducted by Kathleen D. Vohs, Roy F. Baumeister, and others:** Kathleen D. Vohs et al., "Engaging in Self-Control Heightens Urges and Feelings," working paper.

60 **"Ego depletion may not change":** Ibid., 5.

64 **"In other words, every eight hours":** Daniel Gilbert, *Stumbling on Happiness* (New York: Vintage Books, 2006), 17.

65 **"Americans of all ages expect":** Ibid., 19.

65 **Emily Pronin, Daniel Lin, and Lee Ross:** Emily Pronin, Daniel Y. Lin, and Lee Ross, "The Bias Blind Spot: Perception of Bias in Self Versus Others," *Personality and Social Psychology Bulletin* 8 (2002): 369–381.

65 **"We don't always see ourselves as *superior*":** Gilbert, *Stumbling on Happiness*, 252.

66 **Timothy Wilson and Daniel Gilbert delineate four aspects:** Timothy D. Wilson and Daniel T. Gilbert, "Affective Forecasting," *Advances in Experimental Social Psychology* 35 (2003): 346–411.

66 **people tend to oversimplify:** Ibid., 348.

67 **Researchers Julia Woodzicka and Marianne LaFrance first asked:** Julia A. Woodzicka and Marianne LaFrance, "Real Versus Imagined Gender Harassment," *Journal of Social Issues* 57, no. 1 (2001): 15–39.

69 **the *impact bias*:** Wilson and Gilbert, "Affective Forecasting," 351.

69 **"the psychological immune system":** Ibid., 380 ff.

71 **psychologists Lauren B. Alloy and Lyn Y. Abramson:** Lauren B. Alloy and Lyn Y. Abramson, "Judgment of Contingency in Depressed and Non-Depressed Students: Sadder but Wiser?" *Journal of Experimental Psychology* 108, no. 4 (1978): 441–485.

71 ***depressive realism*:** Some other points of view on the subject include David Dunning and Amber L. Story, "Depression, Realism, and the Overconfidence Effect: Are the Sadder Wiser When Predicting Future Actions and Events?" *Journal of Personality and Social Psychology* 61, no. 4 (1981): 521–532; Lorraine G. Alan, Shepherd Siegel, and Samuel Hannah, "The Sad Truth About Depressive Realism," *Quarterly Journal of Experimental Psychology* 60, no. 3 (2007): 482–495.

72 **As Timothy D. Wilson writes:** *Strangers to Ourselves: Discovering the Adaptive Unconscious* (Cambridge, MA: Belknap Press of Harvard University, 2002), 140.

72 **"Though I had a million things to do":** Stephenie Meyer, official Web site, "Bio," accessed 16 June 2013, www.stepheniemeyer.com/bio.html.

73 **Psychologists Gabriele Oettingen and Doris Mayer distinguish between:** Gabriele Oettingen and Doris Mayer, "The Motivating Function of Thinking About the Future: Expectations Versus Fantasies," *Journal of Personality and Social Psychology* 83, no. 5 (2002): 1,198–1,212.

74 **One experiment by Oettingen and her colleagues:** Gabriele Oettingen, Hyeon-ju Pak, and Karoline Schnetter, "Self-Regulation of Goal-Setting: Turning Free Fantasies About the Future into Binding Goals," *Journal of Personality and Social Psychology* 80, no. 5 (2001): 736–753.

Chapter Four: A Talent for Quitting

83 **Studies show that while persistence is valuable:** Charles S. Carver and Michael F. Scheier, "Scaling Back Goals and Recalibration of the Affect Systems Are Processes in Normal Adaptive Self-Regulation: Understanding the 'Response-Shift' Phenomena," *Social Science and Medicine* 50 (2000): 1,715–1,722; Carsten Wrosch et al., "Adaptive Self-Regulation of Unattainable Goals: Goal Disengagement, Goal Reengagement, and Subjective Well-Being," *Personality and Social Psychology Bulletin* 29, no. 12 (December 2003):1,494–1,508. For whether quitting can improve your health, see Carsten Wrosch, Gregory E. Miller, Michael F. Scheier, and Stephanie Brun de Pontet, "Giving Up on Unattainable Goals: Benefits for Health?" *Personality and Social Psychology Bulletin* 33, no. 2 (February 2007): 251–265. For how not quitting can also literally make you sick, see Gregory E. Miller and Carsten Wrosch, "You've Gotta Know When to Fold 'Em: Goal Disengagement and Systemic Inflammation in Adolescence," *Psychological Science* 18, no. 9 (2007): 773–777.

85 **one perspective has been suggested by Andrew J. Elliot and Todd M. Thrash:** Andrew J. Elliot and Todd M. Thrash, "Approach

and Avoidance Temperament As Basic Dimensions of Personality," *Journal of Personality* 76, no. 3 (June 2010): 865–906.

86 **Andrew J. Elliot and Harry T. Reis suggest:** Andrew J. Elliot and Harry T. Reis, "Attachment and Exploration in Adulthood," *Journal of Personality and Social Psychology* 85, no. 2 (2003): 317–331.

86 **Attachment theory grew out of a series:** Mary Ainsworth, *Patterns of Attachment: A Psychological Study of the Strange Situation* (Hillsdale, NJ: Lawrence Erlbaum Associates, 1978).

87 **fascinating experiment called the *visual cliff*:** The original study measured depth perception in infants. E. J. Gibson and R. D. Walk, "The Visual Cliff," *Scientific American* 202, no. 4 (1960): 67–71.

88 **visual cliff experiment conducted by James F. Sorce and others:** James F. Sorce, Robert N. Emde, Joseph Campos, and Mary D. Klinnert, "Maternal Emotional Signaling: Its Effect on the Visual Cliff Behavior of 1-Year-Olds," *Developmental Psychology* 21, no. 1 (1985): 195–200.

88 **Elliot and Ries hypothesized:** Elliot and Ries, "Attachment and Exploration," 319.

90 **An in-depth analysis by Philip R. Shaver and Mario Mikulincer:** Philip R. Shaver and Mario Mikulincer, "Attachment-Related Psychodynamics," *Attachment and Human Development* 4 (2002): 133–161.

91 **A study by Heather C. Lench and Linda J. Levine:** Heather C. Lench and Linda J. Levine, "Goals and Responses to Failure: Knowing When to Hold Them and When to Fold Them," *Motivation and Emotion* 32 (2008): 127–140.

91 **"Ironically," the authors explain, "their focus on avoiding":** Ibid., 137.

91 **"Counterintuitively, people who focused on the potential failure":** Ibid., 139.

92 **A fascinating study by Elliot and Thrash:** Andrew J. Elliot and Todd M. Thrash, "The Intergenerational Transmission of Fear of Failure," *Personality and Social Psychology Bulletin* 30, no. 8 (August 2004): 957–971.

92 **"failure per se that is feared":** Ibid., 958.

93 **"Most who use it are simply":** Ibid., 959.

94 **in a study of patients in therapy:** Andrew J. Elliot and Marcy A. Church. "Client-Articulated Avoidance Goals in the Therapy Context," *Journal of Counseling Psychology* 49, no. 2 (2002): 243–254.

94 **Some examples from the study make the difference clear:** Ibid., table, 244.

96 **If, as Carsten Wrosch and others argue:** Carsten Wrosch, Michael F. Scheier, Charles S. Carver, and Richard Schulz, "The Importance of Goal Disengagement in Adaptive Self-Regulation: When Giving Up Is Beneficial," *Self and Identity* 2 (2003): 1–20.

97 **psychological theory called *personality systems interactions*:** Nicola Baumann and Julius Kuhl, "Intuition, Affect, and Personality: Unconscious Coherence Judgments and Self-Regulation of Negative Affect," *Journal of Personality and Social Psychology* 83, no. 5 (2002): 1,213–1,225; Nicola Baumann and Julius Kuhl, "Self-Infiltration: Confusing Tasks As Self-Selected in Memory," *Personality and Social Psychology Bulletin* 29, no. 4 (April 2003): 487–497; Sander L. Koole, Julius Kuhl, Nils B. Jostmann, and Kathleen D. Vohs, "On the Hidden Benefits of State Orientation: Can People Prosper Without Efficient Affect-Regulation Skills?" in *Building, Defending, and Regulating the Self*, ed. Abraham Tesser, Joanne Woods, and Diederik Stapel (New York: Psychology Press, 2005), 217–244; Nils B. Jostmann and Sander L. Koole, "When Persistence Is Futile: A Functional Analysis of Action Orientation and Goal Disengagement," in *The Psychology of Goals*, ed. Gordon B. Moskowitz and Heidi Grant (New York: Guilford Press, 2009), 337–361. See also Nils B. Jostmann, Sander L. Koole, Nickie Y. Van Der Wulp, and Daniel A. Fockenberg, "Subliminal Affect Regulation: The Moderating Role of Action versus State Orientation," *European Psychologist* 10, no. 3 (2005): 209–217.

98 **As James M. Diefendorff and others have noted:** James M. Diefendorff, Rosallie J. Hall, Robert G. Ord, and Mona L. Strean, "Action-State Orientation: Construct Validity of a Revised Measure and Its Relationship to Work-Related Variables," *Journal of Applied Psychology* 85, no. 2 (2000): 250.

100 **When action and state orientations are measured:** Julius Kuhl's scale is shown in Nils B. Jostmann and Sander L. Koole, "When Persistence Is Futile," in *The Psychology of Goals*, ed. Gordon B.

Moskowitz and Heidi Grant (New York: Guilford Press, 2009). The examples used here on shown on page 345.

100 **These orientations appear to be shaped:** Sander L. Koole, Julius Kuhl, Nils B. Jostmann, and Catrin Finkenauer, "Self-Regulation in Interpersonal Relationships: The Case of Action Versus State Orientation," in *Self and Relationship*, ed. Kathleen D. Vohs and E. J. Finkel (New York and London: Guilford Press, 2006), 360–386.

101 **An experiment conducted by researchers in Amsterdam:** Sander L. Koole and Nils B. Jostmann, "Getting a Grip on Your Feelings: Effects of Action Orientation on Intuitive Affect Regulation," *Journal of Personality and Social Psychology* 87, no. 6 (2004): 974–990.

102 **their orientation can stand them in good stead:** James M. Diefendorff, "Examination of the Roles of Action-State Orientation and Goal Orientation in the Goal-Setting and Performance Process," *Human Performance* 17, no. 4 (2004): 375–395.

103 **A series of experiments by Sander L. Koole and David A. Fockenberg:** Sander L. Koole and Daniel A. Fockenberg, "Implicit Emotional Regulation Under Demanding Conditions: The Mediating Role of Action Versus State Orientation," *Cognition and Emotion* 25, no. 3 (2011): 440–452.

Chapter Five: Managing Thoughts and Emotions

107 **what John D. Mayer and Peter Salovey have called *emotional intelligence*:** John D. Mayer and Peter Salovey, "What Is Emotional Intelligence?" in *Emotional Development and Emotional Intelligence*, ed. Peter Salovey and D. J. Sluyter (New York: Basic Books, 1997), 3–31.

107 **Daniel Goleman's enormously popular and culturally influential book:** Daniel Goleman, *Emotional Intelligence: Why It Can Matter More than IQ* (New York: Bantam Books, 1994).

107 **but they have publicly disavowed:** John D. Mayer, Peter Salovey, and David R. Caruso, "Emotional Intelligence: New Ability or Eclectic Traits?" *American Psychologist* 65, no. 7 (September 2008): 515.

107 **"the ability to perceive emotions":** Mayer and Salovey, "What Is Emotional Intelligence?" 5. The levels of emotional intelligence described here are based on their chapter, and the phrases used to describe the levels are drawn from their table 1.1.

108 **Because all of this happens in early childhood:** Daniel J. Siegel and Mary Hartzell, *Parenting from the Inside Out* (New York: Jeremy P. Tarcher/Penguin: 2003), 203–205.

111 **A study by Lisa Feldman Barrett and others:** Lisa Feldman Barrett, James Gross, Tamlin Conner Christensen, and Michael Benvenuto, "Knowing What You're Feeling and Knowing What to Do About It: Mapping the Relation Between Emotion Differentiation and Emotion Regulation," *Cognition and Emotion* 15, no. 6 (2001): 713–724.

113 **The Marshmallow and You:** Yuichi Shoda, Walter Mischel, and Philip K. Peake, "Predicting Adolescent Cognitive and Self-Regulatory Competencies from Preschool Delay of Gratification: Identifying Diagnostic Conditions," *Developmental Psychology* 16, no. 6 (1990): 978–986.

114 **The researchers concluded:** Ibid., 985.

119 **women are more likely to ruminate than men:** Lisa D. Butler and Susan Nolen-Hoeksema, "Gender Differences in Response to Depressed Mood in a College Sample," *Sex Roles* 30, no. 5–6 (1994): 331–346.

119 **Studies show that mothers tend to teach their male infants:** Katherine M. Weinberg, Edward Z. Tronick, Jeffrey F. Cohn, and Karen L. Olson, "Gender Differences in Emotional Expressivity and Self-Regulation During Early Infancy," *Developmental Psychology* 35 (1999): 175–188.

120 **In addition, mothers talk to daughters:** Robyn Fivush, "Exploring Sex Differences in the Emotional Context of Mother-Child Conversations About the Past," *Sex Roles* 20, no. 11–12 (1989): 675–695.

120 **Nolen-Hoeksema and Benita Jackson:** Susan Nolen-Hoeksema and Benita Jackson, "Mediators of the Gender Difference in Rumination," *Psychology of Women Quarterly* 25 (2001): 37–47.

121 **"Setting Free the Bears":** Daniel M. Wegner, "Setting Free the Bears: Escape from Thought Suppression," *American Psychologist* (November 2011): 671–679.

Chapter Six: Taking Stock

127 **Did You See the Gorilla?:** Christopher Chabris and Daniel J. Simons, *The Invisible Gorilla: How Our Intuitions Deceive Us* (New

York: Broadway Paperbacks, 2011); Daniel J. Simons and Christopher Chabris, "Gorillas in Our Midst: Sustained Inattention Blindness," *Perception* 28 (1999): 1,059–1,074.

128 **One of the researchers, Simons:** Daniel J. Simons and Daniel T. Lewin, "Failure to Detect Changes to People During a Real-World Interaction," *Psychonomic Bulletin and Review* 5, no. 4 (1998): 644–649.

130 **in a follow-up experiment by Daniel T. Levin:** Daniel T. Levin, Nausheen Momek, Sarah B. Drivdahl, and Daniel J. Simons, "Change Blindness Blindness: The Metacognitive Error of Over-estimating Change-Detection Ability," *Visual Cognition* 7, no. 1–3 (2000): 397–412.

131 **"Goals Gone Wild":** Lisa D. Ordóñez, Maurice E. Schweitzer, Adam D. Galinsky, and Max H. Bazerman, "Goals Gone Wild: The Systematic Side Effects of Over-Prescribing Goal Setting," Working Paper 09-083, Harvard Business School, Boston.

131 **an important summary by Edwin A. Locke and Gary P. Latham:** Edwin A. Locke and Gary P. Latham, "New Directions in Goal-Setting Theory," *Current Directions in Psychological Science* 15, no. 5 (October 2006): 265–268.

132 **MBAs who embraced broader learning goals:** Ibid., 266.

132 **Numerous studies, including one by Anat Drach-Zahavy:** Anat Drach-Zahavy and Miriam Erez, "Challenge Versus Threat Effects on the Goal Performance Relationship," *Organizational Behavior and Human Decision Process* 88 (2002): 667–682.

133 **the short and long of the Pinto story:** Ordóñez et al., "Goals Gone Wild," 4.

134 **The Pinto is only one of several examples:** Ibid., 10–11.

134 **The rejoinder to "Goals Gone Wild":** Edwin A. Locke and Gary P. Latham, "Has Goal Setting Gone Wild, or Have Its Attackers Abandoned Good Scholarship?" *Academy of Management Perspectives* 23, no. 1 (2009): 27–23. See also the spirited answer to the accusation: Lisa D. Ordóñez, Maurice E. Schweitzer, Adam D. Galinsky, and Max H. Bazer, "On Good Scholarship, Goal Setting and Scholars Gone Wild," Working Paper 09-122, Harvard Business School, Boston.

136 **"The Superstitious Pigeon":** B. F. Skinner, "Superstition in the Pigeon," *Journal of Experimental Psychology* 38 (1938): 168–172.

138 **the article published in the *Atlantic*:** Anne-Marie Slaughter, "Why Women Still Can't Have It All," *Atlantic*, July–August 2012, www .theatlantic.com/magazine/archive/2012/07/why-women-still-cant -have-it-all/309020.

144 **That's the point William Bridges makes:** William Bridges, *Transitions: Making Sense of Life's Changes* (New York: Da Capo Press, 2004), 116–117.

146 **why it's so hard to clear your mind:** Ezequiel Morsella, Avi Ben-Zeev, and Meredith Lanska, and John A. Bargh, "The Spontaneous Thoughts of the Night: How Future Tasks Breed Intrusive Cognitions," *Social Cognition*, 28, no. 5 (2012): 640–649.

148 **what science knows about moods, especially mystery moods?:** N. Pontus Leander, Sarah G. Moore, and Tanya L. Chartrand, "Mystery Moods: Their Origins and Consequences," in *The Psychology of Goals*, ed. Gordon B. Moskowitz and Heidi Grant (New York and London: Guilford Press, 2009), 480–504.

148 **what Tanya Chartrand and her colleagues call a "nonconscious" goal:** Tanya L. Chartrand, Clara Michelle Cheng, Amy L. Dalton, and Abraham Tesser, "Nonconscious Incidents or Adaptive Self-Regulatory Tool?" *Social Cognition* 28, no. 5 (2010): 569–588.

Chapter Seven: Mapping Your Goals

151 **For years, many books and talks:** The scoop on this is reported by Sid Savara, "Writing Down Your Goals: The Harvard Written Goal Study; Fact or Fiction?" Personal Development Training with Sid Savara, Web page, accessed 17 June 2013, http:// sidsavara.com/personal-productivity/fact-or-fiction-the-truth -about-the-harvard-written-goal-study.

151 **a study done in 2011 at McGill and Toronto Universities:** Dominique Morisano et al., "Setting, Elaborating, and Reflecting on Personal Goals Improves Academic Performance," *Journal of Applied Psychology* 85, no. 2 (2010): 255–264.

154 **As described by psychologists Richard M. Ryan and his colleagues:** Richard M. Ryan, Kennon M. Sheldon, Tim Kasser, and Edward L. Deci, "All Goals Are Not Created Equal: An Organismic Perspective on the Nature of Goals and Their Regulation," in *The Psychology of Action*, ed. Peter M. Gollwitzer and John A.

Bargh (New York and London: Guilford Press, 1996), 1–26. See also Kennon M. Sheldon, Richard M. Ryan, Edward L. Deci, and Tim Kasser, "The Independent Effects of Goal Contents: It's Both What You Pursue and Why You Pursue It," *Personality and Social Psychology Bulletin* 30, no. 4 (April 2004): 475–486; Edward L. Deci and Richard M. Ryan, "The 'What' and 'Why' of Goal Pursuits: Human Needs and the Self-Determination of Behavior," *Psychological Inquiry* 13, no. 4 (2000): 227–268.

154 In a study called "Further Examining the American Dream": Tim Kasser and Richard M. Ryan, "Further Examining the American Dream: Differential Correlates of Intrinsic and Extrinsic Goals," *Personality and Social Psychology Bulletin* 22, no. 3 (March 1996): 280–287.

160 One such principle is that of *flow*: Mihaly Csikszentmihalyi, *Flow: The Psychology of Optimal Experience* (New York: Harper Perennial/Modern Classics, 2008).

161 the "autotelic experience": Ibid.,67.

162 "if they are lucky": Ibid.

162 The optimal experience of flow: Ibid., 53–66.

164 The skill we should rely on: Gabriele Oettingen and Peter M. Gollwitzer, "Strategies of Setting and Implementing Goals: Mental Contrasting and Implementation Intentions," in *Social Psychological Foundations of Clinical Psychology*, ed. J. E. Maddux and J. P. Tanguy (New York: Guildford Press, 2010), 114–135.

165 both indulging and dwelling yield only moderate goal commitment: Gabriele Oettingen et al., "Turning Fantasies about Positive and Negative Futures into Self-Improvement Goals," *Motivation and Emotion* 29, no. 4 (December 2003): 237–267.

167 Using brain imaging: Anja Achtziger et al., "Strategies of Intention Formation Are Reflected in Continuous MEG Activity," *Social Neuroscience* 4, no. 1 (2009): 11–27.

168 "suggesting that mental contrasting": Ibid., 23.

168 In a study of self-talk, Ibrahim Senay: Ibrahim Senay, Dolores Abarracin, and Kenji Noguchi, "Motivating Goal-Directed Behavior Through Introspective Self-Talk: The Role of the Interrogative Form of Simple Future Tense," *Psychological Science* 21, no. 4 (2010): 499–504.

Chapter Eight: How to Quit Well

173 **As Roy Baumeister and his colleagues write:** Roy F. Baumeister, Ellen Bratslavsky, Catrin Finkenauer, and Kathleen Vohs, "Bad Is Stronger than Good," *Review of General Psychology* 5, no. 4 (2001): 323–370. The quotation is on page 323.

179 **As Dutch psychologists Marcel Zeelenberg:** Marcel Zeelenberg and Rik Pieters, "A Theory of Regret Regulation 1.0," *Journal of Consumer Psychology* 17, no. 1 (2007): 3–15; Rik Pieters and Marcel Zeelenberg, "A Theory of Regret Regulation 1.1," *Journal of Consumer Psychology* 17, no. 1 (2007): 29–35.

179 **One of the first theories about regret:** Daniel Kahneman, *Thinking, Fast and Slow* (New York: Farrar, Straus and Giroux, 2011), 346ff.

180 **In his book *Thinking, Fast and Slow*:** Ibid., 348.

180 **But this theory was challenged:** Thomas Gilovic and Victoria Husted Medvec, "The Experience of Regret: What, When, and Why," *Psychological Review* 102, no. 2 (1995): 379–395.

181 **(The disagreement between Kahneman and Gilovic and Medvec:** Thomas Gilovic, Victoria Husted Medvec, and Daniel Kahneman, "Varieties of Regret: A Debate and Partial Resolution," *Psychological Review* 105, no. 3 (1995): 602–605.

182 **Regrettable actions become less painful:** Gilovic and Medvec, "The Experience of Regret," 387.

183 **their *decision justification theory*:** Terry Connolly and Marcel Zeelenberg, "Regret in Decision Making," *Current Directions in Psychological Science* 11, no. 6 (December 2002): 212–216.

183 **someone who drives home from a party:** Ibid., 213.

183 **researchers Todd McElroy and Keith Dows found that action-oriented individuals:** Todd McElroy and Keith Dows, "Action Orientation and Feelings of Regret," *Judgment and Decision Making* 2, no. 6 (December 2007): 333–341.

184 **Colleen Saffrey and her colleagues:** Colleen Saffrey, Amy Summerville, and Neal J. Roese, "Praise for Regret: People Value Regret Above Other Negative Emotions," *Motivation and Emotion* 31, no. 1 (March 2008): 46–54.

185 **originally developed by Barry Schwartz:** Barry Schwartz et al., "Maximising Versus Satisficing: Happiness Is a Matter of Choice,"

Journal of Personality and Social Psychology 63, no. 5 (2002): 1,178–1,197.

185 **The participants were administered a regret scale:** Ibid., 53.

186 **believing that regret is positive may well be just a coping mechanism:** Ibid., 52.

186 **the *psychological immune system*:** Daniel Gilbert, *Stumbling on Happiness* (New York: Vintage Books, 2007), 177–178.

187 **Counterfactual thinking is different:** Kai Epstude and Neal J. Roese, "The Functional Theory of Counterfactual Thinking," *Personality and Social Psychology Review* 12, no. 2 (May 2008): 168–192.

188 **In an interesting meta-analysis:** Neal J. Roese and Amy Summerville, "What We Regret Most . . . and Why," *Personality and Social Psychology Bulletin* 31, no. 9 (September 2008): 1,273–1,285.

189 **"Opportunity breeds regret":** Ibid., 1274.

189 **Marcel Zeelenberg and Rik Pieters:** Rik Pieters and Marcel Zeelenberg, "A Theory of Regret Regulation 1.1," 33.

191 **A study on rumination:** Annette van Randenborgh, Joachim Hüffmeier, Joelle LeMoult, and Jutta Joormann, "Letting Go of Unmet Goals: Does Self-Focused Rumination Impair Goal Disengagement?" *Motivation and Emotion* 34, no. 4 (December 2010): 325–332.

192 **we've all got to put down the duckie:** In case you don't know the segment, treat yourself here: "Sesame Street (Vintage): Put Down the Duckie," YouTube, uploaded by Hellfrick, 24 August 2007, www.youtube.com/watch?v=SMAixgo_zJ4.

Chapter Nine: Resetting Your Inner Compass

193 **As Charles S. Carver and Michael F. Scheier note:** Charles S. Carver and Michael F. Scheier, *On the Self-Regulation of Behavior* (Cambridge and London: Cambridge University Press, 1998), 348.

194 **As Robert A. Emmons explains, human beings don't experience:** Robert A. Emmons, "Striving and Feeling: Personal Goals and Subjective Well-Being" in *The Psychology of Action*, ed. Peter Gollwitzer and John A. Bargh (New York and London: Guilford Press, 1996), 314.

194 **"people are more than just collections":** Ibid., 331.

194 **"the search for meaningfulness":** Ibid., 333.

195 **In his book *Flow*:** Mihaly Csikszentmihalyi, *Flow: The Psychology of Optimal Experience* (New York: Harper Perennial/Modern Classics, 2008), 158–159.

196 **Psychologist Patricia Linville:** Patricia W. Linville, "Self-Complexity and Affective Extremity: Don't Put All of Your Eggs in One Cognitive Basket," *Social Cognition* 1, no. 1 (1985): 94–120.

197 **Linville hypothesizes:** Ibid., 97.

198 **self-complexity as a cognitive buffer:** Patricia W. Linville, "Self-Complexity As a Cognitive Buffer Against Stress-Related Illness and Depression," *Journal of Personality and Social Psychology* 12, no. 4 (1987): 663–676. See also Erika J. Koch and James A. Shepherd, "Is Self-Complexity Linked to Better Coping? A Review of the Literature," *Journal of Personality* 72, no. 4 (August 2004): 727–760.

198 **"the negative affect and self-appraisal":** Ibid., 663.

199 **In their classic book on self-regulation:** Carver and Scheier, *On the Self-Regulation of Behavior*, 348.

200 **"a relatively stable, generalized expectation that good outcomes will occur":** Carsten Wrosch and Michael F. Scheier, "Personality and Quality of Life: The Importance of Optimism and Goal Adjustment," *Quality of Life Research* 12, suppl. 1 (2003): 59–72.

201 **Life Orientation Test:** Charles S. Carver, "LOT-R (Life Orientation Test—Revised)," University of Miami, Department of Psychology, Coral Gables, FL, accessed 1 July 2013, www.psy.cmu .edu/faculty/scheier/scales/LOTR_Scale.pdf.

201 **Wrosch and Scheier assert:** Ibid., 69.

202 **A highly influential argument by Peter M. Gollwitzer:** Peter M. Gollwitzer, "Action Phases and Mindsets," in *Handbook of Motivation and Cognition: Foundation of Social Behavior*, ed. E. Tory Higgins and Richard M. Sorrentino (New York and London: Guilford Press, 1990), 2: 53–92.

204 **The researchers had participants name two personal problems:** Peter M. Gollwitzer, Heinz Heckhausen, and Heike Katajczak, "From Weighing to Willing: Approaching a Change Decision Through Pre- or Postdecisional Mentation," *Organizational Behavior and Human Decision Processes* 45 (1990): 41–65. See also Inge Schweiger Gallo and Peter M. Gollwitzer, "Implementation

Intentions: A Look Back at Fifteen Years of Progress," *Psicothema* 19, no. 1 (2007): 37–42.

206 **"nonconscious" thinking that sometimes gets in the way:** Peter M. Gollwitzer, "Implementation Intentions: Strong Effects of Simple Plans," *American Psychologist* 54, no. 7 (1999): 493–502. The quotation is on page 496.

206 **As Gollwitzer, Ute C. Bayer, and Kathleen C. Molloch note:** Peter M. Gollwitzer, Ute C. Bayer, and Kathleen Molloch, "The Control of the Unwanted" in *The New Unconscious*, ed. Ran R. Hassin, James S. Uleman, and John A. Bargh (New York: Oxford University Press, 2006), 485–515.

206 **the road to happiness:** Sonja Lyubomirsky, Kennon M. Sheldon, and David Schkade, "Pursuing Happiness: The Architecture of Sustainable Change," *Review of General Psychology* 9, no. 2 (2005): 111–131.

207 **"These relatively weak associations":** Ibid., 117.

207 **"the hedonic adaptation tends to shuttle":** Ibid., 118.

208 **Sheldon and Lyubomirsky tested this hypothesis:** Kennon M. Sheldon and Sonja Lyubomirsky, "Achieving Sustainable Gains in Happiness: Change Your Actions, Not Your Circumstances," *Journal of Happiness Studies* 7 (2006): 55–86.

208 **"only to the extent that one takes action":** Ibid., 80.

Bibliography

Achtziger, Anja, Thorsten Fehr, Gabriele Oettingen, Peter M. Gollwitzer, and Brigitte Rockstroh. "Strategies of Intention Formation Are Reflected in Continuous MEG Activity." *Social Neuroscience* 4, no. 1 (2009): 11–27.

Ackerman, Joshua M., Noah J. Goldstein, Jenessa R. Shapiro, and John A. Bargh. "You Wear Me Out: The Vicarious Depletion of Self-Control." *Psychological Science* 70, no. 3 (2009): 327–332.

Ainsworth, Mary. *Patterns of Attachment: A Psychological Study of the Strange Situation*. Hillsdale, NJ: L. Laurence Erlbaum Associates, 1978.

Alan, Lorraine G., Shepherd Siegel, and Samuel Hannah. "The Sad Truth About Depressive Realism." *Quarterly Journal of Experimental Psychology* 60, no. 3 (2007): 482–495.

Alloy, Lauren B., and Lyn Y. Abramson. "Judgment of Contingency in Depressed and Non-Depressed Students: Sadder but Wiser?" *Journal of Experimental Psychology* 108, no. 4 (1978): 441–485.

Bargh, John A., and Tanya L. Chartrand. "The Unbearable Automaticity of Being." *American Psychologist* 54, no. 7 (July 1999): 462–479.

Bargh, John A., Mark Chen, and Lara Burrows. "Automaticity of Social Behavior: Direct Effects of Trait Construct and Stereotype Activation on Actions." *Journal of Personality and Social Psychology* 71, no. 2 (1996): 230–244.

Bargh, John A., Peter Gollwitzer, Annette Lee-Chai, Kimberly Barndollar, and Roman Trötschel. "The Automated Will: Nonconscious Activation and Pursuit of Behavior Goals." *Journal of Personality and Social Psychology* 81, no. 6 (2001): 1,014–1,027.

Bargh, John A., and Ezequiel Morsella. "The Unconscious Mind." *Perspectives on Psychological Science* 3, no. 1 (2003): 73–79.

Barrett, Lisa Feldman, James Gross, Tamlin Conner Christensen, and Michael Benvenuto. "Knowing What You're Feeling and Knowing

What to Do About It: Mapping the Relation Between Emotion Differentiation and Emotion Regulation." *Cognition and Emotion* 15, no. 6 (2001): 713–724.

Baumann, Nicola, and Julius Kuhl. "How to Resist Temptation: The Effects of External Control Versus Autonomy Support on Self-Regulatory Dynamics." *Journal of Personality* 73, no. 2 (April 2005): 444–470.

———. "Intuition, Affect, and Personality: Unconscious Coherence Judgments and Self-Regulation of Negative Affect." *Journal of Personality and Social Psychology* 83, no. 5 (2002): 1,213–1,225.

———. "Self-Infiltration: Confusing Tasks As Self-Selected in Memory." *Personality and Social Psychology Bulletin* 29, no. 4 (April 2003): 487–497.

Baumeister, Roy F., Ellen Bratslavsky, Mark Muraven, and Dianne M. Tice. "Ego Depletion: Is the Active Self a Limited Resource?" *Journal of Personality and Social Psychology* 74, no. 5 (1998): 1,252–1,265.

Baumeister, Roy F., Ellen Bratslavsky, Catrin Finkenauer, and Kathleen Vohs. "Bad Is Stronger than Good." *Review of General Psychology* 5, no. 4 (2001): 323–370.

Baumeister, Roy F., and John Tierney. *Willpower: Rediscovering the Greatest Human Strength.* New York: Penguin Books, 2011.

Bridges, William. *Transitions: Making Sense of Life's Changes.* New York: Da Capo Press, 2004.

Butler, Lisa D., and Susan Nolen-Hoeksema. "Gender Differences in Response to Depressed Mood in a College Sample." *Sex Roles*, 30: 331–346.

Carver, Charles S. "Approach, Avoidance, and the Self-Regulation of Affect and Action." *Motivation and Emotion* 30 (2006): 105–110.

———. "Negative Affects Deriving from the Behavior Approach System." *Emotion* 4, no. 1 (2004): 3–22.

Carver, Charles S., and Michael F. Scheier. *On The Self-Regulation of Behavior.* Cambridge and London: Cambridge University Press, 1998.

———. "Scaling Back Goals and Recalibration of the Affect Systems Are Processes in Normal Adaptive Self-Regulation: Understanding The 'Response-Shift' Phenomena." *Social Science and Medicine* 50 (2000): 1,715–1,722.

Chabris, Christopher, and Daniel Simons. *The Invisible Gorilla: How Our Intuitions Deceive Us.* New York: Broadway Paperbacks, 2011.

Chartrand, Tanya L., and John A. Bargh. "The Chameleon Effect: The Perception-Behavior Link and Social Interaction." *Journal of Personality and Social Psychology* 76, no. 6 (1999): 893–910.

Chartrand, Tanya L., Rick B. van Baaren, and John A. Bargh. "Linking Automatic Evaluation to Mood and Information Processing Style: Consequences for Experienced Affect, Impression Formation, and Stereotyping." *Journal of Experimental Psychology* 35, no. 1 (2006): 70–79.

Chartrand, Tanya L., Clara Michelle Cheng, Amy L. Dalton, and Abraham Tesser. "Nonconscious Incidents or Adaptive Self-Regulatory Tool?" *Social Cognition* 28, no. 5 (2010): 569–588.

Connolly, Terry, and Marcel Zeelenberg. "Regret in Decision Making." *Current Directions in Psychological Science* 11, no. 6 (December 2002): 212–216.

Csikszentmihalyi, Mihaly. *Flow: The Psychology of Optimal Experience.* New York: Harper Perennial/Modern Classics, 2008.

Deci, Edward L., and Richard M. Ryan. "The 'What' and 'Why' of Goal Pursuits: Human Needs and the Self-Determination of Behavior." *Psychological Inquiry* 13, no. 4 (2000): 227–268.

Diefendorff, James M. "Examination of the Roles of Action-State Orientation and Goal Orientation in the Goal-Setting and Performance Process." *Human Performance* 17, no. 4: 375–395.

Diefendorff, James M., Rosalie J. Hall, Robert G. Ord, and Mona L. Strean. "Action-State Orientation: Construct Validity of a Revised Measure and Its Relationship to Work-Related Variables." *Journal of Applied Psychology* 85, no. 2 (2000): 250–261.

Drach-Zahavy, Anat, and Miriam Erez. "Challenge Versus Threat Effects on the Goal Performance Relationship." *Organizational Behavior and Human Decision Process* 88 (2002): 667–682.

Duhigg, Charles. *The Power of Habit: What We Do in Life and Business.* New York: Random House, 2012.

Dunning, David, Dale W. Griffin, James D. Mikojkovic, and Lee Toss. "The Overconfidence Effect in Social Prediction." *Journal of Personality and Social Psychology* 58, no. 4 (1990): 568–581.

Dunning, David, and Amber L. Story. "Depression, Realism, and the Overconfidence Effect: Are the Sadder Wiser When Predicting

Future Actions and Events?" *Journal of Personality and Social Psychology* 61, no. 4 (1981): 521–532.

Elliot, Andrew J. "A Hierarchical Model of Approach-Avoidance Motivation." *Motivation and Emotion* 29 (2006): 111–116.

Elliot, Andrew J., and Todd M. Thrash. "Approach-Avoidance Motivation in Personality: Approach and Avoidance Temperaments and Goals." *Journal of Personality and Social Psychology* 82, no. 5 (2002): 804–818.

————. "Approach and Avoidance Temperament As Basic Dimensions of Personality." *Journal of Personality* 78, no. 3 (June 2010): 865–906.

————. "The Intergeneration Transmission of Fear of Failure." *Personality and Social Psychology Bulletin* 30, no. 8 (August 2004): 957–971.

Elliot, Andrew J., and Marcy A. Church. "Client-Articulated Avoidance Goals in the Therapy Context." *Journal of Counseling Psychology* 49, no. 2 (2002): 243–254.

Elliot, Andrew J., and Harry T. Reis. "Attachment and Exploration in Adulthood." *Journal of Personality and Social Psychology* 85, no. 2 (2003): 317–331.

Elliot, Andrew J., and Kennon M. Sheldon. "Avoidance Achievement Motivation: A Personal Goals Analysis." *Journal of Personality and Social Psychology* 73, no. 1 (1997): 151–185.

Elliot, Andrew J., Todd M. Thrash, and Jou Murayama. "A Longitudinal Analysis of Self-Regulation and Well-Being: Avoidance Personal Goals, Avoidance Coping, Stress Generation, and Subjective Well-Being." *Journal of Personality* 73, no. 3 (June 2011): 643–674.

Emmons, Robert A., and Laura King. "Conflict Among Personal Stirrings: Immediate and Long-Term Implications for Psychological and Physical Well-Being." *Journal of Personality and Social Psychology* 54, no. 6 (1988): 1,040–1,048.

Epstude, Kai, and Neal J. Roese. "The Functional Theory of Counterfactual Thinking." *Personality and Social Psychology Review* 12, no. 2 (May 2008): 168–192.

Fivush, Robyn. "Exploring Sex Differences in the Emotional Context of Mother-Child Conversations About the Past." *Sex Roles* 20, nos. 11–12 (1989): 675–695.

Friedman, Ron, Edward L. Deci, Andrew J. Elliot, Arlen C. Moller, and Henk Aarts. "Motivational Synchronicity: Priming Motivation

Orientations with Observations of Others' Behaviors." *Motivation and Emotion* 34 (2010): 34–38.

Gable, Shelley L. "Approach and Avoidance Social Motives and Goals." *Journal of Personality* 74, no. 1 (February 2006): 175–222.

Gallo, Inge Schweiger, and Peter M. Gollwitzer. "Implementation Intentions: A Look Back at Fifteen Years of Progress." *Psicothema* 19, no. 1 (2007): 37–42.

Gibson, E. J., and R. D. Walk. "The Visual Cliff." *Scientific American* 202, no. 4 (1960): 67–71.

Gilbert, Daniel T. *Stumbling on Happiness*. New York: Vintage Books, 2007.

Gilbert, Daniel T., Erin Driver-Linn, and Timothy D. Wilson. "The Trouble with Vronsky." In *The Wisdom in Feeling: Psychological Processes in Emotional Intelligence*, ed. Lisa Feldman Barrett and Peter Salovey. New York: The Guilford Press, 2002.

Gilbert, Daniel T., and Jane E. J. Ebert. "Decisions and Revisions: The Affective Forecasting of Changeable Outcomes." *Journal of Personality and Social Psychology* 82, no. 4 (2002): 503–514.

Gilbert, Daniel T., Carey K. Morewedge, Jane L. Risen, and Timothy D. Wilson. "Looking Forward to Looking Backward." *Psychological Science* 15, no. 5 (2004): 346–350.

Gilovic, Thomas, and Victoria Husted Medvec. "The Experience of Regret: What, When, and Why." *Psychological Review* 102, no. 2 (1995): 379–395.

Gilovic, Thomas, Victoria Husted Medvec, and Daniel Kahneman. "Varieties of Regret: A Debate and Partial Resolution." *Psychological Review* 105, no. 3 (1995): 602–605.

Goleman, Daniel. *Emotional Intelligence: Why It Can Matter More than IQ*. New York: Bantam Books, 1994.

Gollwitzer, Peter M. "Implementation Intentions; Strong Effects of Simple Plans." *American Psychologist* 54, no. 7 (1999): 493–502.

———. "Action Phases and Mindsets." In *Handbook of Motivation and Cognition: Foundation of Social Behavior*, edited by E. Tory Higgins and Richard M. Sorrentino, 2:53–92. New York and London: Guilford Press, 1990.

Gollwitzer, Peter M., Heinz Heckhausen, and Heike Katajczak. "From Weighing to Willing: Approaching a Change Decision Through

Pre- or Postdecisional Mentation." *Organizational Behavior and Human Decision Processes* 45 (1990): 41–65.

Gollwitzer, Peter M., Ute G. Bayer, and Kathleen Molloch. "The Control of the Unwanted." In *The New Unconscious*, edited by Ran R. Hassin, James S. Uleman, and John A. Bargh, 485–515. New York: Oxford University Press, 2006.

Gollwitzer, Peter M., and John A. Bargh, eds. *The Psychology of Action: Linking Cognition and Motivation to Behavior.* New York: Guilford Press, 1996.

Heatherton, Todd, and Patricia A. Nichols. "Personal Accounts of Successful Versus Failed Attempts at Life Change." *Personality and Social Psychology Bulletin* 20, no. 6 (December 1994): 664–675.

Henderson, Marlone D., Peter M. Gollwitzer, and Gabriele Oettingen. "Implementation Intentions and Disengagement from a Failing Course of Action." *Journal of Behavior Decision Making* 20 (2007): 81–102.

Houser-Marko, Linda, and Kennon M. Sheldon. "Eyes on the Prize or Nose to the Grindstone: The Effects of Level of Goal Evaluation on Mood and Motivation." *Personality and Social Psychology Bulletin* 34, no. 14 (November 2008): 1,556–1,569.

Inzlicht, Michael, and Brandon J. Schmeichel. "What Is Ego Depletion? Toward a Mechanistic Revision of the Resource Model of Self-Control." *Perspectives on Psychological Science* 7, no. 5 (2012): 450–463.

Johnson, Joel T., Lorraine M. Cain, Toni L. Falker, Jon Hayman, and Edward Perillo. "The 'Barnum Effect' Revisited: Cognitive and Motivational Factors in the Acceptance of Personality Descriptions." *Journal of Personality and Social Psychology* 49, no. 5 (1985): 1,378–1,391.

Jostmann, Nils B., Sander L. Koole, Nickie Y. Van Der Wulp, and Daniel A. Fockenberg. "Subliminal Affect Regulation: The Moderating Role of Action Versus State Orientation." *European Psychologist* 10 (2005): 209–217.

Kahneman, Daniel. "A Perspective on Judgment and Choice: Mapping Bounded Rationality." *American Psychologist* 85, no. 9 (September 2003): 692–720.

———. *Thinking, Fast and Slow.* New York: Farrar, Straus and Giroux, 2011.

Kahneman, Daniel, and Amos Tversky. "Prospect Theory: An Analysis of Decision Under Risk." *Econometrica* 47, no. 2 (March 1979): 263–291.

Kasser, Tim, and Richard M. Ryan. "Further Examining the American Dream: Differential Correlates of Intrinsic and Extrinsic Goals." *Personality and Social Psychology Bulletin* 22, no.3 (March 1996): 280–287.

———. "The Dark Side of the American Dream: Correlates of Financial Success As a Central Life Aspiration." *Journal of Personality and Social Psychology* 65, no. 3 (1993): 410–422.

Kay, Aaron C., S. Christian Wheeler, John A. Bargh, and Lee Ross. "Material Priming: The Influence of Mundane Physical Objects on Situational Construal and Competitive Behavior Choice." *Organizational Behavior and Human Decision Process* 93 (2004): 83–96.

Klinger, Eric. "Consequences of Commitment to and Disengagement from Incentives." *Psychological Review* 82, no. 2 (1975): 1–25.

Koch, Erika J., and James A. Shepherd. "Is Self-Complexity Linked to Better Coping? A Review of the Literature." *Journal of Personality* 72, no. 4 (August 2004): 727–760.

Koole, Sander L., Julius Kuhl, Nils B. Jostmann, and Catrin Finkenauer. "Self-Regulation in Interpersonal Relationships: The Case of Action Versus State Orientation." In *Self and Relationship*, edited by Kathleen D. Vohs and E. J. Finkel, 360–386. New York and London: The Guilford Press, 2006.

Koole, Sander L., and Nils B. Jostmann. "Getting a Grip on Your Feelings: Effects of Action Orientation on Intuitive Affect Regulation." *Journal of Personality and Social Psychology* 87, no. 6 (2004): 974–990.

———. "On the Waxing and Waning of Working Memory: Action Orientation Moderates the Impact of Demanding Relationship Primers on Working Memory Capacity." *Social Psychology Bulletin* 32, no. 12 (December 2006): 1,716–1,728.

Koole, Sander L., and Daniel A. Fockenberg. "Implicit Emotional Regulation Under Demanding Conditions: The Mediating Role of Action Versus State Orientation." *Cognition and Emotion* 25, no. 3 (2011): 440–452.

Koole, Sander L., Julius Kuhl, Nils B. Jostmann, and Kathleen D. Vohs. "On the Hidden Benefits of State Orientation: Can People Prosper

Without Efficient Affect-Regulation Skills?" In *Building, Defending, and Regulating the Self,* edited by Abraham Tesser, Joanne Woods, and Diederik Stapel, 217–244. New York: Psychology Press, 2005.

Kruger, Justin. "Lake Wobegon Be Gone! The 'Below-Average Effect' and the Egocentric Nature of Comparative Ability Judgments." *Journal of Personality and Social Psychology* 77, no. 2 (1999): 221–232.

Kuhl, Julius. "Motivational and Functional Helplessness: The Moderating Effect of State Versus Action Orientations." *Journal of Personality and Social Psychology* 40, no. 1 (1981): 155–170.

Lench, Heather C., and Linda J. Levine. "Goals and Responses to Failure: Knowing When to Hold Them and When to Fold Them." *Motivation and Emotion* 32 (2008): 127–140.

Levin, Daniel T., Nausheen Momek, Sarah B. Drivdahl, and Daniel J. Simons. "Change Blindness Blindness: The Metacognitive Error of Overestimating Change-Detection Ability." *Visual Cognition* 7, nos. 1–3 (2000): 397–412.

Linville, Patricia W. "Self-Complexity and Affective Extremity: Don't Put All of Your Eggs in One Cognitive Basket." *Social Cognition* 1, no. 1 (1985): 94–120.

———. "Self-Complexity As a Cognitive Buffer Against Stress-Related Illness and Depression." *Journal of Personality and Social Psychology* 12, no. 4 (1987): 663–676.

Locke, Edwin A., and Gary P. Latham. "Has Goal Setting Gone Wild, or Have Its Attackers Abandoned Good Scholarship?" *Academy of Management Perspectives* 23, no. 1 (February 2009): 27–23.

———. "New Directions in Goal-Setting Theory." *Current Directions in Psychological Science* 15, no. 5 (October 2006): 265–268.

Loewenstein, George F., and Drazen Prelec. "Preferences for Sequences of Outcomes." *Psychological Review* 100, no. 1 (1993): 91–108.

Lovallo, Dan, and Daniel Kahneman. "Delusions of Success: How Optimism Undermines Executives' Decisions." *Harvard Business Review* (July 2003), 56–63.

Lyubomirsky, Sonja, Kennon M. Sheldon, and David Schkade. "Pursuing Happiness: The Architecture of Sustainable Change." *Review of General Psychology* 9, no. 2 (2005): 111–131.

Masicampo, E. J., and Roy F. Baumeister. "Consider It Done! Plan Making Can Eliminate the Cognitive Effects of Unfulfilled Goals."

Journal of Personality and Social Psychology (June 2, 2011), advance online publication. DOI:10.1037/ 90024192.

Mayer, John D., Peter Salovey, and David R. Caruso. "Emotional Intelligence: New Ability or Eclectic Traits." *American Psychologist* 65, no. 7 (September 2008): 515.

McElroy, Todd, and Keith Dows. "Action Orientation and Feelings of Regret." *Judgment and Decision Making* 2, no. 6 (December 2007): 333–341.

Mikulincer, Mario, Philip R. Shaver, and Dana Pereg. "Attachment Theory and Affect Regulation: The Dynamics, Development, and Cognitive Consequences of Attachment-Related Strategies." *Motivation and Emotion* 27, no. 2 (June 2003): 77–102.

Miller, Gregory E., and Carsten Wrosch. "You've Gotta Know When to Fold 'Em: Goal Disengagement and Systemic Inflammation in Adolescence." *Psychological Science* 18, no. 9 (2007): 773–777.

Morisano, Dominique, Jacob B. Hirsh, Jordan B. Peterson, Robert O. Pihl, and Bruce M. Shore. "Setting, Elaborating and Reflecting on Personal Goals Improves Academic Performance." *Journal of Applied Psychology* 85, no. 2 (2010): 255–264.

Morsella, Ezequiel, Avi Ben-Zeev, Meredith Lanska, and John A. Bargh. "The Spontaneous Thoughts of the Night: How Future Tasks Breed Intrusive Cognitions." *Social Cognition* 28, no. 5 (2010): 640–649.

Moskowitz, Gordon B., and Heidi Grant, eds. *The Psychology of Goals.* New York: Guilford Press, 2009.

Muraven, Mark, Dianne M. Tice, and Roy M. Baumeister. "Self-Control As Limited Resource: Regulatory Depletion Patterns." *Journal of Personality and Social Psychology* 74, no. 3 (1998): 774–789.

Nolen-Hoeksema, Susan, and Benita Jackson. "Mediators of the Gender Difference in Rumination." *Psychology of Women Quarterly* 25 (2001): 37–47.

Oettingen, Gabriele. "Future Thought and Behaviour Change." *European Review of Social Psychology* 23, no. 1 (2012): 1–63.

Oettingen, Gabriele, and Doris Mayer. "The Motivating Function of Thinking About the Future: Expectations Versus Fantasies." *Journal of Personality and Social Psychology* 83, no. 5 (2002): 1,198–1,212.

Oettingen, Gabriele, and Peter M. Gollwitzer. "Strategies of Setting and Implementing Goals: Mental Contrasting and Implementation

Intentions." In *Social Psychological Foundations of Clinical Psychology*, edited by J. E. Maddux and J. P. Tanguy, 114–135. New York: Guildford Press, 2010.

Oettingen, Gabriele, Doris Mayer, Jennifer S. Thorpe, Hanna Janetzke, and Solvig Lorenz. "Turning Fantasies About Positive and Negative Futures into Self-Improvement Goals." *Motivation and Emotion* 29, no. 4 (December 2003): 237–267.

Oettingen, Gabriele, Hyeon-ju Pak, and Karoline Schnetter. "Self-Regulation of Goal-Setting: Turning Free Fantasies About the Future into Binding Goals." *Journal of Personality and Social Psychology* 80, no. 5 (2001): 736–753.

Ordóñez, Lisa D., Maurice E. Schweitzer, Adam D. Galinsky, and Max H. Bazerman. "Goals Gone Wild: The Systematic Side Effects of Over-Prescribing Goal Setting." Working Paper 09-083, Harvard Business School, Boston, 2009.

———. "On Good Scholarship, Goal Setting and Scholars Gone Wild." Working Paper 09-122, Harvard Business School, Boston, 2009.

Pieters, Rik, and Marcel Zeelenberg. "A Theory of Regret Regulation 1.1." *Journal of Consumer Psychology* 17, no. 1 (2007): 29–35.

Pronin, Emily, Daniel Y. Lin, and Lee Ross. "The Bias Blind Spot: Perceptions of Bias in Self Versus Others." *Personality and Social Psychology Bulletin* 28, no. 3 (March 2002): 369–381.

Reid, R. L. "The Psychology of the Near Miss." *Journal of Gambling Behavior* 2, no. 1 (1986): 32–39.

Roese, Neal J., and Amy Summerville. "What We Regret Most . . . and Why." *Personality and Social Psychology Bulletin* 31, no. 9 (September 2008): 1,273–1,285.

Ryan, Richard M., and Edward L. Deci. "Intrinsic and Extrinsic Motivations: Classic Definitions and New Directions." *Contemporary Educational Psychology* 25 (2000): 54–67.

Saffrey, Colleen, Amy Summerville, and Neal J. Roese. "Praise for Regret: People Value Regret Above Other Negative Emotions." *Motivation and Emotion* 31, no. 1 (March 2008): 46–54.

Salovey, Peter, and D. J. Sluyter. *Emotional Development and Emotional Intelligence.* New York: Basic Books, 1997, 3–31.

Samuelson, William, and Richard Zeckhauser. "The Status Quo Bias in Decision-Making." *Journal of Risk and Uncertainty* 1 (1988): 7–59.

Schmeichel, Brandon J., and Kathleen Vohs. "Self-Affirmation and Self-Control: Affirming Core Values Counteracts Ego Depletion." *Journal of Personality and Social Psychology* 96, no. 4 (2009): 770–782.

Schwartz, Barry, Andrew Ward, John Monterosso, Sonja Lyubomirsky, Katherine White, and Darrin R. Lehrman. "Maximizing Versus Satisficing: Happiness Is a Matter of Choice." *Journal of Personality and Social Psychology* 83, no. 5 (2002): 1,178–1,197.

Senay, Ibrahim, Dolores Abarracin, and Kenji Noguchi. "Motivating Goal-Directed Behavior Through Introspective Self-Talk: The Role of the Interrogative Form of Simple Future Tense." *Psychological Science* 21, no. 4 (2010): 499–504.

Shaver, Philip R., and Mario Mikulincer. "Attachment-Related Psychodynamics." *Attachment and Human Development* 4 (2002): 133–161.

Sheldon, Kennon M., and Sonja Lyubomirsky. "Achieving Sustainable Gains in Happiness: Change Your Actions, Not Your Circumstances." *Journal of Happiness Studies* 7 (2006): 55–86.

Sheldon, Kennon M., and Tim Kasser. "Pursuing Personal Goals: Skills Enable Progress But Not All Progress Is Beneficial." *Personality and Social Psychology Bulletin* 24, no. 12 (1998): 1,319–1,331.

Sheldon, Kennon M., Tim Kasser, Kendra Smith, and Tamara Share. "Personal Goals and Psychological Growth: Testing an Intervention to Enhance Goal Attainment and Personality Integration." *Journal of Personality* 70, no. 1 (February 2002): 5–31.

Sheldon, Kennon M., Richard M. Ryan, Edward L. Deci, and Tim Kasser. "The Independent Effects of Goal Contents: It's Both What You Pursue and Why You Pursue It." *Personality and Social Psychology Bulletin* 30, no. 4 (April 2004): 475–486.

Shoda, Yuichi, Walter Mischel, and Philip K. Peake. "Predicting Adolescent Cognitive and Self-Regulatory Competencies from Preschool Delay of Gratification: Identifying Diagnostic Conditions." *Developmental Psychology* 16, no. 6 (1990): 978–986.

Siegel, Daniel J., and Mary Hartzell. *Parenting from the Inside Out.* New York: Jeremy P. Tarcher/Penguin: 2003.

Simons, Daniel J., and Christopher Chabris. "Gorillas in our Midst: Sustained Inattention Blindness." *Perception* 28 (1999): 1,059–1,074.

Simons, Daniel J., and Daniel T. Lewin. "Failure to Detect Changes to

People During a Real-World Interaction." *Psychonomic Bulletin and Review*, 5, no. 4 (1998): 644–649.

Skinner, B. F. "Superstition in the Pigeon." *Journal of Experimental Psychology* 38 (1938): 168–172.

Slaughter, Anne-Marie. "Why Women Still Can't Have It All." *Atlantic*, July/August 2012. www.theatlantic.com/magazine/archive/2012/07/ why-women-still-cant-have-it-all/309020.

Sorce, James F., Robert N. Emde, Joseph Campos, and Mary D. Klinnert. "Maternal Emotional Signaling: Its Effect on the Visual Cliff Behavior of 1-Year-Olds." *Developmental Psychology* 21, no. 1 (1985): 195–200.

Staw, Barry M. "The Escalation of Commitment to a Course of Action." *Academy of Management Review* 6, no. 4 (October 1981): 577–587.

Thrash, Todd M., and Andrew J. Elliot. "Implicit and Self-Attributed Achievement Motives: Concordance and Predictive Validity." *Journal of Personality* 70, no. 5 (October 2002): 729–755.

Tversky, Amos, and Daniel Kahneman. "Availability: A Heuristic for Judging Frequency and Probability." *Cognitive Psychology* 4 (1973): 207–232.

Vallone, Robert P., Dale W. Griffin, Sabrina Lin, and Lee Ross. "Overconfident Prediction of Future Actions and Outcomes by Self and Others." *Journal of Personality and Social Psychology* 58, no. 4 (1990): 582–591.

van Randenborgh, Annette, Joachim Hüffmeier, Joelle LeMoult, and Jutta Joormann. "Letting Go of Unmet Goals: Does Self-Focused Rumination Impair Goal Disengagement?" *Motivation and Emotion* 34, no. 4 (December 2010): 325–332.

Vohs, Kathleen D., and Todd Heatherton. "Self-Regulatory Failure: A Resource Failure Approach." *Psychological Science* 11, no. 3 (May 2000): 249–254.

Vohs, Kathleen D., Roy F. Baumeister, Nicole L. Mead, Wilhelm Hoffman, Suresh Ramanathan, and Brandon J. Schmeichel. "Engaging in Self-Control Heightens Urges and Feelings." Working Paper.

Wagner, Dylan D., and Todd F. Heatherton. "Self-Regulatory Depletion Increases Emotional Reactivity in the Amygdala." *Social, Cognitive and Affective Neuroscience* (August 27, 2012). DOI:10/ 1093scan/ nss082.

Wegner, Daniel M. *The Illusion of Conscious Will.* Cambridge, MA: MIT Press, 2002.

———. "Ironic Processes of Mental Control." *Psychological Review* 101, no. 1 (1994): 34–52.

———. "Setting Free the Bears: Escape from Thought Suppression." *American Psychologist* (November 2011): 671–679.

———. *White Bears and Other Unwanted Thoughts: Suppression, Obsession, and the Psychology of Mental Control* (New York and London: Guilford Press, 1994), 70.

———. "You Can't Always Think What You Want: Problems in the Suppression of Unwanted Thoughts." *Advances in Experimental Psychology* 25 (1992): 193–225.

Wegner, Daniel M., David J. Schneider, Samuel R. Carter III, and Teri L. White. "Paradoxical Effects of Thought Suppression." *Journal of Personality and Social Psychology* 53, 1 (1987): 5–13.

Weinberg, Katherine M., Edward Z. Tronick, Jeffrey F. Cohn, and Karen L. Olson. "Gender Differences in Emotional Expressivity and Self-Regulation During Early Infancy." *Developmental Psychology* 35 (1999): 175–188.

Wilson, Timothy D. *Strangers to Ourselves: Discovering the Adaptive Unconscious.* Cambridge, MA: Belknap Press of Harvard University, 2002.

Wilson, Timothy D., and Daniel T. Gilbert. "Affective Forecasting." *Advances in Experimental Social Psychology* 35 (2003): 346–411.

Woodzicka, Julie A., and Marianne LaFrance. "Real Versus Imagined Gender Harassment." *Journal of Social Issues* 57, no. 1 (2001): 15–39.

Wrosch, Carsten, and Michael F. Scheier. "Personality and Quality of Life: The Importance of Optimism and Goal Adjustment." *Quality of Life Research* 12, suppl. 1 (2003): 59–72.

Wrosch, Carsten, Gregory E. Miller, Michael F. Scheier, and Stephanie Brun de Pontet. "Giving Up on Unattainable Goals: Benefits for Health?" *Personality and Social Psychology Bulletin* 33, no. 2 (February 2007): 251–265.

Wrosch, Carsten, Michael F. Scheier, Gregory E. Miller, Richard Schulz, and Charles S. Carver. "Adaptive Self-Regulation of Unattainable Goals: Goal Disengagement, Goal Reengagement, and Subjective Well-Being." *Personality and Social Psychology Bulletin* 29, no. 12 (December 2003): 1,494–1,508.

Wrosch, Carsten, Michael F. Scheier, Charles S. Carver, and Richard Schulz. "The Importance of Goal Disengagement in Adaptive Self-Regulation: When Giving Up Is Beneficial." *Self and Identity* 2 (2003): 1–20.

Zeelenberg, Marcel, and Rik Pieters. "A Theory of Regret Regulation 1.0." *Journal of Consumer Psychology* 17, no. 1 (2007): 3–18.

Index